ENGLISHNESS AND NATIONAL CULTURE

'Nation' is probably the strongest of all forms of group identity. Over and above its expression in symbols such as flags, leaders and national icons, national identity also works at a less visible, more fascinating level – in the forms of discourse specific to a nation: not what we say so much as how we say it.

In this compelling study, Antony Easthope argues that the typical discourses of Englishness are structured by a deep-rooted philosophic tradition: empiricism. He sustains his lively polemic through appeal to a wide array of instances from high and popular culture, ranging from philosophical and literary works to the daily press and aspects of the English sense of humour.

Englishness and National Culture asserts a profound continuity running through from the seventeenth century until now. Today's journalists, historians, novelists, poets, comedians and politicians may imagine they are speaking as themselves. They are mistaken; 'ancestral voices' speak through them.

Antony Easthope is Professor of English and Cultural Studies at Manchester Metropolitan University, and is the author of *Literary into Cultural Studies* (Routledge, 1991).

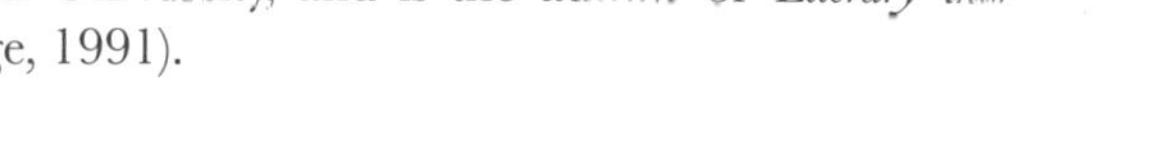

ENGLISHNESS AND NATIONAL CULTURE

Antony Easthope

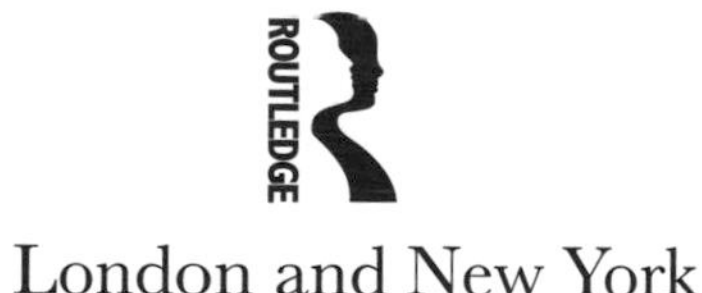

London and New York

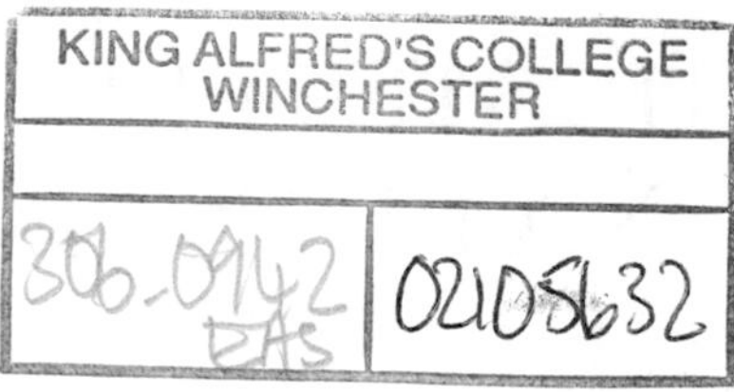

First published 1999
by Routledge
11 New Fetter Lane, London EC4P 4EE

Simultaneously published in the USA and Canada
by Routledge
29 West 35th Street, New York, NY 10001

Typeset in Baskerville by Routledge
Printed and bound in Great Britain by
T.J. International Ltd, Padstow, Cornwall

British Library Cataloguing in Publication Data
A catalogue record for this book is available from the British Library

Library of Congress Cataloguing in Publication Data
Easthope, Antony.
Englishness and national culture / Antony Easthope.
Includes bibliographical references and index.
1. National characteristics, English. 2. England–Civilization.
I. Title.
DA118.E23 1999
942–dc21 98–35349

ISBN 0–415–19687–6
ISBN 0–415–19688–4

FOR MY FATHER,
KELYNGE EASTHOPE

When in doubt, the English imagine a pendulum.

Raymond Williams

CONTENTS

FIGURES

PREFACE

Culture and Society by Raymond Williams was published in 1958. Since then, analysis which began by thinking about social groups in terms of class developed to consider gender and ethnicity (among others); it now needs to be directed at the most powerful collective identity to emerge with modernity: nation.

My argument begins by justifying an understanding of nation in terms of collective identification; in conclusion I return to some of the unwelcome but ineluctable implications of recognising that human groups are organised on a basis which is unconscious as well as conscious.

National collectivities identify with the overt symbols of nationhood (flags, presidents) but my proposal is that a much deeper effect is achieved through identification with a discursive formation specific to a particular nation. If two strangers from the same nation meet and talk casually for half an hour, there would be a number of ways to analyse their exchange. I shall address the level at which the conversation would enact national identity, not just in what was said but in *how* it was said (typical tropes, shifts of tone, jokes employed, the conception of truth appealed to). To support this I shall take Englishness as my example.

From the New Left of the 1960s I have retrieved the proposal that the English tradition is essentially *empiricist*. It would have been possible to justify that argument by tracing a history of empiricism in English writing from 1600: my approach has been to establish a sense of the empiricist tradition from the seventeenth century and then look in detail at four examples of contemporary discursive forms.

Englishness and National Culture aims to demonstrate a profound and hardly acknowledged continuity between the seventeenth century and today. This means that often when English people (journalists, historians, novelists, poets, comic writers and others) think they are speaking in their own voices, in fact the discourse of an empiricist tradition is speaking for them.

I am deeply grateful to people who found time to read this manuscript and from whose criticisms I have learned a great deal and tried to improve the argument accordingly. Fred Botting, Huw Jones, Willy Maley, Steve Rigby, Michael Westlake and Scott Wilson all commented on the theoretical section, while Martin Bell, Anthony Mellors and Ian Parker discussed particular chapters. I must also express my keen admiration for the anonymous reader for Routledge who understood what the book was trying to do better than I did. I am very pleased to thank Talia Rodgers for keeping faith with the project throughout. Finally, I would like to express my sincere gratitude to Eric Lupton, without whom this book could not have been written.

Some of the material that went towards Chapters 1, 2 and 4 has appeared elsewhere: in *Contemporary Writing and National Identity*, edited by Tracey Hill and William Hughes (Bath: Sulis Press, 1995); in 'The Question of National Culture: Thinking about Englishness' in *Moving the Borders*, edited by Marialuisa Bignami and Caroline Patey (Milan: Unicopli, 1996); and 'Culture and Nation: Englishness' in *Litteraria Pragensia/Perspectives*, edited by Susan Bassnett and Martin Procházka (Prague: British Council, 1997). An earlier version of part of Chapter 6 was published as 'Romancing the Stone: History-Writing and Rhetoric' in *Social History*, 18 (2) (May 1993). 'How Good is Seamus Heaney?' from *English*, 184 (Spring 1997) was revised to make up part of Chapter 8.

For giving permission to use copyright material I would like to thank: Steve Bell and the *Guardian* newspaper for 'Dr Tate's Patent School-room', 16 January 1996; Illingworth and Solo Syndication Ltd, London, for 'What, me? No I never *touch* goldfish!', 17 November 1939; Faber & Faber Ltd for an extract from 'The Waste Land' from *Collected Poems 1909–1962* by T.S. Eliot; extracts from 'The Whitsun Weddings' from *Collected Poems* by Philip Larkin; 'The Hawk in the Rain' from *The Hawk in the Rain* by Ted Hughes and an extract from 'Hawk Roosting' from *Lupercal* by Ted Hughes; extracts from 'The Grauballe Man' from *New Selected Poems 1966–1987* by Seamus Heaney; Grafton Books for 'Shoes' from *tottering state* (copyright Tom Raworth).

While every attempt has been made where appropriate to trace the copyright holders of the above material, the author and publisher would be pleased to hear from any interested parties.

I have marked '*sic*' only for the first instance when a cited text uses a masculine term to mean men and women.

Part I

NATION

1

NATION, IDENTITY, DISCOURSE

> I am determined to talk about France as if it were another country, another fatherland, another nation.
>
> (Fernand Braudel 1988, 1, p. 15)

> Britain…treated as if it were a foreign country.
>
> (Gregory Elliott 1995, p. 7)

National identity is a product of modernity. It is therefore comparable to another exemplary version of the modern experience though one that rarely gets serious attention: driving a car.

The one thing everybody says about driving is that you don't learn how to do it until after you've passed your test. You know how to drive when it has become a habit, a pre-conscious integration of perception and movement. Without reflection, from the whole field of vision I immediately pick out the signs that matter (that car's flashing light 50 metres away means it is turning left) and co-ordinate them with motor response (foot off accelerator and over brake). Driving is a matter of submitting to rules, something you are reminded of every time you approach a crossroads (are the lights red or green?).

Driving offers us two radically different positions. In one I have exceptional individual mastery. I see the world with almost all-round vision through a wide-screen windscreen as well as via two side-view mirrors and one rear-view mirror. Besides physical controls (operated with minimum physical exertion) I have ready access to a display of dials, gauges and one-touch switches. Driving seems an almost spontaneous extension of my bodily self – I inhabit it, I live it, it is a disposition so effectively assimilated that I say 'I drive', ignoring the car I do the driving with.

On the other hand, although notorious as 'private, enclosed' and 'individual' (Williams 1975, p. 356), car driving is a stunning instance of the dependence of the self on other people. To drive means that every micro-second I consign my life to the rationality, competence and good intentions of the Other. I have to trust that they will read the signs, obey the rules and observe the conventions as much as they trust I will do the same, checking the mirror before pulling out, stopping at red lights, and so on. To do it at all I have to believe I'm driving the car but it is as true to say that the car and the roadway system drive me.

A car driver, then, has a self he or she knows about yet that depends on another identity in which they are situated and positioned in ways they know little about. This book will explore national identity not as a set of images, figures and practices of which we are more or less conscious but rather as an unconscious structure. It is, in a sense, a post-colonial study of Englishness. While various Brits have been happy to write about other countries and cultures in the context of post-colonial theory, few such dispassionate eyes have been turned on the motherland. I shall try to write about English culture as if it were foreign to me.

In January 1996 Dr Nicholas Tate, Chief Executive of the School Curriculum and Assessment Authority, argued the need for schools to teach a particular 'canonical' account of English national history, giving a clear priority to the action of monarchs, prime ministers and military heroes in shaping the nation's destiny (this, by the way, was to be taught with an emphasis on strong narrative, simple use of biography, and confidence that history consisted of the communication of facts). The effect of the proposal to define Englishness like this was sardonically exposed by a cartoon published in the *Guardian* on 16 January. In a gloomy schoolroom a blackboard carried this parody of the Lord's Prayer:

> Our Churchill which art in Nelson
> Hallowed be thy Rhodes. Thy Gradgrind come.
> Thy Smiles be done in Kent as it is in Surrey.
> Give us this day our Daily Mail,
> And forgive us our Socialists, as we
> forgive them that organise against us (Not!)
> And lead us not into Trade Unionism,
> but deliver us from Scargill.
> For thine is the Jingo
> the Land of Hope and Glory,
> For ever and ever,
> School without Roof
> Amen.

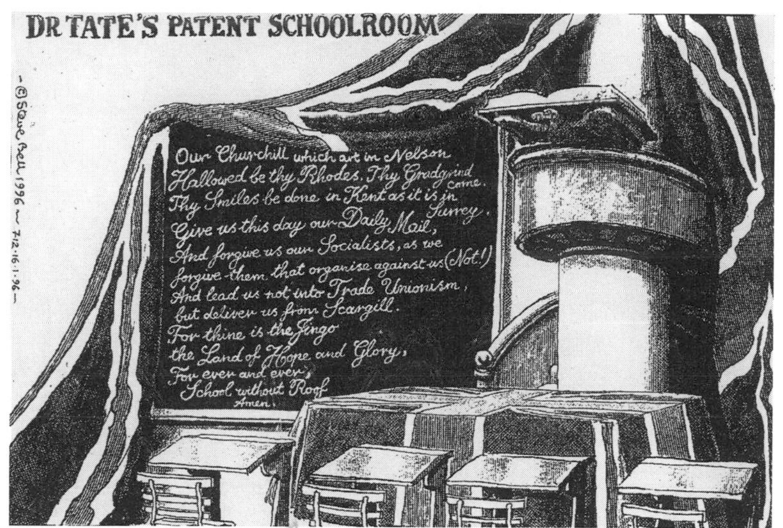

Figure 1.1 Steve Bell cartoon, 'Dr Tate's Patent Schoolroom'
Source: *Guardian*, 16 January 1996.

Tate's interpretation of English national identity and this mocking counter-interpretation show clearly how nation is imbricated with loaded definitions of class, region, gender, ethnicity and culture (see, for example, Parker *et al*. 1992) – this is nation at the same level at which the car driver knows about driving. But I want to explore the conjecture that national identity also works at deeper strata than simply the *content* of the various overtly national practices, narratives, discourses, symbols and tropes through which national identity is conventionally presented and where it always appears one-sided and in dispute. I am interested in nation as an identity that can speak us even when we may think we are speaking for ourselves.

Consider the following case. Two people from the same country meet abroad and talk for half an hour. They might be of the same class, gender, religious affiliation, ethnic background or they might be alike in none of these. Now there would be a number of ways of analysing their exchange. One would be to consider its particular content; another, the various class, gender and other identities which come into play for the conversants; or the aspects in which the conversation reflects international identities (as European, say, or Islamic).

From these various co-existent possibilities I shall concentrate on how the text of their exchange might follow the procedures of a national discourse, procedures which include:

- the assignment of priorities, both thematic and discursive;
- strategies for managing agreement and disagreement;
- the notion of truth presumed;
- how the serious and less serious are defined against each other;
- control of tone, transition between topics;
- tropes and figures used;
- jokes (these might be especially significant).

If after their chat the couple felt that they had shared in a common national identity, it would not be so much because of what they said but because of how they said it. My methodological principle here is close to that of the linguist, Ferdinand de Saussure, when he set out to examine language not in the infinity of particular utterances (*parole*) but as an underlying system (*langue*). How far can we understand nation as a particular discursive formation?

Three difficulties in analysing nation

Current debate places a number of obstacles in the path of an approach to nation; especially (and significantly) in an English context these are all founded in a belief that nation is somehow not material, not real.

Nation as class dominance

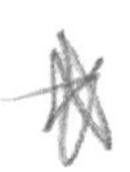

In the first place there is a widely held belief that nation is a form of ideology, that is, a way of thinking designed to promote the interests of a particular social group. According to this view, the idea of nation, the national state and national unity is a hegemonic deception perpetrated by the ruling class in order to mask its own power ('The working people have no country', as the *Communist Manifesto* famously proclaims, Marx and Engels 1950, 1, p. 44, and see also Davis 1978 and Nimni 1994). So national identity is not real because it's really just an exercise in class domination. As Raymond Williams asserts, with typical bluntness, 'The building of states, at whatever level, is intrinsically a ruling-class operation' (1983, p. 181).

It was Tom Nairn, who, drawing on Fanon's discussion of 'National Culture', in a path-breaking work of 1977, *The Break-Up of Britain*, opposed this one-sided and reductive view of nation. Contrasting 'negative' and 'positive' nationalism – on the one hand, Nazism soaked in the worst excesses of barbarism, on the other, the Vietnamese struggle for independence – Nairn argued that national identity was not just imposed from above but spontaneously supported from below, not just an ideology but something actually lived into, for example, in the fight for national liberation.

Since all nations must have a moment of origin, there is a respect in which nation derives from an exercise of force rather than democratic enactment. This emerged clearly when the new South Africa was founded, in fraught circumstances. On 2 May 1994 when Nelson Mandela first spoke as elected President of the new democracy, addressing himself to 'My fellow South Africans,' he affirmed, 'We might have our differences, but we are one people with a common destiny in our rich variety of culture, race and tradition' (see *Guardian*, 3 May 1994). In an essay on Nelson Mandela published seven years earlier Jacques Derrida had looked forward to this very moment.

Asserting that all human institutions originate in an act of violence Derrida suggests that probably 'such a *coup de force* always marks the foundation of a nation, state or nation-state' (1987, p. 18) but in a way which anticipates legitimacy, democracy and 'the general will' (p. 19). A particular rhetorical form suits this anticipatory mode. Mandela's assertion that 'we are a people with a common destiny', though it looks like a statement, is in fact a performative act, Derrida argues, 'recording what *will have been there*, the unity of a nation, the founding of a state, while one is in the act of producing that event' (p. 18). And the 'originating violence' attending the foundation of the nation-state 'is forgotten only under certain conditions' (p. 18).

In this account the violence inhering in state power never goes away but becomes forgotten – overlooked – in so far as the unity of a nation becomes a matter of the general will, as the state becomes supported by the people. Equation of constitutional legality with the general will is never complete though it will always remain a promise as to what will have been.

The birth of the new South Africa and Mandela's speech provide another insight into how nation can produce a largely involuntary consensus. On 22 May 1994 this letter from M.E. Jones appeared in the Natal *Sunday Tribune* (I am grateful to Michael Green of the University of Natal for showing it to me):

> I would like to extend my heartfelt thanks to President Nelson Mandela for a gift I didn't even know I wanted, until May 10, 1994.
>
> As part of probably one of the smallest minorities in this vast country (I am a white, suburban, thirty-something mother) I have never understood, let alone had any feelings of, nationalism

> and patriotism. I have never known what it is to identify with and feel part of a larger whole.
>
> For the first time in my life I am moved when I hear our anthem being played, or see that multicoloured horizontal Y fluttering in the breeze. I have been moved to tears more often this week than in my entire life; and those tears have been of profound joy at finally having a country to claim as my own.
>
> I would like to give a big thank you, from the bottom of my previously cynical and unpatriotic heart, to Mr Mandela, the African National Congress and all those wonderful South Africans who made it happen, for giving me a country to love.
>
> The depth and intensity of my national pride and love has taken me completely by surprise, but what a warm, wonderful, heart-stirring feeling it is.

How far this is an untypical or extravagant reaction time will tell but the new country will not break up while there is a widespread identification with it as strong as that expressed in this letter. To try to understand the nation-state *exclusively* in terms of class power exercised through the state is simplistic and reductive.

Nation as 'imagined community'

Marxist theories of nation are deficient not only in believing nation is imposed from the top but because in believing this they have assumed nationalism is an ideology and therefore, in some sense, just not real. Besides Tom Nairn, Benedict Anderson has done much to combat the view that nationalism should be classified 'as *an* ideology' when it is in fact a much wider, lived experience in a relation between social structures and subjectivity, more like kinship or religion or gender than something that should be treated as if it belonged 'with "liberalism" or "fascism"' (1991, p. 5).

However, Anderson is not able to come up with the account of nation as collective identity which his rejection of nation as ideology had shown to be necessary. In the absence of this he is driven to promulgate merely another version of nation as unreal when he claims they are 'imagined communities' (a view which has become something of an orthodoxy for theories of nation). Anderson is of course right to stress that nation, like the rest of human culture, is 'imagined' in the sense that it is constructed rather than the result of a natural process but this notion of 'imagined communities' is unsatisfactory, for two reasons.

Anderson cannot extricate himself from the conventional contrast of 'traditional' and 'modern' societies as an opposition between the real and the fake. The nation, he writes, is 'an imagined political community', '*imagined* (italics original) because the members of even the smallest nation will never know most of their fellow-members, meet them, or even hear of them, yet in the minds of each lives the image of their communion' (p. 6). Here 'the imaginary' is defined in a way which appears familiar and unremarkable to an English reader because it is empiricist – thus imaginary supposed in opposition to personal knowledge, direct encounter and being within actual earshot of another person (the kind of thing, in other words, that is sometimes thought to be so attractive about small and ancient 'organic' groupings).

But now the argument cuts back in a different direction, for Anderson goes on to assert that 'all communities larger than primordial villages of face-to-face contact (and perhaps even these) are imagined' (p. 6). The parenthesis '(and perhaps even these)' is obscure, and the generalisation itself evades the problem of what it is about human collectivities that might properly be described in terms of an opposition between real and imaginary. In the next sentence Anderson simply sidesteps the issue with an explicit statement that, 'Communities are to be distinguished, not by their falsity/genuineness, but by the style in which they are imagined' (p. 6). This conceptual muddle would not matter so much if his account subsequently went on to make clear what is meant by 'style' (if he means 'discourse', one might ask how he understands the concept). But his various explanations of nation as culture and 'style' (national language and print culture are important, nations take the place of a declining religion, and so on), suggestive as they are in a descriptive way, remain *ad hoc*, opportunistic and undertheorised.

This view of the pre-national community as real face-to-face contact contrasted with unreal national societies is embedded deep within British culture. It is starkly apparent when, for example, Raymond Williams comments that:

> 'Nation' as a term is radically connected with 'native'. We are *born* into relationships which are typically settled in a place. This form of primary and 'placeable' bonding is of quite fundamental human and natural importance. Yet the jump from that to anything like the modern nation-state is entirely artificial.
>
> (1983, p. 180)

And it is repeated by others – by Eric Hobsbawm when he refers to 'the unavailability of *real* human communities' and asks why having lost these, people should 'wish to imagine' nations as their replacement (1992, p. 46), by a leading theorist of nation, Anthony D. Smith, who replying to Anderson's arguments, goes along with the bland assumption that 'all communities larger than villages are imagined' (1993, p. 17).

This attitude to nation underwrites a nostalgic and sentimental desire to believe that face-to-face contact is real, free from interference by signs, language, 'writing', while opposed to this the larger, more impersonal groupings constructed by modernity are imaginary, false, unreal. In the pre-national culture, the lost organic community where everyone knows everyone else, people are supposedly directly present to each other without mediation while in the nation they are not.

That binary opposition cannot be sustained, as Jacques Derrida demonstrates with withering authority in his discussion of Rousseau and Lévi-Strauss. In a vigorous struggle to elude modernity, Rousseau puts forward the impossible idea of a community (in Derrida's words) which is 'immediately present to itself, without difference, a community of speech where all the members are within earshot' (1976, p. 136). But, alas, it is the case for every speaking subject that immediacy, spontaneity and direct presence are necessarily deflected and betrayed by the universalising, classificatory force of language. Alienation of this kind is inescapable in every human culture there has ever been. Any theoretical opposition which would contrast some notion of authentic identity with the inauthenticity of national identity has to be rejected.

Second, Anderson compounds his mistaken idea of nation as somehow fictional because he makes no attempt to theorise what might count as a materialist explanation of the nature and function of collective identity (of which national identity is his major instance). Who would disagree with Anderson when he observes that our feeling for organisations such as the Labour Party or Amnesty International, groups we can 'join or leave' at will (1991, p. 144) has very little charge compared to our love of nation, a group we have not chosen to join? Common sense furnishes him with no analysis of *why* this is so. Etienne Balibar makes a definitive comment on the limitations of Anderson when he proposes that we should

> dispense right away…with the antithesis between the 'real' and the 'imaginary' community. *Every social community reproduced by the functioning of institutions is imaginary*, that is to say, it is based on the projection of individual existence into the weft of a collective narrative, on the recognition of a common name and on the traditions lived as the trace of an immemorial past.
>
> (1991, p. 93)

For a better account of nation we need to understand collectivity, how individual existence is 'projected' into the collective.

Nation as real versus nation as spirit

A third problem for analysing nation follows from the prevalence of a binary opposition between objective and subjective aspects of historical development. One side of that binary, widely supported among sociologists and historians, affirms that economic, social and political forces are real while discourse, culture and identity are less so; they are spiritual, subjective, and so outside serious discussion.

In an introductory chapter to his magisterial collection on *Patriotism* Raphael Samuel treats the same binary as received opinion when he writes that: 'The idea of the nation, though a potent one, belongs to the realm of the imaginary rather than the real. It occupies a symbolic rather than territorial space' (1989, 1, p. 16).

In this domain of empiricist history-writing, where a theoretical perspective is assumed as already given, there is no place for discussion of problematic questions of the nature of collective identity issuing in nation or the difficulties that must arise from the presumed difference between nation as 'real' (equated with 'territorial space') and nation as 'imaginary' (inhabiting 'symbolic space'). Instead, over Samuel's four volumes there is a worthy but uninteresting preoccupation with such topics as 'Edwardian Militarism' or 'Kipling and Masculinity'.

One more brief but representative example. Linda Colley's recent book on the development of national feeling especially during the Napoleonic wars, *Britons: Forging the Nation, 1787–1837*, has received much acclaim. The characteristic inadequacy it represents lies in the assurance it shows in discussing what it treats as 'objective' factors in the forging of Britain during the period as against the incoherence and lack of serious theoretical interest it reveals when it comes (as it must) to a review of 'subjective' factors. In 'Conclusions' Colley asserts that war, liberty and Protestantism encouraged an impressive number of Britons to 'make the step from a passive awareness of nation to an energetic participation on its behalf' (1992, p. 371). For this to carry its intended weight we would need a clear understanding of exactly what distinction is being made between 'passive' and 'active', and between 'awareness' and 'participation' (at issue, then, is a change in people, in subjects and subjectivity). That discussion is not forthcoming. Lacking an explicit theory of a historicised subjectivity, work in this vein must rely by default on some unacknowledged idea of universal human nature.

These are instances of what could be called the 'left' deviation in nation theory, a belief that the economic and political are real while culture and identity are not (or not so real). Its contrary takes the form of the rightist view that national culture is *only* moral, spiritual and subjective. Here is one instance of how not to think about national identity. Jung wrote a classification of national character by listing the inherent characteristics of (for example) 'the Jew' and 'the German'. It was his view that 'the "nation" (like the "state") is a personified concept that corresponds in reality only to a specific nuance of the individual psyche…[The nation] is nothing but an inborn character' (1953–77, 10, p. 921).

And here is another, from an applied politics. On 24 March 1990 Mrs Thatcher, then Prime Minister, met with her Foreign Secretary and six academics (including Oxford professors) to discuss 'the German national character' with the aim of preventing German re-unification (another failed Thatcher project). Their procedure was to list defects in 'the German national character' in alphabetical order, beginning with 'aggressiveness', then running on through '*angst*', 'assertiveness', 'bullying', 'egotism', 'inferiority complex', until they reached 'sentimentality' where they gave up long before reaching 'xenophobia' or ever realising they might well have been talking about the English. The assembled experts were obviously unaware that the thinker best known for promoting belief in national culture as a purely ideal formation was himself a German. George Wilhelm Friedrich Hegel presumably tacked together his idea that nation was the highest realisation of Spirit on one of those afternoons when he was not overcome by *angst*, egotism or sentimentality.

My aim here will be to breach any inherited binary between objective and subjective, material and ideal. National cultures are material in that they are produced through institutions, practices and traditions which historians and sociologists can describe. But national cultures are also reproduced through narratives and discourses about which those social sciences feel inhibited but which recent work in theory makes a matter of coherent analysis.

Identity

Rastko Močnik (a former friend and intellectual colleague of Slavoj Žižek) writes that 'if you want to have a fair social science, then don't enter into the question of the individual subject; but you won't have a social science until you solve this very question' (1993, p. 139). The double bind he's pointing to is that the social sciences, including history, have generally established themselves as disciplines by putting in the foreground of their analysis an objective concern with institutions, practices, events, and all this would be prejudiced by opening the question of subjectivity; but how can these disciplines continue to claim status as science or systematic knowledge while ignoring a question they can't escape? All those who address nation, that crucial and problematic formation of human collectivity, must by necessity proceed on the assumption that subjects in some way can constitute themselves into groups. Here are some examples:

> a nation is a community which normally tends to produce a state of its own.
>
> (Weber 1948, p. 179)

> A portion of mankind may be said to constitute a Nationality if they are united among themselves by common sympathies which do not exist between them and any others.
>
> (Mill 1910, p. 359)

> A state is a legal and political organisation, with the power to require obedience and loyalty from its citizens. A nation is a community of people, whose members are bound together by a sense of solidarity, a common culture, a national consciousness.
>
> (Seton-Watson 1977, p. 1)

> A nation can therefore be defined as *a named human population sharing an historical territory, common myths and historical memories, a mass, public culture, a common economy and common legal rights and duties for all its members.*
>
> (Smith 1991, p. 14)

> I propose the following definition of the nation: it is an imagined political community – and imagined as both inherently limited and sovereign.
>
> (Anderson 1991, pp. 5–6)

Instead of these casual presumptions about collective identity, so close in their 'obviousness' to common sense, a proper analysis of nation requires some explicit analysis of what it means to be 'united...by common sympathies', 'bound together by a sense of solidarity', capable of 'sharing' memories, culture, etc., constituted as a 'community'. My own version of how a group works may not be acceptable to everyone but it does at least offer to explain collectivity identity and how it works. It is also explicit, and so may be disputed by those prepared to be equally explicit about their own conception of the group.

Some brief preliminaries. The human species, as Freud pointedly remarks, is 'more closely related to some species and more distant to others' (1953–74, 17, p. 141). On the one hand, no matter how kindly you nurture a baby chimpanzee you cannot install him or her into the human community as a speaking subject because, for all its closeness to *Homo sapiens*, even a chimpanzee does not have quite the same genes as we do. On the other hand, genes alone are not enough, as evidenced by those rare but documented cases of human infants reared by animals (pigs and wolves being the most usual foster parents). Not surprisingly, missing human culture, these feral children act, behave and sound like the animals they live with (see Hirst and Woolley 1982, pp. 44–60). A specific genetic inheritance and human culture are both necessary conditions for the development of human identity.

The Darwinian argument is that, in order to succeed, a species must develop not only instincts for survival, which (as many people know) Darwin monumentalised in *The Origin of Species* (1859) but also instincts for reproduction, which (not so well known) he wrote up in *The Descent of Man and Selection in Relation to Sex* (1871). Corresponding to the two instincts (German: *Instinkt*) for survival and reproduction Freud theorised narcissism and sexual desire as forms of drive (*Trieb*), instinct, that is, which has become signified or represented.

For Hegel identity unfolds in a dialectic with the Other, culminating in absolute self-consciousness in what is essentially an internal process of self-identification. To this idealist tradition, which conceives subjectivity as transcendental, psychoanalysis offers a radical alternative. Freud affirms that 'the ego has to be developed' (1973–86, 11, p. 69) and sets out a detailed account of the mechanisms through which the process takes place (mainly) as a form of narcissism. Along with the instincts for survival and reproduction, members of the human species evidence an equally strong drive to achieve a sense of individual identity – as G.A. Cohen argues, 'nothing is more essentially human' than 'the need for self identity' (1985, p. 154).

Since Freud, Jacques Lacan has emphasised the development of the ego as consequence of a process of internalisation in which the subject finds itself by identifying with the Other (one might think of a baby surrounded by loving adults desiring the best for it so that in response the little he or she can only want to be that best). In his discussion of the mirror stage as exemplifying the construction of identity Lacan points to what a toddler experiences between the ages of six and eighteen months, noting that the human infant responds to its mirror image 'with a flutter of jubilant activity' (1977a, p. 1) while other animals treat it with indifference. In its reflected image the subject aspires to an ideal of unity and permanence which it feels will make good its lack (*manque à être*), and identifies itself there. 'This form', Lacan proposes, 'situates the agency of the ego, before its social determination, in a fictional direction' (p. 2); that is, from its very inception the ego consists of an external image internalised and treated as the self in a process of misrecognition (the mirror stage anticipates the structure of lack and desire, which will be discussed in more detail in the next chapter).

Thus feral children become like the animals who nurture them, and, as is well known, children who are loved come to love themselves while those who are hated, hate themselves. Robert, in a case cited by Lacan, was born from an absent father and a mother who from the first neglected to wash, dress or feed him. He became so ill he was hospitalised, then returned to his mother, who abandoned him. Unremittingly violent towards others and towards himself, at the age of three years his main expression was to shout 'Wolf!'. Abhorred, he became this abhorrence. On one occasion '*seeing his own image in the glass, he hit it, crying out –* Wolf! Wolf!' (1988a, p. 95).

Those not already familiar with this psychoanalytic theory of the formation of identity might like to think of the mirror stage in relation to car driving. Thus a process (the car and road system) operates to produce a position and identity for the car driver; but the driver disavows the prior existence of this process, identifying rather with an idealised image of themselves as a full subject controlling a car. Lacan's account of how identity is borrowed from the Other and becomes the self would explain why children born in England generally grow up to be English while those born in Russia turn out to be Russian, and so on. And the same processes are at work in both the construction of individual and collective identity.

Collective identity

In his short book of 1921 on *Group Psychology and the Analysis of the Ego* Freud begins by noting that collective identity (including national identity) is precisely that, a group identity defined over and against what differs from it. Even individuals who like each other show some mutual hostility but in the collective that kind of intolerance vanishes: 'individuals in the group behave as though they were uniform, tolerate the peculiarities of its other members, equate themselves with them, and have no feeling of aversion towards them' (1973–86, 11, pp. 131–2).

It is as though the group is in possession of 'a sort of collective mind' (p. 99), what Freud later specifies as '*Gemeingeist*' (p. 152).

Although rational factors of interest and self-advantage help to produce this group effect, Freud wants to understand the 'emotional ties' and what he calls 'love instincts' (p. 120) at work in groups over and above rational factors. He argues that these are forms of drive which work through narcissism or self-love – members of a group identify with the same object and therefore enter into a common identification with each other. (By 'object' psychoanalysis does not mean a discrete entity in the everyday world but rather something which has become charged with unconscious significance for someone and so figures as possible satisfaction for a form of drive.)

Because his argument is that groups are founded in a version of self-love and because such narcissistic feeling is separate from sexual desire, Freud insists that collectivities are by nature non-sexual:

> In the great artificial groups, the Church and the army, there is no room for woman as a sexual object. The love relation between men and women remains outside these organisations. Even where groups are formed which are composed of both men and women the distinction between the sexes plays no part. There is scarcely any sense in asking whether the libido which keeps groups together is of a homosexual or of a heterosexual nature, for it is not differentiated according to the sexes.
>
> (p. 175)

Freud's explicit implication is that an individual must fall out of a group to return to his or her sexuality. Almost every English Second World War film presents a moment when a uniformed couple (invariably heterosexual) are thrown accidentally into close bodily contact by enemy action; as the 'All Clear' sounds they look into each other's eyes and discover a new meaning in their embrace; they then return to their duties.

In order to support his account of the group Freud reaches for an analysis of the individual subject. At first the infant subject identifies with its objects, and, as the child moves out of its first unity, it seeks to hold on to an idea of this former self at one with the world. This sense of yourself as you were and would like to be develops into the ego ideal, 'a critical agency within the ego' (p. 139). Division of the self between ego and ego ideal together with the tendency to regress to identification between subject and object – an effect Lacan takes as constitutive for the ego – can be illustrated through a number of not-unfamiliar psychological effects.

One is hypnosis, in which an object (the hypnotist) comes to take the place of the ego ideal, so the I follows commands coming from there. Another is melancholy, resulting perhaps from the death of a loved one, as in, say, the case of Hamlet and his father; the lost object may be kept alive for the subject if the I identifies itself with that object, though the condition for this is that the ego ideal (forerunner of the superego, the 'voice of conscience') becomes active in criticising and judging the I (Hamlet is given over to self-criticism). A third is what Freud calls 'being in love' and formulates as the principle that the object (the loved one) '*has been put in the place of the ego ideal*' (p. 144); in a young man's sentimental passion, for instance, 'the ego becomes more and more unassuming and modest, and the object more and more sublime and precious, until at last it gets possession of the entire self-love of the ego' (p. 143).

For Freud the non-rational aspect of a collective identity such as national identity works like hypnotism or falling in love. Individuals in a group '*have put one and the same object in the place of their ego ideal*' and have '*consequently identified themselves with one another in their ego*' (p. 147, italics original). He offers the diagram in Figure 1.2 (p. 147).

Freud discusses two examples. In a military organisation the common soldier takes the leader of the army as his ideal and identifies with his equals, in the Christian Church the ordinary Christian both idealises and identifies with Jesus. The external object need not be a person since, as Freud suggests, 'an idea, an abstraction' will do as well and may be the sign of a more advanced culture (p. 129) (Serge Moscovici has an extended and not unsympathetic account of Freud's theory but misses the view that an idea or abstraction may serve as a point of identification; see 1985, pp. 219–88).

The seeming fullness of collective identity in Freud's account is as much structured by lack as any individual identity. It is underwritten by

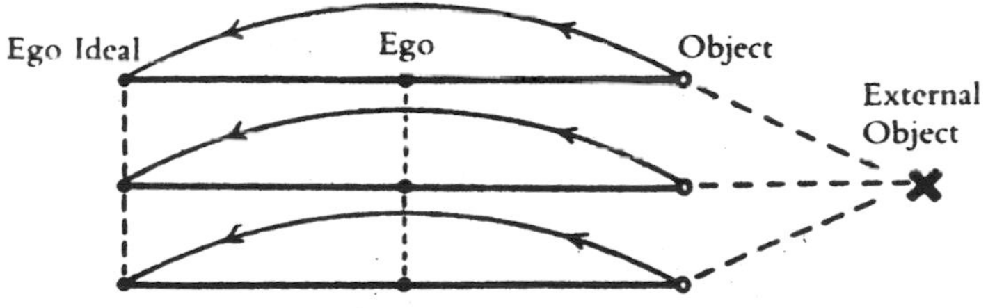

Figure 1.2 Diagram, from Freud's *Group Psychology and the Analysis of the Ego*

Jacques Lacan (who reproduces Freud's diagram with approval, 1977b, p. 272) because it substantiates his own analysis of the constitution of subjectivity. The object (say, the idea of nation) reflects a desired identity for the subject, as does the idealised image of unity and permanence found in the mirror in the mirror stage. Thus the object functions as the other, a place for recognition and identification, providing the subject with national identity in a double process: (1) through identification with the idea of nation; and (2) a simultaneous identification with others. In collective identification you feel you know what is expected of you.

John Ford's 1939 epic film, *Drums along the Mohawk*, which traces the struggle of the early immigrants to found the United States, ends with a variegated group – settlers, rootless Native Americans, farmers, soldiers and others – watching while a flag is paraded into their stockade. A man asks one of the soldiers what's going on and is told that the parading of the flag is a result of 'Cornwallis's surrender to Washington at Yorktown'. He says, 'So that's our new flag – the thing we've been fighting for' and learns that the thirteen stripes are for the colonies, the thirteen stars are for the union.

Another soldier appears and asks to take the flag for a minute; he climbs to the bell-tower at the top of the stockade and displays it there. Three different sets of figures look up at the flag – an elderly black servant, a white settler and his wife (Henry Fonda and Claudette Colbert, the main figures in the film's narrative), a Native American. Each of the figures is shown separately from a high-angle camera position, all are placed on the right of the screen looking up to the left out of shot. The interpretation is unmistakable. Since the national flag has become a common object for all of them, they are equated in a shared identification with each other.

Freud remarks that 'an idea, an abstraction' can easily constitute the object of common identification. My contention will be that *in addition* to all the well-known practices and institutions securing what Freud refers to as the 'rational' interests of members of a nation, and in addition to all the more evident objects of national identification (Nelson Mandela and 'that multicoloured horizontal Y' for the South African woman, a flag in *Drums along the Mohawk*, in the case of England, say, the monarchy), what at a less conscious level incites identification with nation is a particular and distinct discursive formation. Against the view of someone who might argue that identification with a form of discourse is labile, tenuous and weak, I would urge that it is in fact immensely strong since it is cognate with those primordial movements, constitutive for the species, in which the subject strives to win a place for itself within language and so become a speaking subject. And of course because collective identification is an active process, there can be no question that any individual subject's identification would ever be even or completed.

Identity and discourse

In default of a viable conception of the subject as self-unfolding, self-discovering and – ultimately – self-constituting, theoretical concern, especially since the 1960s, has explored various ways of thinking the subject as 'constructed' as an effect of discourse. I don't think I need to do more than touch on some of the main arguments here, as they follow particularly from Louis Althusser's well-known essay on ideology of 1970. Althusser asserts that all ideology has the function of '*"constituting" concrete individuals as subjects*' (1977, p. 160). By 'concrete individuals' Althusser means new-born babies; these are 'interpellated' by the practices and discourses of the particular culture they arrive into so that, as speaking subjects, they come to see its constructedness as obvious and natural. It is important to add to Althusser's analysis the qualification that the process of interpellation is never perfectly achieved.

How discourse affords an identity or position to its participant becomes a main emphasis in some versions of feminist theory which argue the importance of the possibilities of an *écriture féminine*. Perhaps more directly relevant for the analysis of a social formation, nation, are the accounts of how the form, operation and assumed parameters of certain discourses exert an unacknowledged power over and above any explicit content. One of the first of these is given in Edward Said's *Orientalism*.

The words for 'Orient' and 'Occident' originate simply in the Latin words for sun rising (*oriens*) and sun setting (*occidens*) so that strictly understood 'orient' and 'occident' are entirely relative to the position of the observer. However, as Said explains, a huge and embedded discursive regime, upheld by 'not only scholarly works but also works of literature, political tracts, journalistic texts, travel books, religious and philological studies' (1985, p. 23), has taken this necessarily mobile and relational positioning and transformed it into a fixity, specifying the 'Middle' and 'Far East' in relation to an originary point in Europe. From this imaginary centre Europe claims to be a subject able to know the non-European world, the 'Orient', as an object (in his epigraph to the book Said cites Marx, 'They cannot represent themselves; they must be represented').

This discursive structuring secures a particular notion of identity for the West: 'European culture gained in strength and identity by setting itself off against the Orient as a sort of surrogate and even underground self' (p. 3). Said refers to the apogee of Orientalist confidence with this sardonic summary:

> On the one hand there are Westerners, and on the other there are Arab-Orientals; the former are (in no particular order) rational, peaceful, liberal, logical, capable of holding real values, without natural suspicion; the latter are none of these things.
>
> (p. 49)

That is: the discursive formation of Orientalism establishes the Western subject in identification with a good image of itself ('rational, peaceful', etc.) through a process by which other feelings not compatible with this ideal are disavowed and projected on to an Oriental Other.

Other writers have followed Said's precedent in showing how, behind our backs, discourse acts as bearer of identity. H.L. Gates provides a major instance from discursive forms which were officially condemned and yet were actually transformed and transmitted into Modern English, a language different from those in which they originated. In *The Signifying Monkey* Gates argues for a continuity between forms of discourse from what is now known as West Africa and contemporary African-American rituals, linguistic practices, performative speech patterns and writing, specifically in the tradition of 'Signifyin(g)'. The two-mouthed divine trickster figure called Esu-Elegbara in Nigeria and Legba among the Fon in Benin, and the figure of the Signifying Monkey preside over a rhetorical and narrative tradition characterised by self-reflection and indeterminacy (*guije* or *jigue* in Afro-Cuban mythology represents, Gates remarks, 'a fascinating conflation of the Monkey and Esu'; 1988, p. 17).

'Everything that must be excluded for meaning to remain coherent and linear comes to bear in the process of Signifyin(g),' writes Gates, citing with approval the jazz musician Mezz Mezzrow's account of Signifyin(g) as a 'mode of "verbal horseplay"...which could apply equally to verbal texts and musical texts' (p. 69), as well as the work of the anthropologist Roger D. Abrahams, who lists nine features of Signifyin(g). Gates concludes that this mode consists of a 'language of trickery', a 'set of words or gestures which arrives at "direction through indirection"' (Gates 1988, p. 74). I shall resist the temptation to quote from Gates' examples of Signifyin(g), though it is not easy. Appearing both in the popular and high cultural tradition, Signifyin(g) corresponds to a discursive line running from sources in West African culture, through nineteenth-century African-American texts to a wide range of contemporary instances, as Gates shows. It is both consciously named tradition and informal inheritance.

Signifyin(g) bestows identity but without in any way claiming that identity as an essence. Since it is made available only in and through a discursive formation, it cannot belong to anyone: Signifyin(g) 'is a principle of language use and is not in any way the exclusive province of black people, although blacks named the term and invented the rituals' (p. 90). Gates invites others to appropriate his theoretical paradigm, mentioning in an aside that 'Perhaps critics of other literature will find this theory useful as they attempt to account for the configuration of texts in their traditions' (pp. xxiv–xxv). It is an invitation I shall accept in thinking about Englishness.

Identity unified or plural?

To approach nation as a form of identity made available in and through discourse (and so structured around lack) immediately puts in question one of the most insistent desires articulated about the idea of nation, that above all else nation constitute a *unity*. In a recent essay Jacques Derrida has stressed how a desire for circularity and self-enclosure may organise a nation's sense of itself. He opens up the question of national consciousness in terms of philosophy by proposing that a nation posits itself 'not only as a bearer of philosophy but of an exemplary philosophy, i.e. one that is both particular and potentially universal' (1992c, p. 10).

Derrida illustrates his argument with a close reading of Fichte's *Addresses to the German Nation* (1807–8) and particularly a passage in the seventh discourse:

> In the nation which to this day calls itself *the* people, or Germans, originality has broken forth into the light of day in modern times, at any rate up to now, and the power of creating new things has shown itself. Now, at last, by a philosophy that has become clear in itself, the mirror (the mirror the clarity of which the philosophy has achieved) is being held up to this nation, in which it may recognise and form a clear conception of that which it has hitherto become by nature without being distinctly conscious of it, and to which it is called by nature; and a proposal is being made to this nation to make itself wholly and completely what it ought to be, to do

> this according to that clear conception and with free and deliberate art, to renew this alliance, and to close the circle.
>
> (cited Derrida 1992c, p. 11)

The nation is called 'to make itself wholly and completely what it ought to be' not through a process of transition from one radically separate state to another but, as Derrida explains, merely by a shift in awareness so that what was already there 'by nature' becomes 'distinctly conscious'. This 'relation between unconscious philosophy and conscious philosophy is a *circular* relation' (p. 12, italics original), a nation imagining itself as an absolute and undivided self-presence (this is one reason why Derrida remarks elsewhere 'there is no nationality or nationalism that is not religious or mythological, let us say "mystical" in the broad sense', 1994, p. 91).

The unity which nation, on this showing, conceives itself to be is impossible. Within the register of philosophic discourse (more or less) Derrida could refer the impossibility of any such self-presence to the priority of difference as its condition of existence. But that impossibility can be demonstrated, perhaps even more compellingly, according to the logic of subjectivity preferred here. National unity, nation as unity, is an effect. It is an effect, first of all, of the process of collective identification with a common object which is accompanied by identification of individuals with each other. And, as a pre-condition for this effect, there is already the process within the individual subject in which an identity, mirrored from the Other and never more than provisionally fixed, is treated as the self (it is interesting that Fichte also reaches for the image of the mirror to exemplify the achieved unity of the nation). Unity of identity is an imaginary consequence of the symbolic process which produces it, like that in which the car driver overlooks the road system believing that he or she drives the car. Similarly, a sense of national identity comes about when a set of signifiers are endowed by fantasy with meaning.

Identity, in this conceptualisation of identity, arises as a necessary coherency which can never escape the operation of which its temporary fixity is an effect. In this sense all identity is plural and disjunct; all identity (one might say) is queer identity, including national identity. Slavoj Žižek puts it very well when he says, 'the final answer is of course that *nobody* is fully English, that every empirical Englishman contains something "non-English" – Englishness thus becomes an "internal limit", an unattainable point which prevents empirical Englishmen from achieving full identity-with-themselves' (1991b, p. 110). Englishwomen too, onc may add. And in *Strangers to Ourselves* Julia Kristeva calls on the theory of the unconscious to lead her argument to the conclusion that 'The foreigner is within me, hence we are all foreigners' (1991, p. 192) (and it should not be missed that this argument also cuts against any belief that groups have a real and authentic identity in comparison with which national identity can be measured and dismissed as 'artificial').

If identity is conferred in and by discourse and since discourse is by nature differential, dispersed and plural, it would follow that, no matter what national identity claims for itself, it can never be more than one among many. Empirically it seems obviously the case that each of us performs a number of identities. Besides the family, identities extend in overlapping circles into work and leisure, ethnic and sub-cultural identities as well as local and regional ones and, above the national register, continental and potentially international identities. This is certainly Freud's view when he writes in *Group Psychology*:

> Each individual is a component part of numerous groups, he is bound by ties of identification in many directions, and he has built up his ego ideal upon the most various models. Each individual therefore has a share in numerous groups' minds – those of his race, of his class, of his creed, of his nationality, etc.
>
> (1973–86, II, p. 161)

The individual, then, is an effect of multiple identifications.

Noam Chomsky introduced the idea of linguistic competence: to become competent in some of the forms of a national discourse, to become familiar and habituated to that discourse is, I suggest, to become competent in that identity, unconsciously taking on something of it as oneself, just as an identity as a car driver is acquired not by passing a test but by doing it until you hardly think about it any more. Surely, then, all such identities are multiple? If I was born and brought up in England I may mainly identify myself as English; but if as a child I am taken for some time to Ireland I will have to live into that identity; later, spending two years teaching in the United States I will become versed in American discourse; offered the chance to work for six months in Kenya I come back with part of myself Kikuyu; if I learn Italian and go on holiday to Italy in the summer, to that extent I become Italian; and so on.

Paul Gilroy writes: 'I am not against the nation…I am against the rhetoric of cultural insiderism, because I think it is too readily limited to unacceptable ideas of homogeneous national culture and exclusionary national or ethnic belonging' (1993, p. 72).

If identity is understood as an effect of discourse, national identity in a national culture can never achieve the unified homogeneity it wishes for itself. It may be less heartening to admit that the same line of argument entails there can be no escape from identity (except into psychosis or death); and further that all identity defines itself precisely by establishing an inside and an outside so that *all* identity to a degree practises insiderism together with an exclusionary force. These are questions I will come back to in a final chapter.

Language versus discourse

Although the connection between national identity and a national language seems obvious, in fact the relation is not straightforward at all (in the first place some nations – Canada, Switzerland – have more than one national language). The affinity between Englishness and English has tempted writers to claim a special genius for the English language. G.C. Swayne, for example, fancied that the English language itself was constructed on empiricist principles, 'like the English constitution…and perhaps also the English Church, full of inconsistencies and anomalies, yet flourishing in defiance of theory' (cited Crowley 1989, p. 78).

Such views do not make linguistic sense. The foundation of any language is a particular and limited selection of sounds which are defined through contrastive opposition to each other. These phonemes, smallest unit systematised by a language, have an entirely arbitrary relation to meaning. The phonemes or signifiers of a language do not provide the basis for any claims at all about the 'nature' of that language.

Nevertheless, there is a respect in which someone's first or native language does confer a sense of national identity. In 1862 Edward Lear sent a nonsense letter to Evelyn Baring, beginning, 'Thrippsy pillivinx, Inky tinky pobblebockle abblesquabs?' and ending, 'ramsky damksy crocklefether squiggs'. Jean-Jacques Lecercle points out that even though he may not understand what this means, he knows it is written using the phonemes peculiar to Modern English.

Because of habit and use these sounds become specific to a person who learns them as their first language (and may in turn influence palatal development). Of his Lear example Lecercle admits that, even 'if I pronounced it in my best Maurice Chevalier accent, I would be conscious of letting the text down' because it takes 'a lifetime of pronouncing "th" sounds, to utter "crocklefether squiggs" in the correct fashion' (1990, p. 2). And if Lecercle fears his version of the English 'th' would reveal he did not practise it from the cradle, so, with greater reason, might the Irish Mr Graves in Beckett's novel, *Watt*: 'Mr. Graves pronounced his *th* charmingly. Turd and fart, he said, for third and fourth. Watt liked these venerable Saxon words' (1963, p. 142). The lifetime needed to speak your own language (or languages) begins at birth.

As Lecercle goes on to remark, a first language differs from any other second or acquired language because we picked it up 'naturally', without formal instruction, at an age when it could become intimately associated with our earliest identifications. In principle nothing distinguishes the signifiers of Modern English from those of any other language but contingently, for native speakers, they mean the 'mother tongue'.

All my examples occur in Modern English and come from printed sources, and most (but not all) take the form of Standard English. Neither of these linguistic features – Modern English, Standard English – are neutral, for they have accumulated cultural force by being promoted over a denigrated other. Thus Modern English began as the East Midland dialect of Middle English which, because of the rise of London, triumphed over the Southern, Northern and West Midland dialects (just as – I guess – the Southern Californian accent is emerging via CNN as the likely world media accent of the English language). Later, as part of the idea of England-as-Britain, Modern English wins out against the Welsh language or Gaelic (Scots or Irish).

Operating with a uniform spelling, and a consistent vocabulary and syntax, Standard English exercises a hegemony over regional varieties as well as other class or ethnic dialects. It does so precisely because it appears to suppress linguistic features marked in these varieties. Consequently it can affirm itself as uniformly English, equal to and measured against similarly delimited notions of the French or Italian language. Standard English becomes the vehicle of the English literary canon which (give or take a few strange Elizabethanisms in Shakespeare) accordingly would prove its Englishness because it is in Standard English.

But if we thought the national language as Standard English was sufficient to define national identity we would be stuck with an idea of nation as partial and imposed hegemony corresponding to the theoretical error of understanding nation as class dominance. Preoccupation with language in thinking about nation obscures the crucial distinction between *language* and *discourse*.

As Emile Benveniste points out, 'Sentences have neither distribution nor use…with the sentence we leave the domain of language as a system of signs and enter into another universe…whose expression is discourse' (1971, p. 110). While the notion of 'language' governs the ordering of phonemes, morphemes and words (lexemes), and their syntactical organisation into correctly formed sentences, the concept of 'discourse' is directed at the way sentences become linked together to form a consecutive and cohesive order, taking part in a greater whole which is homogeneous as well as heterogenous. While language specifies usage up to the level of the *sentence*, discourse is concerned with how one sentence follows another.

Englishness, so I shall argue, is inscribed in the various national discourses which *run across* Modern English whether it occurs in a written or oral form, as Standard English or 'deviations' from it (at least two of my examples are non-Standard). Evidence for the non-correlation between language and discourse comes from the history of Modern English and its rapid ascendency towards becoming the world language.

In 1500 about 4 million people spoke English, rising to around 30 million in 1800. Today one in five of the world's population can speak Modern English. Modern English already occurs variously in United States, Australian, Canadian, Indian, Kenyan and South African versions, as well as many, many others, with only small local variations in vocabulary and pronunciation. But each of these uses of a common language embodies a particular national culture in a specific discursive formation. I suspect that English empiricism has some degree of overlap with the pragmatism of the United States, and that the deployment of irony in English humour has a cognate relation to the harsh irony in Australian national culture. Differences remain, however, and it is these I want to bring to prominence, differences which are carried in the more intimate, lived and apparently trivial aspects of our identity and experience, those present, say, in the contrast between 'Bugs Bunny' and 'Winnie the Pooh'. Beyond questions of language it is the discursive formation that matters and that should be the object of critical study.

'This sceptr'd isle' and other questions

Successfully invaded in 1066 by 'a class of rulers already organised as a cohesive political-military unit' (Wood 1991, p. 27), England was soon established as a unified state with a common law and administration, a common coinage, and, increasingly after the fourteenth century, a common language. England, not Britain. When John of Gaunt in Shakespeare's play of the 1590s speaks glowingly of England as a 'sceptr'd isle' he silently incorporates Wales and Scotland into his 'England'. Rebuffed during the sixteenth and early seventeenth century in its attempts to advance into continental Europe, England turned north and west, to colonise the Scots and complete colonisation of the Welsh, moving on then to Ireland (1536: Wales united to England in matters of law; 1707: Act of Union with Scotland; 1801: Act of Union with

Ireland). This territory became Britain, its island borders clearly demarcating its conveniently small territorial limits, easy to protect with naval power. This left Ireland worryingly both inside and outside the mainland, an always uncertain backdoor as far as the English perceived it.

Imperialist cultures must claim they are doing what they have to do in the name of some universal idea rather than a narrow, national interest (for illustration one might recall the United States' contribution to 'Band Aid' in 1985: a group of Americans singing 'We are the world'). So, to become an imperial power, a nation must sacrifice part of its national particularity. This is what happened when the idea of 'Britain' became promoted as a more general name to include the other nations subjected by the colonising power of England – something of Englishness had to be given up.

Some time after 1973 I went to a Chile Solidarity meeting at which exiled Chileans wore national costume, danced national dances and sang national songs. How, it made me wonder, if I was ever forced into political exile, would I perform my Englishness? Under the conditions of modernity people need a national identity and so a desirable side-effect of my analysis here will be to isolate and retrieve aspects of a specifically English identity.

Even after the Norman Conquest England did not acquire a system of jurisprudence based on a written legal code (and derived ultimately from Roman law). English common law in the form of case law prevailed. Whether or not that helps to explain the origins of the English tradition as empiricist, it is to a notion of empiricism I shall turn as a way to offer a definition of the English discursive formation. During the 1960s the New Left worked out a critique of the English tradition on the basis of its empiricism. This analysis has not really been followed through as it deserves.

Given the preceding theoretical commitments and limited parameters, a comparative study would be preferable – of the national cultures of, say, England, France and the United States. I'm going to have to leave that to others. Nor, in concentrating on the English tradition, am I going to run past a succession of well-known mileposts along the line followed by Raymond Williams in *Culture and Society* (1961, from Burke to Bentham and Coleridge, to Carlyle and Arnold, and on to Eliot and Orwell) or, in another accent, by Basil Willey in *The Seventeenth-Century Background* (1962a), *The Eighteenth-Century Background* (1962b) and *Nineteenth-Century Studies* (1964). Another slog through 'the English moralists' would be neither interesting or instructive, and demonstrating their commitment to empiricism would be repetitive and perhaps too easy.

It is important that my corpus for analysis should consist of other kinds of more varied and informal discourses than the serious and high-flown. At the same time I want to engage with the contemporary in order to make some intervention in the present. So, after a general chapter on nation, there will be a section on the mainstream tradition of English empiricist writers (Bacon, Hobbes and Locke) in Chapter 3, followed by another more wide-ranging discussion of English discursive forms in Chapter 4. All of this will be set up as a template against which to measure and assess a number of texts from contemporary discourses, two areas which are (roughly) factual (history-writing and journalistic literary criticism) and two fictional (two modern novels, one tragic and one comic, followed by the dominant mode in contemporary English poetry). I shall be concerned mainly with a discursive formation as the *practice* of a form of discourse (through attempted transparency, irony, etc.) but also with the explicit *idea* of a discourse of that kind (Locke, for example, exemplifies clarity of style while advocating it).

Ellen Meiksins Wood (and she is not the first) implies 'that British political culture has remained rooted in the seventeenth century' (1991, p. 69). By picking up the two ends I anticipate showing there is a link, a deep, underground continuity, between textual innovations of the period 1650–1700, the great foundational moment for Englishness, and contemporary forms; that Pope's ironies are alive and well in higher journalism today, Miltonic pathos in George Orwell, Dryden's comic satire in David Lodge. One might expect that a culture which has not experienced traumatic disruption since 1660 would retain the structure of its signifying chains unaltered into the present. How we might reconsider a persisting matrix of this kind will be a topic for the conclusion.

Nation beyond analysis?

Derrida asserts that nationality is religious, mythological or ' "mystical" in the broad sense': it is only too easy to adduce evidence that many people, including some who should know better, have gone along with the idea of nation as absolutely ineffable, unsayable, beyond analysis:

> Charles Maurras remarked that no Jew, no Semite, could understand or handle the French language as well as a Frenchman proper; no Jew, he remarked, could appreciate the beauties of Racine's line in *Bérénice*: '*Dans l'orient désert quel devint mon ennui*'.
>
> (cited Kedourie 1961, p. 72, no source given; the verse occurs at line 234 in the play)

> I stand for an Irish civilisation based on the people and embodying and maintaining the things – their habits, ways of thought, customs – that make them different – the sort of life I was brought up in.... Once, years ago, a crowd of us were going along the Shepherd's Bush Road when out of a lane came a chap with a donkey – just the sort of donkey and just the sort of cart that they have at home. He came out quite suddenly and abruptly and we all cheered him. Nobody who has not been an exile will understand me, but I stand for that.
>
> (Michael Collins, cited Minogue 1967, pp. 22–3)

> [the effect of] the words 'Earth to earth, ashes to ashes, dust to dust' ... comes from an as-it-were ancestral 'Englishness'.... The passage [from Thomas Browne's *Urne-Buriall*] can bring goose-flesh to the napes only of English-readers.
>
> (Benedict Anderson 1991, pp. 145, 146)

> I have lived through some of these disasters. Like many other people, I was brought face to face with these questions in that summer of 1940 – which by an irony of fate was gloriously hot, radiant with sunshine, flowers and joie de vivre. We the defeated, trudging the unjust road towards a suddenly-imposed captivity, represented the lost France, dust blown by the wind from a heap of sand. The real France, the France held in reserve, *la France profonde*, remained behind us. It would survive, it did survive.... Ever since those days, already so long ago, I have never ceased to think of a France buried deep inside itself, within its own heart, a France flowing along the contours of its own age-long history, destined to continue, come what may.
>
> (Fernand Braudel 1988, 1, pp. 24–5)

There is a great deal that might be said about the effects and rhetoric, the references and tropes, that these citations draw upon in their open-mouthed attention to an event that defies explanation, the truth about a nation which survives invisibly (no matter what), and, significantly, how a native responds with peculiar insight to a special kind of language. All I want to claim is that nation, even in its most apparently profound and inexpressible moments, cannot escape expression in signifiers, and the signifier is susceptible to rational analysis. If nation is the collective identity we incur from modernity, surely we should not continue to think about it in pre-modern modes?

Nation and the present writer

It is no surprise that the topic of nation comes so close to those who write about it that they feel compelled to break the usual decorum of academic impersonality and say something about themselves. In the examples I have collected these lapses into autobiography also illustrate how plural national identity is:

> At this point the author must admit that there are limits to the detachment which is his usual aim. Descended from generations of Scots and Irish, but with a working life lived, like that of my parents, mostly in England, I cannot think that the break-up of Britain could be anything but a disaster.
>
> (Seton-Watson 1977, p. 487, fn. 19)

> The present author, for instance, is identified as a Londoner when in the north of England, an Englishman when in Scotland, a European when in Africa, a Canadian when crossing the 49th parallel, a white when in Harlem, and a middle-class male almost everywhere.
>
> (Birch 1989, p. 6)

> Perhaps someone who is part Welsh, part English, Transatlantic in lifestyle and European by choice – as well as British – may be allowed to express the hope that, if Britishness survives (and it may not), it will in the future find a more pragmatic and more generous form.
>
> (Colley 1992, p. 9)

> The present writer recalls being submitted to such a piece of (unsuccessful) political invention in an Austrian primary school of the middle 1920s, in the form of a new national anthem desperately attempting to convince children that a few provinces left over when the rest of a larger Habsburg empire seceded or was torn from them, formed a coherent whole, deserving love and patriotic devotion.
>
> (Hobsbawm 1992, p. 92)

To these I add my own contribution:

> My father was English but my mother was Irish, born in Tralee, Co. Kerry. To escape the bombing in 1943 I was taken

> to Ireland. One of my earliest memories is being hunted down the street by a gang of kids chanting 'Proddy-Woddy Good God' (this was how I learned that I was a Protestant). In Ireland I was mocked for my English accent; a year later back in England for my Irish accent. At university when I read Jean-Paul Sartre saying that identity was a role we each impersonate I embraced it as simple common sense.

My own positioning, secure neither within Englishness nor Irishness, helps me put nation at an appropriate critical distance, though it would be a mistake to go on from there to think one could write as though one stood securely outside nation. And in a study which aims to show that Englishness is carried and reproduced by a specific form of discourse, the question of chosen stylistic is one of some delicacy. Would it be possible to construct the whole argument in a high-theoretical or 'Althusserian' style? Or should I aim for a kind of sci-fi cyberspeak as though the text were generated by a desiring machine? In fact, I have found it impossible to escape the very modes I identify as English – including some particular binary oppositions, a certain kind of colloquialism together with 'empiricist' irony. In hoping for accessibility this study risks complicity with the very discourse it would criticise.

Derrida has words of comfort for those in this situation. 'The movements of deconstruction', he writes, 'do not destroy structures from the outside'; it is not possible to work 'except by inhabiting those structures' but the aim must be to inhabit them '*in a certain way*'; because of course 'one always inhabits, and all the more when one does not suspect it' (1976, p. 24). This is reassuring but it should alert one to effects of signification which can so easily slip past, in particular *tone*.

A traumatic experience is one the subject repeats because he or she cannot work it through. Today, more than one nation carries something on its back it cannot see: Germany (Nazism), Russia (Stalin), France (Vichy), the United States (Vietnam). England still can neither face nor forget the Empire and loss of Empire. In what I shall later argue is a very English mode, the English continue to repeat Empire through irony – an irony which recognises its inevitability and at the same time mourns the loss.

As so often sport, because it is informal and unofficial, provides the revealing instance. In the summer of 1996, during the European Football Championships held in Britain, the *Radio Times* for 15–21 June produced a cover advertising the key match between England and Scotland to be played on Saturday 15 June 1996 under the headline, ENGLAND EXPECTS. A couple of days later, at the other end of the newspaper market, the *Guardian* (20 June 1996) contrasted Italy's failure to qualify with England's hopes from the semi-final with the phrase, 'As England expects, Italy laments'.

The words retrace the memory of Nelson's famous signal to his ships at Trafalgar: 'England expects this day that every man shall do his duty'. But they retrace them with an irony which combines admission that Empire is rightly gone for good with a certain covert nostalgia. In writing about Englishness I shall call on that sense of critical distance from the Imperial Nation which is available – and obligatory – at the *fin de millénaire*. And I shall be alert to preventing the other side of the discourse from coming through. This strategy may not wholly succeed.

My purpose is to exhibit national identity as a discursive effect and so as part of culture, not nature. At this point it is usual to run up once more against the idea that compared with historical institutions, for example, language and discourse are temporary, fragile and evanescent, like a sentence from yesterday's newspaper. That may be true at the level of content. But at its deeper levels, in the way things are said and written, in its *formal* operations, discourse is as solid as a rock, substantial, massively resistant to change, so that if it is transformed, huge areas of historical experience are transformed along with it.

Jacques Lacan proposes that 'the slightest alteration in the relation between man (*sic*) and the signifier…changes the whole course of history (*le cours de son histoire*, "the course of his history") by modifying the moorings that anchor his being' (1977a, p. 171). In this respect (and drawing on another register) it may be appropriate to think of discourse as what Wittgenstein has in mind when he writes of a language as 'a form of life' (1968, para. 19). This present study will tend to confirm a view of the signifier as an anchor rather than a flag.

2

NATIONAL DESIRE

> The idea of the nation is the most materialist of ideas.
>
> (Régis Debray 1977, p. 29)

Nineteenth-century commentators on the national question – Lord Acton, Ernest Renan, John Stuart Mill – have nothing like the authority of (say) Marx for political economy or Peirce for semiology. In the nineteenth century the question of nation 'never produced its own grand thinkers' (Anderson 1991, p. 5) because it was not then a crucial political issue. In the last decade of the twentieth century we are better placed – beyond the great epoch of European nations, after two World Wars fought largely around the principle of the nation-state, followed, in the period from 1945, by a world-wide anti-colonial movement whose liberationary struggles were powerfully nationalist in inspiration. The owl of Minerva flies only in the dusk, after the event; Charles Tilly points out, 'as is so often the case, we only begin to understand this momentous historical process – the formation of national states – when it begins to lose its universal significance' (1994, p. 254). Care needs to be taken here, however; it may not be the nation-state as such but only the *formation* of nations and the period of their triumphalist self-acclamation which, having passed, permit us a retrospective understanding.

Currently, books on nation appear at the rate of almost one a week (see, for example, Hutchinson and Smith 1994, Balakrishnan 1996). And yet, for reasons anticipated in Chapter 1, these generally do not – or do not satisfactorily – address what seems to me the inescapable question: the passion and desire which lie at the heart of nation (the word 'desire' itself is enough to strike terror into the heart of any decent-minded sociologist or historian). Yet historical study would be failing in its task of affording historical understanding if it cannot provide a satisfactory analysis of the causes, meanings and effects of a text such as the following, Stendhal writing of the year 1794 in his *Life of Napoleon*:

> In our eyes, the inhabitants of the rest of Europe who fought to keep their chains were pitiable imbeciles, or rascals in the pay of the despots who attacked us. *Pitt* and *Coburg*, whose names are still heard repeated in the old echo of the Revolution, seemed to us the leaders of those scoundrels and the personification of everything that was treacherous and stupid in the world. Everything was then dominated by a deep feeling of which I can no longer see any trace. If he is less than 50, let the reader imagine to himself, according to the books, that in 1794 we had no sort of religion at all; our deep and inner feelings were compounded in this one idea: *being useful to our country*.
>
> Everything else – clothing, food, promotion – were in our eyes only miserable and ephemeral details. As there was no society, being *socially successful*, so important an element in the character of our nation, did not exist for us.
>
> In the street, our eyes would fill with tears on coming across a wall inscription in honour of the young drummer boy Barra (who got himself killed at thirteen years of age rather than stop beating his drum, in order to prevent a surprise attack). For us who knew no other social world, these were festivals, numerous and touching ceremonies, which came along to nourish the sentiment which dominated everything in our hearts.
>
> It was our religion. When Napoleon appeared to put an end to the continual blunders to which the dreary government of the Directory exposed us, we saw in him only the *military utility* of dictatorship. He gave us victories, but we judged all his actions by the rules of the religion which, from our first childhood, made our hearts beat faster. We saw nothing admirable in it but *utility to our country*.
>
> (Stendhal, *Vie de Napoléon*, cited Minogue 1967, pp. 49–50)

Although Stendhal writes with ironic detachment about his younger self – and a self caught up in violent action – his words pose vividly the question of nation and national identity. What is the content and force of this repeated 'we' in which 'we' are defined by excluding 'them' ('everything that was treacherous and stupid'), an identification with the idea of the nation ('*being useful to our country*') which entails common identification of one with another (ending in communal tears for 'the young drummer boy')? What is this desire for nation which supplants and surpasses other collective identities as a totalising and overriding preoccupation, becoming 'our religion' so we 'knew no other social world'? How should we understand this process of identification national desire incites? How to make sense of a collective identity which so ruthlessly demarcates an inside from an outside?

An Anglo-Saxon willingness to treat such questions on the basis of a set of oppositions in which objective/subjective is equated with fact/fiction may itself count as evidence of the empiricism this present study would illustrate – in the English tradition such assumptions have an ancestry stretching back to Hobbes (a topic for Chapter 3). Symptomatic of the strength of this inheritance is the frequency with which Ernest Renan as a theorist of nation falls on the sharp edge of these binary oppositions, is named and then dismissed with ironic contempt as someone who just cannot be serious.

Renan's lecture, 'What is a nation?', delivered in Paris in 1882, begins by listing possible common features in a nation – origin in conquest by a dynasty, race, language, religion, community of material interest, geography. Each of these Renan discards, affirming instead that a nation is 'a soul, a spiritual principle', defined by two things:

> One is the possession in common of a rich legacy of memories; the other is present-day consent, the desire to live together, the will to perpetuate the value of the heritage that one has received in an undivided form.
>
> (1990, p. 19)

Renan, in other words, defines nation primarily in terms of culture, both as a national narrative ('memories') and as an effect of common identification which provokes 'the desire to live together'.

Historians in Britain typically discard Renan's doctrine as 'inadequate' (Kedourie 1961, p. 81), 'a definitional defeat' (Minogue 1967, p. 11), 'purely subjective' and thus 'not very helpful' (Birch 1989, p. 6); his views constitute 'a metaphysical abstraction unembodied in time and space' (Royal Institute of International Affairs (RIIA) 1963, p. 261). Following similar logic, the communal feeling for nation is said elsewhere to be 'the abstraction of the nation' into a 'fantasy' that has only a 'tenuous connection with the concrete national life' (p. 23); another writer maintains that the 'symbols' for a national group are 'fictional' and matter 'little compared to the fact that the group exists' (Harris 1992, p. 11); it is claimed that any attempt to analyse desire for nation in terms of 'the need for identity' should be rejected on the grounds that it merely 'posits a universal, non-rational entity' (Breuilly 1982, p. 33).

This attitude is well epitomised when one commentator remarks in a derisive tone that the feeling for nation is like 'falling in love' (Harris 1992, p. 15). To this I would reply that falling in love is as real and material as anything else human beings do, point out Benedict Anderson's assertion that 'nations inspire love' (1991, p. 141), and recall that Freud discusses 'being in love' as an effect structured in the same way as collective identification, for in both cases an object (the loved one, nation) is put in the place of an ego ideal. If, as the passage from Stendhal strongly implies, the passionate desire for nation is like falling in love, there is no avoiding some attempt to say what is at stake in the psychoanalytic understanding of desire. While the conventional view is that desire is a matter of pleasure and satisfaction, desire considered as a unconscious effect is defined by a lack which cannot be made good.

Lacan offers to describe Being and Meaning as opposites excluding each other in a Venn diagram (1977b, p. 211), see Figure 2.1.

A new-born infant is completely at one, oblivious of any difference between itself and the surrounding world, so presumably locked within being. Growing into language, however, the subject accedes to the world of meaning, which is the possession of other people, the Other. If I stayed within being I would remain completely myself but my life would have no meaning; entering language I begin to have meaning but only because my being disappears into language – I can only say things that *anyone* could say.

The relation between being and meaning (my being, my search for meaning) is dynamic, it is one of desire. The individual subject tries to refind within meaning that most intimate and real part of itself that seemed present to it in being but which got lost in the transition to

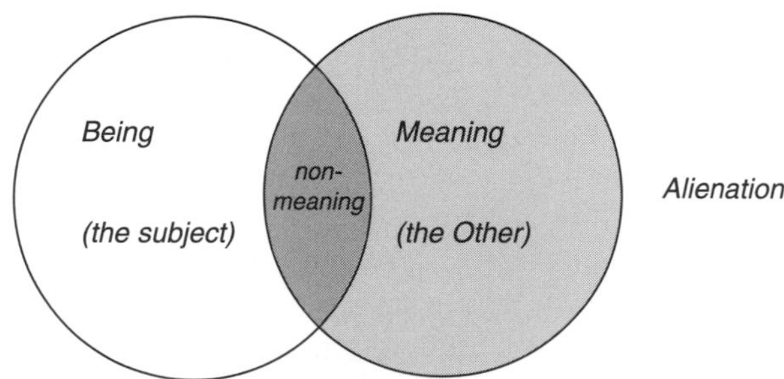

Figure 2.1 Venn diagram of 'Being' and 'Meaning'
Source: From Lacan's *Four Fundamental Concepts of Psychoanalysis.*

meaning (it survives, Lacan suggests, in the unconscious, represented in the diagram by the cross-hatched area of 'non-meaning'). This lack in being (*manque-à-être*) is the cause of desire, which can never be satisfied because it is constituted as desire for what is missing. In this definition national desire is desire for a being nation seems to offer but can never provide.

A recent discussion has remarked that:

> One of the basic challenges still confronting theories of the nation is to bring together the subjective with the objective, that is, to synthesize an understanding of national consciousness, nationality and nationalism as entailing certain forms of subjectivity, with an approach to the nation, the nation-state, and the nationalist movement as objective forms of social relations.
>
> (James 1996, p. 7)

We do indeed need to move beyond accounts based in a crippling opposition between the categories of the objective and the subjective. While it would not be wrong to think of psychoanalytic theory as positing analysis of a universal, non-rational identity, it is also crucial to recognise that subjectivity is always specified and realised historically. While turning to a summary of theories of nation as an objective, historical phenomenon, I shall be ready to recall the explanation of collective identity offered in the previous chapter. I shall propose, in fact, that this account is necessary to explain the intense and sometimes devastating force of national desire as it emerges with modernity, produced in a relay between subjectivity and historical events, practices and institutions.

Historical definition of nation

To develop an argument around the idea of nation one does not need an essential definition of nation since a bundle of features showing a family resemblance will do. Nor does one have to have universal agreement about what constitutes a nation; there is more than one acceptable narrative of the development of nation, and all that is needed is a workable definition, one which yields a coherent view of nation and so will aid understanding of how it works. My account will have to work its way through some existing debates about the historical development of nations, including (1) the distinction between tribe and nation and (2) the relation between state and culture, in order to reach (3), the topic of nationalism, the peculiar intensity which characterises national desire.

'The overwhelming majority of the world's people have lived until recently without the need to be members of national groups' (Harris 1992, p. 2): nations are a recent and historically unprecedented invention, only one of the many forms of collectivity in which human beings have identified themselves. Hunter–gatherer groups, clans, tribes, empires: collective identity took several different forms before there were ever nations. Anthony D. Smith refers to such an ethnic community by the French term *ethnie* and lists a number of attributes an *ethnie* may share:

> a collective proper name
> a myth of common ancestry
> shared historical memories
> one or more differentiating elements of common culture
> an association with a specific 'homeland'
> a sense of solidarity for significant sectors of the population.
> (1991, p. 21)

Historically, an existing pre-national cultural identity provides a very good basis for the development of a nation in the modern sense, which almost everyone agrees, is a post-Renaissance phenomenon. But what distinguishes the pre-national group from nation proper?

With characteristic dogmatism Joseph Stalin asserted that a nation must have four things: a common language, a common territory, a common economic life and a common psychological make-up (see 1973, pp. 57–61). More loosely, one might characterise a nation as sharing the following cluster of features, in no significant order:

> customs
> ethnic similarity
> language
> political organisation
> religion
> territory.

That same cluster could also identify a clan or tribe. However, common usage suggests that a tribe is an older and more primitive collectivity than a nation. Anthony Smith describes how a tribe maintains inequality in role and status while in a nation citizenship is equal (1973). Ernest Gellner notes that 'some pre-modern loyalty-evoking political units have embraced populations and covered territories similar to those which one would expect to be produced by modern nationalism', and wonders whether these units 'so close to nationalism' contradict the theory of nationalism as a post-Renaissance development (1964, p. 173). His slightly uneasy answer is that they do not, on the grounds that it is 'worth separating' modern nationalism, distinguished from tribalism by (he lists) 'citizenship through education, group *differentiae* in terms of the language of instruction, and unmediated membership of mass co-cultural societies' (p. 173).

Citizenship, some kind of formal education system, mass society: what lies behind these details, providing a not-too-surprising way to discriminate tribe and nation, is the idea that nation is a form of collective identity which becomes possible only in the conditions of *modernity*. Since it would not be possible to define modernity apart from the existence of the modern state, all those writers whose accounts of nation invoke the modern form of the state presuppose modernity as precondition for nation; those few exceptions, who want to distinguish between state and nation, tend to offer definitions of nation assuming some form of modern state organisation (see, for example, Smith 1991).

Defining nation in relation to modernity becomes even more persuasive when one turns to historical periodisation. In a first phase – for example, England between 1500 and 1642 – nation and modern state begin to grow through 'identification of the nation with the person of the sovereign' (Carr 1945, p. 2) – it was, as Perry Anderson, asserts, 'the Absolute monarchies' which 'introduced standing armies, a permanent bureaucracy, national taxation, a codified law, and the beginnings of a unified market' (1979, p. 17). In other words, the beginnings of the modern state, and so the modern nation. Here one should not underestimate the extent to which the modern nation-state succeeded because of its efficiency in establishing and defending itself militarily, nor least because it was usually able to recruit personnel for an army and navy through conscription (for the role of the military in the construction of the nation-state, see Giddens 1985).

The second, determining period for the discovery of nation in the West lies between 1750 and 1800, comprehending 1776 and 1789, the American and French Revolutions. These explicitly pronounce that:

1 Political sovereignty rests with the people not a monarch.
2 The new state is independent and self-governing.
3 The political entity of the state is to be identified with the national culture, 'nation' *is* 'the people'.

The United States' Declaration of Independence epitomises these three principles. Appealing to 'self-evident truths' and a temporal moment which is 'necessary', it proclaims that sovereignty comes 'from the consent of the governed'; it claims to speak in the name of a nation whose separate identity gives it the right 'to dissolve the political bands which have connected them with another'; and (deliberately avoiding the federalist connotations of the word 'nation') it elides the state with culture by referring to 'one people' (even though, as Derrida points out, this people 'does not exist' before the Declaration; 1984, p. 21). In 1811 when Venezuelan revolutionaries drew up a constitution for the First Venezuelan Republic, they borrowed 'verbatim from the Constitution of the United States of America' (Gerhard Masure, cited Anderson 1991, p. 192).

It is of course in its commitment to an idea of the people against any form of autocratic power that the overwhelmingly democratic tendency of nation is realised. Although empirically nations are not always democracies or fully democratic, that impulse is inscribed in the very structure of the institution, can never be eradicated, is always liable to break out from any constraint.

In a third phase nation spreads with modernity around the world, even at the core of the process of colonialism, until in 1922 the founding of the 'League of Nations' acknowledges nation as a global norm, one confirmed in 1945 by the United Nations' Charter (Chapter 1, Article 2) which demands 'respect for the principle of equal rights and self-determination of peoples'. It is both sad and salutary to remark that a recent collection of essays on nation (Hutchinson and Smith 1994) contains an extract from a paper published in 1985 with references to internal dissensions in Rwanda, one on the Soviet Union published in 1985, another on Yugoslavia (also published in 1990) – all these written before the names Tutsi and Hutu, Chechenia and Bosnia-Herzogovina passed into international currency as testimony to the fragility of the modern nation-state. At the same time conflict elsewhere is driving towards nation (in 1999 one might name Nigeria, Burma and East Timor).

Though I would not go along with his view that nationalism is an ideology in the sense that it is an imposed way of thinking, it is hard to disagree with Anthony Birch when he announces the success of nation:

> Nationalism emerged as an ideology as a consequence of the French Revolution. Two hundred years after that revolution, it can be recognised as the most successful ideology the world has ever known. Empires and other pre-national forms of political organisation have come to an end, save for one or two small remnants such as Gibraltar and New Caledonia. The

> whole land surface of the world, with the single exception of Antarctica, is now divided between the jurisdictions of nation-states. The formal independence and equality of these states are recognised in international law and in the organisation of the United Nations and its agencies. In short, nationalism has triumphed.
>
> (1989, p. 221)

And Anthony Smith advances the following resounding (if slightly ungrammatical) conclusion:

> Of all the collective identities in which human beings share today, national identity is perhaps the most fundamental and inclusive. Not only has national*ism*, the ideological movement, penetrated every corner of the globe; the world is divided, first and foremost, into 'nation-states' – states claiming to be nations – and national identity everywhere underpins the recurrent drive for popular sovereignty and democracy, as well as the exclusive tyranny that it sometimes breeds. Other types of collective identity – class, gender, race, religion – may overlap or combine with national identity but they rarely succeed in undermining its hold, though they may influence its direction.
>
> (1991, p. 143)

Marx believed that the form of collective identity produced by modernity was class, but as Ernest Gellner wittily points out, history sent the message to another address, not to class but to nation. Virginia Woolf famously asserted that 'As a woman, I have no country' because her country was 'the whole world' (1992, p. 313) but so far no collective international sense of gender identity has emerged with a force and substance which can rival nation.

Smith's qualification of nation-states as 'states claiming to be nations' is crucial. Elsewhere he recalls that:

> Walker Connor's estimate in the early nineteen-seventies showed that only about 10 per cent of states could claim to be true 'nation-states', in the sense that the state's boundaries coincide with the nation's and that the total population of the state share a single ethnic culture.

Yet Smith agrees with Walker Connor's view that now 'most states aspire to become nation-states in this sense (cited Smith 1991, p. 15). In other words: although only a small number of nations so far are nation-states, nation today defines itself in an all-but-universal *wish* that nation as territorial state and nation as culture should coincide.

Nation as state, nation as culture

One acceptable but by no means incontrovertible definition of a modern state would be to say it consists of political apparatuses with supreme jurisdiction over a territorial area backed up by a claim to monopoly of coercive power and some degree of democratic support from the people. National culture has been described as 'a community of people, whose members are bound together by a sense of solidarity, a common culture, a national consciousness' (Seton-Watson 1977, p. 1); the theoretical emphasis preferred in this present study would define culture as an organisation of signifying practices, whose main function is to reproduce and transform meanings and, with these meanings, subjectivities.

State and culture are necessarily distinct in principle. Historically, empirically, nation as state and nation as culture have not always occurred together (and this disjunction has preoccupied discussion to the exclusion of other issues, as we shall see). Seton-Watson is right to observe:

> The distinction between states and nations is fundamental.... States can exist without a nation, or with several nations, among their subjects; and a nation can be coterminous with the population of one state, or be included together with other nations within one state, or be divided between states.
>
> (1977, p. 1)

There are three possibilities:

1 A homogeneous and identifiable culture can be larger than any one state (German culture in the eighteenth century and after).
2 A polity can be larger than the various distinct cultures it contains (the Roman Empire).
3 State and culture can be congruent in the so-called nation-state (classically, the United States, France).

In practice the picture is complex. 'The Habsburg Empire was a most powerful state, yet it was not a "nation"; Prussia was the state at its most perfect, but it was not a "nation"; Venice was a state which lasted for centuries: was it then a "nation"?', asks Elie Kedourie (1961, p. 77). From the sixteenth century England, France, Scotland, Holland, Castile and Sweden became nation-states; Spain did not. It is questionable whether the term 'nation-state' should be used of Poland or Hungary before 1945. Although many Catalan, Scots, and Flemish nationalists want 'home rule and cultural parity' they do not necessarily seek the 'outright independence' they would get with a nation-state (Smith 1991, p. 74).

As Eric Hobsbawm declares, nation 'is a social entity only insofar as it relates to a certain kind of modern territorial state, the "nation-state", and it is pointless to discuss nation and nationalism except insofar as both relate to it' (1992, pp. 9–10), pointless because any cultural grouping might claim to be a nation but would not be recognised as such unless it achieved state and territorial realisation. For over two centuries the organisation of groups and collectivities into nations has spread across the globe. Historically, then, the evidence is very strong that it is the idea of the nation-state, realised in the United States of America in 1776 and France in 1789, which provides the ideal and model for collective identity at the end of the twentieth century.

On this basis it becomes possible to distinguish two historically different conditions of the nation, under the signs of the French and the American. On the one hand there are, typically, the European nation-states which came about in the effort to achieve and defend a state ('Nationalism…is an ideological movement for attaining and maintaining the *autonomy*, *unity* and *identity* of a nation'; Smith 1991, p. 74); on the other, there are those which came about in a struggle of national liberation against a colonial power ('Nationalism is a reaction of peoples who feel culturally at a disadvantage'; John Plamenatz, cited Kamenka 1976, p. 24). Benedict Anderson cites a striking example in which the two forms mirror each other, for in 1913 the Dutch colonial regime in Batavia sponsored huge festivities to celebrate the centennial of the 'national liberation' of the Netherlands from French imperialism only for early Javanese–Indonesia nationalists to take over the event and so 'turn Dutch history against the Dutch' (1991, p. 117). In both cases, European and colonial nationalism, 'some form of national culture pre-existed the state' (Hobsbawm 1992, p. 10), and what both share is a drive to bring state and culture into alignment.

Theorising nation as state, nation as culture

Although the idea goes back a little earlier, the German historian Friedrich Meinecke was the first to break down the unified idea of nation when he made a clear and explicit distinction between the two aspects of nation as *Staatsnation* and *Kulturnation*. While developing the right-wing nationalist argument that it is only with the purging of cosmopolitan values that a sovereign nation-state is realised (the example is Germany), Meinecke marks off the 'political nation', which is 'primarily based on the unifying force of a common political history and constitution', from the 'cultural nation', which is 'primarily based on some jointly experienced cultural knowledge' (1970, p. 10). The difference can lead to markedly opposed viewpoints: 'The idea of the nation is the most materialist of ideas' (Debray 1977, p. 29); 'A nation is a soul, a spiritual principle' (Renan 1990, p. 19).

Present-day mainstream debate over the definition of and historical explanation for nation divides between those who give priority to the importance of either state and modernity or culture and tradition. An idealist and Romantic legacy from Herder, Fichte and Hegel thinks of the nation on the organic model as something which grows according to its own internal process, as old as history, 'as natural as a plant' (Herder, cited Guibernau 1996, p. 49). Continuing this attitude in contemporary discussion is Hans Kohn, who writes that 'Although objective factors are of great importance for the formation of nationalities, the most essential element is a living and active corporate will' (1965, p. 10) (Kohn is almost the only modern writer to have a good word for Renan).

Anthony Smith is the strongest advocate for an account of nation which would privilege culture over state:

> nationalism is an ideology of the nation, not the state.... The idea that nations can be free only if they possess their own sovereign state is neither necessary nor universal....Nor has every nationalist movement made the acquisition of a state for its nation a priority.
>
> (1991, p. 74)

Smith emphasises the development of nation from the *ethnie*, though his definition of nation as '*a named human population sharing an historical territory, common myths and historical memories, a mass, public culture, a common economy and common legal rights and duties for all its members*' (p. 14) contains features impossible without a form of modern state organisation (a public culture which is 'mass', legal rights common in the sense that they apply equally to citizens rather then unequally to ranks differentiated by birth).

Ernest Gellner stands at the front of those who argue for nation as a product of modernity, that industrialism requires a certain division of labour and with it a level of education which can only be sustained by a modern, national state (I will have more to say about Gellner's study of nation later on). Among those who have followed Gellner in his concern to define nation principally as a state and political organisation there is John Breuilly, for example, who argues that nationalism is related 'to the objectives of obtaining and using state power' (1982, p. 2), a struggle in which the promotion of national culture is a consequence. Nigel Harris affirms that 'What turns national liberation into a stable nationalism is the accomplishment of State power' (1992, pp. 17–18). And similarly, Anthony Birch is confident that 'The pure theory of nationalism supposes the existence of nations before they acquire political expression, but in reality nations have to be a created by a process which is at least partly political' (1989, pp. 6–7).

The argument between state-led and culture-led accounts of nation can also be ascribed to nation as it developed and was experienced in different parts of Europe: 'Historic territory, legal-political community, legal-political equality of members, and common civic culture and ideology: these are the components of the standard Western model of nation' (Smith 1991, p. 11). Meanwhile Eastern models have encouraged emphasis on culture because of the significance in their development of 'genealogy and presumed descent ties, popular mobilisation, vernacular languages, customs and traditions' (p. 13).

Does a culture produce the state or does the state foster culture? In promoting and reproducing nation the causal relation between political forces, on the one hand, and all that the idea of culture may stand for, on the other, must be two-way and dialectical. It is symptomatic that arguments for a priority remain entirely unresolved and with no foreseeable prospect of resolution, leading one theorist to conclude that 'the concept of nation' is 'inherently unstable and dualist' (Smith 1986, p. 4). The precise nature of the causal interconnection between state and nation tells us less about national identity than the *gap* it seeks to bridge.

Eugene Kamenka proposes that it is the actual 'disparity' between the state and a sense of nation which produces nationalism (1976, p. 14), while in an often-cited statement Gellner concludes that 'Nationalism is primarily a political principle, which holds that the political and national unity shall be congruent' (cited with approval by Hobsbawm 1992, p. 9). 'Shall be', the optative mood, exemplifies a hope for a unity which does not – and cannot – exist in actuality for there is 'always a gulf between political and cultural processes' (Guibernau 1996, p. 5).

'Nation', as the American Declaration assumes, *is* 'the people', not a statement but a demand which E.H. Carr finds in the origin of nation:

> The founder of modern nationalism as it began to take shape in the nineteenth century was Rousseau, who, rejecting the embodiment of the nation in the personal sovereign or the ruling class, boldly identified 'nation' and 'people'; and this identification became a fundamental principle both of the French and of the American revolutions.
>
> (1945, p. 7)

This identification of nation and people is wished for not just in the French and American foundations but appears as the aspiration of all nations since, including those still struggling to become nations.

Representing two different materialities, nation as state and nation as culture are inherently incommensurate. It is in this breach that the desire for nation arises and of which it is a measure. Thus, the seeming oneness of national identity is produced by a process like that which, in the mirror stage, brings about the effect of the individual ego as unified and self-identical. An idea of the unity of the body (Lacan writes of it as '*Gestalt*'; 1977a, p. 2) provokes a horror of self-fragmentation (the 'body in pieces') which in turn is overcome by an 'imaginary' movement towards identification with a unified ideal (in Lacan's terminology 'the imaginary' refers to the order of the ego in contrast to 'the symbolic', the socially determined order of signifiers). Similarly, the disjunction in nation between state and culture (as well as the heterogeneity of each) is disavowed through fantasy identification with a unified identity, state and culture together, just as in the individual the force of the imaginary comes to overlook the differences within which the subject operates (so: 'I drive the car' rather than 'the system drives me').

In nation this function of the imaginary is supported by a kind of tautology: different objects of identification become equated by evidencing common national attributes ('this is peculiarly English', etc.) while those attributes are reciprocally defined by the objects themselves. Derrida draws attention to Fichte's view that nation may 'make itself wholly and completely what it ought to be': through a closed hermeneutic nation tries to define itself in a circularity. In such an alluring plenitude, the unified mirror of national identity, subjects want to find themselves reflected, identifying themselves in it and so with each other: *E pluribus unum*. And it is an important effect of the felt union of state and culture that what appears social and subject to choice, the *Gesellschaft* of the state, is amalgamated with what is more obviously unchosen and assigned, the *Gemeinschaft* of culture.

Heterogeneity in state and culture

National collectivity occasions desire, then, because it is always incomplete, constituting a lack, an actual heterogeneity, whether we think of nation as state or nation as culture. It might seem that the state is more able to provided homogeneity than culture. For the state is able to establish in principle and enforce in practice a high degree of uniformity across its members: by making them subject to equal laws, through a written constitution promising common rights of citizenship to all subjects, by conceding the right to vote, by impartially demanding military service, by making available forms of state education and by paying for the whole package through the imposition of taxes (though not necessarily equally).

Yet the apparently uniform identity as citizen which the state is able to confer is not conferred once and for all, despite the large gestures which usually surround the signing of Constitutions. In England, for example, there has been a continuing fight to win full citizenship, with the gradual extension of the male franchise, first in 1832 and then in 1867, followed by limited female franchise in 1919 and a full adult suffrage only in 1929. England still does not have an entrenched Constitution and its inhabitants are not citizens but *subjects* of Her Majesty the Queen. Sovereignty is still vested in the Prerogative of the Monarch and so Parliament sitting in that right (with the founding of Charter 88 the struggle for full rights and a written Constitution continues).

Even supposing full and consistent rights were actually extended to all members of a nation, citizenship could still not achieve perfect homogeneity. Julia Kristeva has signalled dramatically the hiatus opened by 'the distinction that sets the *citizen* apart from the *man*' (1991, p. 97). She asks:

> is it not true that, in order to found the rights that are specific to the men of a civilization or a nation – even the most reasonable and the most consciously democratic – one has to withdraw such rights from those that are not citizens, that is, other men? The process means – and this is its extreme inference – that one can be more or less a man to the extent that one is more or less a citizen, that he who is not a citizen is not fully a man.…If, consciously, one grants foreigners all the rights of man, what is actually left of such rights when one takes away from them the rights of the citizen?
>
> (pp. 97–8)

By definition citizenship always implicates its repressed other, all those actively *excluded* from citizenship – strangers, foreigners, resident aliens, stateless persons, refugees, asylum-seekers. In demarcating a boundary between those who do and do not qualify for rights as citizens, the national state seems able to coincide with the national culture but only by dividing against itself. Nation as state may claim to arise on the side of *nomos*, of law, culture, artifice, *Gesellschaft*, but as Derrida argues in *Politics of Friendship*, in so far as one is *born* into a citizenship, nation as state relies on *phusis*, the given, nature, the unchosen, *Gemeinschaft* (1997, pp. 91–9). Even citizenship is not consistent and at one with itself.

There are times – temporal moments, say, such as great national events – when a nation does appear unified and homogeneous as a national culture. These times only mask its actual heterogeneity. The English are a mingling of Celts, Romans, Germanic Angles and Saxons, Nordic Jutes, Vikings and Norman French, and that only takes you to 1500. So no one is purely English, not even the Queen ('That dreadful German woman', as a snobbish colleague once described her to me). Cultural and regional difference is pervasive, and Raymond Williams is consistent with his adherence to local and particular loyalties when he argues:

> All the varied people who have lived on this island are in a substantial physical sense still here. What is, from time to time, projected as an 'island race' is in reality a long process of successive components and repressions but also of succession, supersession and relative integrations.
>
> (1983, pp. 193–4)

This is well said; in its culture every nation, including England, is hybridic and heterogeneous.

Founded in what breaks its completeness national desire always seeks to anneal its disparities, heal its wound. This only reveals the impossibility of cultural homogeneity, as one analysis of fascism implies. Fascism, it can be argued, aims to solve the problem of politics by eradicating politics as political conflict; in order to do this it seeks to abolish the necessary and inescapable differences that inhere within even the most apparently unified culture. But as Slavoj Žižek proposes in his brilliant discussion of anti-Semitism, this project of establishing 'a totally transparent and homogeneous society' (1989, p. 172) is condemned to impossibility in advance, and thus, so Žižek argues, contains its own attempted solution in advance: every possible alterity and heterogeneity will be gathered together and projected on to the fantasy image of 'The

Jew', which can then be held responsible for a blockage which is actually fundamental.

In nation the state is not at one, culture is not at one, and each is inherently distanced from the other. Yet national desire is defined in its thirst for unity. It is in this historically determined effect of lack and seeming plenitude that we may find some of the causes for the shattering intensity of national desire.

Nationalism

The term 'nationalism' was used for the first time in 1798 by Augustin Barruel when, in a history of Jacobinism, he recalls that '*Nationalism*, or the love of nation (*l'amour national*) took the place of the love of mankind in general (*l'amour général*)' (cited Kamenka 1976, p. 8), a neutral use of the term. Since then the concept of 'love of nation' has taken on a very different connotation, and many writers attest to the feeling for nation as desire for a single, mastering identity which would entirely dominate other possibilities:

> Nationalism is a state of mind, in which the supreme loyalty of the individual is felt to be due to the nation-state.
>
> (Kohn 1965, p. 9)

> [Nation is] the *ideal*, *natural* or *normal* form of international political organisation, as the focus of men's loyalties.
>
> (Kamenka 1976, p. 6)

> The interests and values of this nation take priority over all other interests and values.
>
> (Breuilly 1982, p. 3)

> A nation is a self-contained group of human beings who place loyalty to the group as a whole above competing loyalties.
>
> (Ruston Dankwart, cited Smith 1973, p. 49)

> [The 'principle' of nationalism] implies that the political duty of Ruritanians to the polity which encompasses and represents the Ruritanian nation, overrides all other public obligations, and in extreme cases (such as wars) all other obligations of whatever kind.
>
> (Hobsbawm 1992, p. 9)

> nationalism *stricto sensu* ... namely, that outlook which gives an *absolute priority to the values of the nation over all other values and interests.*
>
> (Hroch, in Balakrishnan 1996, p. 81)

'We had no religion at all', as Stendhal writes, 'our deep and inner feelings were compounded in this one idea: *being useful to our country.*'

Historical study frequently remarks the passionate subjective response attaching to nation but, in general, has little to say about it except that it is beyond reason and so probably beyond analysis. E.H. Carr, for example, comments that 'the "democratisation" of nationalism imparted to it a new and disturbing emotional fervour'; with the disappearance of the absolute monarch 'the idea of the personality and character of the nation acquired a profound psychological significance' (1945, pp. 8–9). Carr sees how an apparently rational tendency, national democratisation, excites a profoundly irrational effect in which an abstract political entity becomes identified with as though it were an individual with a personality.

The desire for national identity is felt with a categorical and imperative force that can override all other obligations. So far my argument has aimed to demonstrate how the particular structure of nation serves to incite national desire. The idea of nation figures a unity of state and culture though they are distinct and heterogeneous. Absence at the heart of nation intensifies the wish for its presence. This account, however, does not address the question of why that presence should be desired in the first place, what is in it for the subject. I propose that modernity, which makes the nation-state possible, makes national identity desirable.

Nation and modernity: Tönnies, Gellner

Since Weber there have been a number of theorists of modernity. I will concentrate on two, though, as I will suggest, neither adequately theorises modernity because neither has at his disposal an effective account of subjectivity. With modernity it appeared that one entire mode of culture and social structuring replaced another. That perception drew Ferdinand Tönnies in 1887 (1955) to theorise past and present as two structures of collective identity, *Gemeinschaft* and *Gesellschaft* (usually translated as 'community' and 'society').

Tönnies outlines a conceptual opposition between social organisations based on 'natural will' (*Wesenwille*), unconditioned relations such as that in which mother loves infant, and others defined in terms of 'rational will'

(*Kürwille*), relations conditional in that they depend upon individual choice and self-interested exchange. Within community individuals form parts of a totality whose members experience it as a given, supernaturally endowed: in society participants are isolated and think of its authority as the humanly created product of convention and class relationships.

Whereas social relationships characterised by kinship, neighbourliness and friendship are *gemeinschaftlich*, those relying on exchange and rational calculation are *gesellschaftlich*. Community is legitimated through custom, society through legislation; community's central institutions are family law and the kinship group, society's those of the state and capitalist economy. Although Tönnies is explicit that community and society are abstractions, he is also fairly explicit in his view that community is feudal while society, which 'follows a period of *Gemeinschaft*' (p. 270), is bourgeois. On this showing, traditional community, 'a living organism', gives way to the society of modernity, which is in contrast 'a mechanical aggregate and artifact' (p. 39).

Tönnies' account invites us to think of the social relations of modernity as a constructed settlement rather than given inheritance, as nature transformed into culture, as agreement between newly separated and individualised subjects. Tönnies does attempt to theorise the social and the subjective together by finding social correlates for will, both 'natural' and 'rational', but he does not think in terms of subjects and their desire. Change from traditional community to the society of modernity is detailed without asking how the transition from relative stability to relative mobility might affect subjectivity and identity. In *Thought and Change* Ernest Gellner, writing as a sociologist, develops a subtle argument directly relating modernity to nationalism via a conception of identity, though a conception that in my view remains unexamined (see 1964, especially Chapter 7).

Gellner's point of departure is the distinction drawn by anthropologists between 'structure' and 'culture', the first concerning roles in a society (for example, patrilinear property inheritance) whereas culture pertains to associated meanings (for example, ritual dress). In respect of these terms, however, traditional and modern societies differ, since (in the given terminology) traditional society is much more highly structured. Gellner investigates the possibility that structure and culture have an 'inverse relationship' (p. 154) so that in communities where roles are stable and well known, communication is easy, 'shared culture' less important. In modern societies a person is 'not fully identified' with his or her role, relationships are 'ephemeral, non-repetitive and optional', communication is more difficult, and so culture becomes 'of utmost importance' (p. 155).

Structure and culture contrast two notions of individual identity. In the first, identity is ascribed, inhering in the social and family roles the subject occupies, so that binding obligations follow from it; in the second, in principle at least, identity is chosen and responsibilities are freely taken up. Gellner accepts that all social formations afford both identities but with a historical difference. In traditional communities culture reinforces structure, individual decision supports role, whereas 'in modern societies, culture does not so much underline structure: rather, it replaces it' (p. 155). The stability of structures and roles in traditional society is eroded by modern industrial society with a consequence Gellner describes as follows:

> If a man is not firmly set in a social niche, whose relationship as it were endows him with his identity, he is obliged to carry his identity with him, in his whole style of conduct and expression: in other words, his 'culture' becomes his identity.
>
> (p. 157)

As an essential part of this new, portable identity the individual desires nationality.

Committed as it is to tracking some idea of collective identity, Gellner's account is limited by a common-sense notion of subjectivity which it never really explores. Through what psychic mechanism and with what consequences is a subject 'obliged' to have an identity? How does 'a social niche' endow a subject with identity ('as it were')? What kind of subject is it whose culture (in Gellner's usage) becomes his or her identity?

Yet Gellner does discuss nation in relation to modernity, change and identity. Deprived of structure the subject is driven into culture; denied identity fulfilled in a significant role, he or she demands an individuality which will make up for what has been relinquished. This new, mobile, 'pocket' individuality provokes the subject to seek national identity, among others. Before proceeding I want to substantiate, at least in outline, a sense of the forms in which this more isolated individuality began to become historically available (a process which is explained elsewhere and in other terms by Michel Foucault as a transformation of the subject of punishment into the subject of discipline) (1979).

Some identities of modernity

Identity as romantic self

Wordsworth's poem 'A Poet's Epitaph', first published in 1800, begins:

Art thou a Statist in the van
Of public conflicts trained and bred?
– First learn to love one living man;
Then may'st thou think upon the dead.

And so it goes on, listing as dead roles all the career options of the gentry in Wordsworth's time – to the politician here adding the lawyer, academic, military man, doctor, philosopher, and moralist (but not Stamp Distributor for Westmoreland, the sinecure Wordsworth himself finally landed). All are contemptuously discarded in contrast to 'the Poet' as imagined in the final verses:

But who is He, with modest looks,
And clad in homely russet brown?
He murmurs near the running brooks
A music sweeter than their own.

He is retired as noontide dew,
Or fountain in a noon-day grove;
And you must love him, ere to you
He will seem worthy of your love.
(1952–9, 4, pp. 65–7)

Value, having now evaporated from the conventional social roles, is imputed to the lonely, introspective outsider. And in apparently creating for himself this image of 'the Poet', the speaker of the poem finds a reflection in the Other with which he may identify. This strategy, in which a subject seems (impossibly) to construct its own identity for itself, begins to become normalised with the Romantic Movement; the innovation of the romantic self is a sign of a wider metamorphosis of subjectivity with the arrival of modernity.

Identity as reflected in art and nature

It is a truism to note that the category of the aesthetic in the modern sense of a separated and self-sufficient domain accessible to the individual 'imagination' is introduced in the same historical period as the decisive rise of the nation-state, and signalled by the publication in 1790 of Kant's *Critique of Judgement*. In the idea of the aesthetic the subject desires an abstracted and generalised reflection of identity specifically not dependent on a community of other people (art is defined as useless) yet able to confer on the individual a sense that his or her experience has significance and value. It seems that art thus provides a confirming mirror for a separated subjectivity; and a similar effect is extended to the individual's experience of the natural world (Wordsworth's Poet is a lover of nature).

Sexual identity

The work of Thomas Laqueur (1990) argues that in firm continuity from the ancient world to the end of the eighteenth century the belief is repeated that man and woman derive from the same model, woman being a weaker copy of man (weaker because a copy). Around 1800 this begins to change as definitions of sexuality and the gendered body are promoted which stress not the similarity of the sexes but their difference from each other. Sexual identity, identity as masculine or feminine, appears as an opposition in which each excludes the other. Is it not reasonable that this quest for a radically oppositional difference in identity should be understood alongside those other restructurings of the subject in relation to the romantic self and to art? On the terrain of sexuality, modernity seems to foster desire for an identity more starkly distinct and delineated, a more emphatically masculine man over against a more distinctly feminine woman.

Modernity and national desire

Society is always incomplete; with modernity that incompleteness comes to express itself as a radically insistent drama of lack and plenitude, a drama (if the psychoanalytic account is correct) which stages the organisation of the individual subject into collective identity on the basis of common objects of identification. How history and subjectivity dovetail around nation can be summarised schematically and in outline:

1 Lack is universal and constitutive for the speaking subject who must strive to refind his or her being within meaning; any identity which would repair lack is always borrowed from the Other (as the symbolic order the Other is always encountered in a historically specific form).
2 With modernity the subject becomes *more* individualised and isolated (in Gellner's terms moving from 'structure' to 'culture').
3 The subject's relatively secure identity as reflected in community is surrendered for a *less* secure identity as reflected in society.
4 As lack is thus intensified the subject desires identity *more* intensely.
5 All identity is an effect but the *stronger* desire for identity provoked

by modernity tolerates identity which is *more* manifestly an effect, especially if (in view of 2 above) that version of identity can claim an independence from the Other (as romantic self, as reflected in art, as a more distinct and privatised sense of sexuality).

6 As the particular mode of collective identity made available by modernity, national identity is caught up in the new forms of subjectivity: it is desired with special intensity; and that desire overlooks the fact it is *more* manifestly an effect of construction.

Different forms of identity returned to the subject by the Other are played out by tradition and modernity, respectively. In the world of tradition, caught up in a thick and immediate network of intimacies and obligations enacted through the rhythms of public performance in ritual and festival, the individual inhabits a small, relatively closed grouping in which 'everyone knows everyone else'. That communal Other reflects back to the subject a relatively stable and relatively limited sense of who he or she is, one to which few alternatives can be imagined.

Confronted with greater difference in the dispersal and atomisation of industrialisation, urbanisation and the division of labour, the subject finds in the idea of nation the allure of a hypostasised identity which will efface that greater difference. In the relativised society (*Gesellschaft*) of modernity, where value has drained from social roles as they keep changing in themselves and in relation to each other, each individual, as Engels says of the crowd on the pavements in Market Street, Manchester, in 1844, becomes a 'monad' (1969, p. 58) bound to others only by the rule of not bumping into them though free to wander where he or she wants, horizons unlimited. In that very movement by which modernity offers an unprecedented range of possible identities, the subject's need for a secure identity mirrored by the Other becomes more difficult to satisfy and, correspondingly, desire for it more acute, more passionate – the well-known 'irrational' excess of nationalism and national feeling.

Nation as state and nation as culture cannot be fused into an authentic unity. However, because of its force, national desire runs across that disjunction, responding to the promise that all may be synthesised into a single national characterisation, in the case of England, for example, allowing both state and culture – and their mixed components – to be marked as 'English'.

On the side of the state, the nation as 'English' is produced and sustained by a series of institutions and practices, including the Royal Navy, Parliament, Whitehall, the Inland Revenue, the Old Bailey,

Lloyds of London, the Bank of England, ICI, Manchester Metropolitan University, Eton College, the British Broadcasting Corporation, the British Council, and so on, all of which can be defined as in some way characteristically English. At the same time, on the culture side of the division, a notion of Englishness can seem to preside over 'the English language' and English 'way of talking', a canon of literature established as English, English landscape, a certain sense of humour felt to be English, English common sense, and so on and so on. Running across state and culture, this coalescent adjectivalisation provides an apparently unified object, 'Englishness', which invites subjects into identification with it (and so each other) in a process which gives the effect of national identity.

It is not that historians of nation are unaware that modernity effects a profound subjective transformation expressing itself at the level of collective identity in the desire for nation. The case is rather that they generally fail to take these consequences seriously and refuse to try to examine them properly. Kenneth Minogue accurately observes the effect of national desire when he describes how it produces a feeling that 'The "state" might be "them", but the "nation" was "us" ' (1967, p. 11). And Anthony Smith *de facto* refers national desire to a cause in modernity and an effect in imaginary unity when he says of national identity that 'By discovering that culture we "rediscover" ourselves, the "authentic self", or so it has appeared to many divided and disorientated individuals who have had to content with the vast changes and uncertainties of the modern world' (1991, p. 17).

In his account of nation John Breuilly suggests that modern social thought has recognised the problem of creating 'common identity and a sentiment of solidarity' in the face of 'impersonal, abstract, "rational" relationships based on calculation' (1982, p. 30). Nationalism promises to bridge these contrasts:

> On the one hand it is a community myth, with its emphasis upon cultural identity and emotional solidarity. On the other, it projects this myth upon large-scale societies (nations), which it depicts in terms more appropriate (if at all) to village or small-town life. It seeks to exploit the opportunities of modernity, above all by accepting the large-scale mass society which modernity involves, but at the same time to exploit the sense of loss which modernity creates.
>
> (p. 30)

The observation is accurate and perceptive though Breuilly, wedded to a certain, limited theoretical viewpoint, cannot pursue his own insights. For him the desire for nation is a form of ideology, and thus by nature delusory and unreal; so he can offer no serious explanation of what 'common identity' is or how it might work.

In a concluding chapter I shall come back to how we might begin to assess the kind of collective identity afforded by nation. But I shall turn now to offer a demonstration of how national identity is supported by identification with an object. My example is Englishness. From all the many ways in which English national identity is sustained in forms of identification I want to concentrate on one especially crucial and – as I shall hope to show – deep-rooted object of identification: English identity as conferred by a specifically English discursive formation. Like water to the fish, a way of talking and writing is hardly visible but it is almost certainly the more insidiously effective for that reason. The desire for Englishness – the possibility of Englishness – is intimately inscribed in the tradition of English discourse.

Although both synchronic and diachronic, no claim is being made that this discursive formation constitutes an even totality (what holds the discourse together is an organisation of the signifier which is necessarily made up of differences). Nor is it argued that a dominant version occurs in a hegemonic relation to another authentically oppositional form (the examples I've considered from working-class discourse perform in a different class register but do not escape the assumptions of the prevailing mode). Instead of dominant/subordinated any homogeneity is unsettled rather by a distinction between *centre* and *margins*, as will be suggested. The next two chapters will attempt to define a structure for this discursive inheritance via its most conspicuously characteristic feature: empiricism.

Part II

THE ENGLISH TRADITION

3

EMPIRICISM IN ENGLISH PHILOSOPHY

> National character is not an explanation, it is something to be explained.
>
> (Otto Bauer in Balakrishnan 1996, p. 41)

It should cause no surprise to define the discursive formation of Englishness mainly in relation to empiricism. After celebrating the historical realisation of theory and practice by the French Revolution, Hegel turns to ask whether the English were 'too backward' to understand such general principles (1956, p. 454). His response is that the English already had or thought they had a free constitution in 1789 though it was one based on local and particular rights in contrast to the state centralisation of France. 'Consequently,' Hegel concludes, 'abstract and general principles have no attraction for Englishmen' (p. 455).

The Marxist tradition has pursued Hegel's insight while lending it a more substantial explanation. In *The German Ideology* Marx and Engels make it a basis on which to discriminate two otherwise similar national cultures divided by the Channel. These differences derive from the contrasted experiences of 'the bourgeois revolution' in England 1642–60 and in France after 1789. Hobbes and Locke, founders of the English tradition 'had before their eyes both the earlier development of the Dutch bourgeoisies...and the first political actions by which the English bourgeoisie emerged from local and provincial limitations'; French Enlightenment thinkers were confronted by a bourgeoisie 'still struggling for its free development' (1974, p. 111). Hence, Marx and Engels propose, 'the theory which for the English still was simply the registration of fact becomes for the French a philosophical system' (p. 112), and this difference between historical achievement and aspiration, fact and system, explains the development of an English empiricist as against a French rationalist tradition. Whether it does or not, these speculations have been very productive.

During the 1960s the New Left picked up Marx's account of the English philosophic tradition as empiricist, building it on to a more contemporary, Althusserian foundation. On this basis they advanced a historical narrative which, known now as the Nairn–Anderson theses, would explain the backwardness of English economic, political and cultural development and consequent failure of working-class revolution as all due to *empiricism* (see Anderson 1964; Nairn 1964a and 1964b; Anderson 1966 and 1968). With finely Whiggish contempt Anderson writes:

> The hegemony of the dominant bloc in England is not articulated in any systematic major ideology but is rather diffused in a miasma of commonplace prejudices and taboos. The two great chemical elements of this blanketing English fog are 'traditionalism' and 'empiricism': in it, visibility – of any social or historical reality – is always zero.
>
> (1968, p. 40)

Committed to 'blind empiricism', says Nairn, the English bourgeoisie 'could afford to dispense with the dangerous tool of reason and stock the national mind with historical garbage' (1964b, p. 48). Incisive opposition to the Nairn–Anderson theses came from Edward Thompson. He spurned the Nairn–Anderson historical narrative and queried their assessment of empiricism, arguing that it interacted in a largely radical direction with English Protestantism, fostered a tradition of dissent, and encouraged the English line in natural science down to Darwin. Thompson concludes:

> I cannot see empiricism as an *ideology* at all. Anderson and Nairn have confused an intellectual *idiom*, which for various historical reasons has become a national habit, with an ideology. Bacon and Hazlitt, Darwin and Orwell, may all have employed this idiom, but they can scarcely be said to have been attached to the same ulterior ideological assumptions.
>
> (1978, p. 63)

Rejecting empiricism as not scientific, Anderson and Nairn name it as the dominant English ideology; Thompson denies it is an ideology on the grounds that it is 'a national habit'. What needs to be discriminated here is empiricism as *formal philosophic writing* and as more widely dispersed forms of *empiricist discourse*. It will be the purpose of this and the following chapter to clarify and justify that distinction.

Bacon

Not be confused with the 'factual' or the 'empirical', empiricism affirms that reality can be experienced more or less directly by the unprejudiced observer and that knowledge derives more or less directly from that experience: 'Empiricism is the doctrine that all knowledge is acquired through experience' (Priest 1990, p. 53); 'Empiricism specifies every philosophic doctrine accepting that human knowledge deduces (*déduit*) its principles as well as its objects or contents from experience' (Durozoi and Roussel 1987, p. 109). In philosophy a definition, far from ending a debate, initiates one, and a more specific annotation is needed. Empiricism is worked out in England as an explicit philosophy in the writings of Bacon, Hobbes and Locke, and I shall review these here. Berkeley and Hume I omit, partly because they can be claimed by Ireland and Scotland, respectively, partly because what follows is not meant as a history but rather as a preliminary definition of empiricism in England.

If a date needs to be put on the time when an identifiably English empiricist tradition branches off from the European mainline, let it be 1605. A generation earlier, in 1570, in *The Scholemaster* Roger Ascham warns of the harm that comes when educators 'care not for words, but for matter' (1904, p. 265), acknowledging an opposition between rhetoric and logic but urging in humanist fashion the traditional view that eloquence and moral theme should support each other. In contradiction to Ascham, in 1605 Francis Bacon writes that it is 'the first distemper of learning, when men study words and not matter' (1974, p. 26). As will be argued, some such substantial and confidently affirmed distinction between language and meaning is a necessary condition for the empiricist project.

Rejecting aristocratic formalism in favour of bourgeois realism, Bacon pushes for knowledge based on experience and observation as a necessary form of secular power able to transform the natural world, so that the human 'gift of reason' can be turned 'to the benefit and use of men' (p. 36). Arguably, in his conception of the object of knowledge, Bacon's stress falls on reason rather than the evidence of the senses – knowledge comes not from 'impressions' immediately derived from objects but rather from 'abstract notions derived from these impressions' (1857–74, 2, p. 187). While perception is necessary to knowledge, certainty requires inward illumination by reason.

In virtue of its rationality and capacity for empirical observation, the subject for that experienced object is autonomous, free-standing, sovereign. When Bacon writes that 'there is no power on earth which setteth up a throne or chair of estate in the spirits and souls of men, and in their cogitations, imaginations, opinions and beliefs, but knowledge and learning' (1974, p. 57) his Protestant – and democratic – implication is that, although feudalism furnishes abundant instances in which inherited rank decides truth, in principle there should be no such power since in their inward thoughts individuals are free (this democratic tendency soon becomes dispersed). Knowledge of reality, Bacon suggests, can be directly available to the knowing subject because 'the truth of being and truth of knowing are one, differing no more than the direct beam and the beam reflected' (p. 29). Any discourse or means of representation by which truth comes to be represented for the knowing subject interferes with what is thus transmitted or communicated no more than the polished surface of a mirror blocks dazzling sunlight.

The ideal of transparency depends upon a clear distinction between words and meanings, rhetoric and logic, signifier and signified. Bacon takes the distinction as it comes to hand and firms it up as a hardline opposition between 'words' and 'matter' which allows him to contrast and condemn study of 'words and not matter'. What are words then? Bacon remarks casually that 'words are but the images of matter' (p. 26), a position which would tend to dematerialise the signifier by reducing it to exact correspondence with signified meaning. More typical is the view that words do exist materially and can be properly used to persuade but always at the risk that people can – and can choose – to get lost in them. In astrology, for example, observation 'wandereth in words, but is not fixed in inquiry' (p. 162).

In what has become the classic statement, Bacon's own words perform an effect I shall want to claim as exemplary in the tradition. With the humanist revival of Ciceronianism in mind, Bacon writes:

> men began to hunt more after words than matter; more after the choiceness of the phrase, and the round and clean composition of the sentence, and the sweet falling of the clauses, and the varying and illustration of their works with tropes and figures, than after the weight of matter, worth of subject, soundness of argument, life of invention, or depth of judgement.
>
> (p. 26)

You would be hard put to find a sentence which bore signs of a more careful choice of phrase or more attention to rhythm and development in the syntax. But the 'and…and' build-up of the first part of the comparison, with its pleasure in multiplying words and playing with them ('falling of the clauses', etc.), is brought down in the final half by the five curt and emphatic repetitions ('weight of matter', etc.). Rhetoric lingers on phrasing, seducing the reader into it perhaps, but then as words give way to matter, pleasure is to be expelled in favour of a grasp of reality.

Read from a twentieth-century point of view Bacon's own style does not seem very clear. When writing in English his prose is frequently interrupted by rhetorical oppositions, citations (Scripture, Latin classics) and appeals to authority and precedent so that its overall forensic insistence, statement followed by illustration, becomes easily obstructed. The innovative English clarity lies in Bacon's organisation, listing by topics, terms of analysis. Deriving from building, voyaging, growth, water, light, and referring variously to animals, war, health, games, the body, and the garden, Bacon's metaphors might be termed 'empiricist' in that they evince a common-sense world as experienced by an individual.

What, in Bacon's vision, could ever go wrong? If reality can be accurately observed and understood by enlightened reason, and the individual subject is such that for him (or, in principle, her) knowing and being may coincide, and discourse by nature reflects truth like a mirror, what alterity remains to trouble the process of this translucence? Several moves, each symptomatic, aim to exclude any such possibility. Some of Bacon's favoured pejoratives – 'vain', 'frivolous', 'false' – declare everything other as not properly real, as fiction, words not matter. But where do the words come from? One answer is that they come from and pertain to another social class: 'logic handleth reason exact and in truth, and rhetoric handleth it as it is planted in popular opinions and manners' (p. 141), 'eloquence' has the 'fittest and forciblest access into the capacity of the vulgar sort' (p. 25). If Bacon's empiricist reason cannot validate itself simply by claiming a centre in the freely choosing subject, then it is supported and held in place by a social consensus, by a ruling class which behaves according to the procedures Bacon describes and advocates.

But where does the *desire* for words come from? To which the only answer seems to be that it comes from desire, desire which must be got rid of if Bacon's scheme of things is to subsist as he wishes:

> But as both heaven and earth do conspire and contribute to the use and benefit of man; so the end ought to be, from both philosophies to separate and reject vain speculations, and whatsoever is empty and void, and to preserve and augment whatsoever is solid and fruitful: that knowledge may not be as

> a courtesan, for pleasure and vanity only, or as a bond-woman, to acquire and gain to her master's use; but as a spouse, for generation, fruit, and comfort.
>
> (p. 36)

On one side, 'vanity', words, fantasy, self-deception and the courtesan; on the other, 'use', matter, reason, a grasp of reality. But the courtesan is desired for her master's 'use', while the spouse offers only a 'comfort' in which desire is denied. Hindsight shows the metaphor is typical not accidental – this is not the last time in the empiricist tradition that rhetoric, self-deception and sexual pleasure are epitomised (and rejected) in the figure of a desirable woman.

Desire comes from desire: famously Bacon compares scholasticism (and other bad things he wants to renounce) to spiders who 'out of no great quantity of matter' and 'infinite agitation of wit' spin 'laborious webs of learning' (p. 28). Surely this metaphor of shining threads extruded, it seems, from nowhere implies male masturbation, the very model and epitome of fantasy and useless desire (a figure which will rear its head more than once in the pages to come)?

Hobbes, empiricism, and the English Enlightenment

For Hobbes everything is a material process:

> The World, (I mean not the Earth onely, that denominates the Lovers of it *Worldly men*, but the *Universe*, that is, the whole masse of all things that are) is Corporeall, that is to say, Body; and hath the dimensions of Magnitude, namely, Length, Bredth, and Depth: also every part of Body, is likewise Body, and hath the like dimensions; and consequently every part of the Universe, is Body; and that which is not Body, is no part of the Universe: And because the Universe is All, that which is no part of it, is *Nothing*; and consequently *no where*.
>
> (1991, pp. 463)

Everything is material, is body, including, Hobbes adds, spirits, because they are 'really *Bodies*' (p. 463).

Human knowledge of this prior materiality comes about in two ways:

> THERE are of KNOWLEDGE two kinds; whereof one is

> *Knowledge of Fact*: the other *Knowledge of the Consequence of one Affirmation to another*. The former is nothing else, but Sense and Memory, and is *Absolute Knowledge*; as when we see a Fact doing, or remember it done; And this is the Knowledge required in a Witnesse. The later is called *Science*; and is *Conditionall*; as when we know, that, *If the figure showne be a Circle, then any straight line through the Center shall divide it into two equall parts.*
>
> (p. 60)

In this view, knowledge of fact is primary and absolute, knowledge of consequences or the causal relations between facts ('Science' or exact universal knowledge) is secondary and conditional because (so Hobbes claims) it derives from *a priori* definitions.

Reality, the world of fact, conceived essentially as objects in motion, causes sensations in us and these sensations produce images in the mind which are copies of sensation: 'there is no conception in a mans mind, which hath not at first, totally, or by parts, been begotten upon the organs of Sense' (p. 13). Stored in the memory such images can be called up in the imagination, but as ever more crowd in, so the older and more distant ones are crowded out and fade. Copying the world of sensation, imagination consists, therefore, of 'nothing but *decaying sense*' (p. 15). The way in which the external world actively and directly begets on the passive organs of sense a mental image recalls the patriarchal scenario according to which in Milton's *Paradise Lost* God 'begot' the only Son as perfect image of Himself – in Jesus 'all his Father shon/Substantially exprest' – a reproduction which is both caused by and perfectly represents its paternal origin (Book 5, l. 603).

Mental discourse moves across images either in an unguided fashion (in which case ideas will be associated in ways explicable in terms of how they previously occurred in fact) or as regulated by a desire or a design. Just as objects produce sensations, and sensations pass directly into images, so unspoken thought can pass over into language: 'the generall use of Speech, is to transferre our Mentall Discourse, into Verbal' (Hobbes 1991, p. 25). It is the more plausible that language should be able to deliver things in an equal number of words, as Sprat said, because, eschewing notions of language as phonemic or syntactic system, Hobbes thinks of it as founded in the capacity to provide nouns (or names) for objects ('names are, for Hobbes, the bricks out of which language is built'; Watkins 1989, p. 101). And so there is – or should be – no mediation or intervention by any signifier or means of representation in the transfer of signified meaning from one mind to another: 'When a man upon the hearing of any Speech, hath those thoughts which the words of that Speech, and their connexion, were ordained and constituted to signifie; Then he is said to understand it' (Hobbes 1991, p. 30).

Speech (or language) has four uses:

1. To help us remember explanations.
2. To enable us to share explanations with others.
3. To make known our wills.
4. For the pleasure of playing with words.

These imply four correspondent abuses, starting with self-deception which comes about 'when men register their thoughts wrong' (p. 25) by mistaking the meaning of words (other abuses are deceiving others, lying and slandering).

Discourse, realism and pleasure in Hobbes

In principle, then, according to Hobbes's conception, discourse mirrors reality, though this entails a question about what is happening when it fails to reflect accurately and correctly. For Hobbes the scapegoat is the signifier: unless held firmly in place in the form of pleasurable word-play, the signifier can only lead to trouble, to a hunt for 'words' instead of 'matter'. Words as nouns correspond to reality and if they don't, they are but 'insignificant sounds', as for example when the words are new and undefined like those coined in abundance by schoolmen and 'pusled Philosophers' (p. 30). Again and again Hobbes returns to the damage inherent in the 'abuse of words' (p. 58), 'when men speak such words, as put together, have in them no signification at all' (pp. 58–9), words which can represent 'Good, in the likeness of Evill' and 'Evill, in the likeness of Good' (p. 119).

In seeking to contain the work/play of the signifier Hobbes performs manoeuvres endlessly replicated by English culture after him. One takes place round the word 'jargon'. Scholasticism is a main adversarial discourse for *Leviathan* (Chapters 1, 2, 3, 6 and 9 each end with a crack at it), attacked (among other reasons) for holding a theory of abstract essences, such as 'Round*nesse*, Magni*tude*, Quali*ty*'. Mocking these as '*Nesses*, *Tudes*, and *Ties*' (p. 59), Hobbes reduces them to 'insignificant sounds' and later refers to them as '*Jargon*' (p. 463). The word denoted the warbling of birds until 1570 when the *Oxford English Dictionary* (*OED*) records the use of it to mean trivial discourse. With a weak meaning as 'excessive pleasure in verbal play' and a more usual, strong meaning of 'unintelligible language', in the discourse of Englishness 'jargon' remains a highly charged term to the present day. Hobbes remarks that 'a man may play with the sounds' of words but should never do so in public speech or on a serious occasion (such as a sermon) – at these 'there is no Gingling of words that will not be accounted folly' (p. 52). Acting out the delight of '*Nesses*, *Tudes*, and *Ties*', '*Jargon*' and 'Gingling', his own formulations disclose the pleasure they want to deny.

In Hobbes the autonomy of the free-standing individual is assumed almost without discussion. Language produces universals (man, horse, tree) which are merely an effect of speech, 'for the things named, are every one of them Individuall and Singular' (p. 26). For Hobbes the subject is specified in advance by an empiricist epistemology in which a world of individual objects or 'things' is experienced directly (physical sensations passing into mental images) by a correspondingly individualised subject. The priority of reality (over language, over reason) is constituted on the basis of the everyday world of common sense as perceived by the empirical individual, who, in the act of indicating a given reality – 'that is a man', 'this is a house', 'there is a tree' – reciprocally defines his or her own givenness (this is a view Karl Popper refuses when he argues that 'science and scientific objectivity do not (and cannot) result from the attempts of an individual scientist to be "objective", but from the co-operation of many scientists', cited Quinton 1980, p. 32).

Before Defoe's narrativisation in 1719 and long before Marx satirised the bourgeois obsession with Robinson Crusoe, Hobbes dramatises the self-made and self-creating individual:

> There is no other act of mans mind, that I can remember, naturally planted in him, so, as to need no (*sic*) other thing, to the exercise of it, but to be born a man, and live with the use of his five Senses.
>
> (1991, p. 23)

For Hobbes the rejection of innate ideas bears a democratic implication since in natural abilities – as distinct from experience – Hobbes finds 'equality amongst men' (p. 87). As equal individuals each has a natural right of self-preservation and 'of doing any thing he liketh' (p. 92) only to be restrained by law. Accordingly, law and order is to be established in a contract between self interested individuals to yield sovereignty to a state power which will keep the peace for them and over them.

The centre, the foundation for the Hobbesian universe, is the prudent individual made such through experience seconded by reason. While Bacon makes claims for a degree of shared rationality, Hobbes maintains a reduced and instrumental notion of reason subordinate to experience and desire. Deprived of right reason, what validates and sustains these subjects alone with their five senses?

In the Hobbesian anthropology self-deception is instinctive and endemic, born with self-interest and the right to self-preservation. Almost as soon as we are told there is no mental conception that has not been begotten on the organs of sense, we learn that people measure 'all other things, by themselves' (p. 15), and, later, that good and evil are 'ever used with relation to the person that useth them' (p. 39). If this is so, one is entitled to inquire about the book's own voice. What authorises the truth of *Leviathan* as a text and what preserves it from folly, fancy and gingling?

Consistent with its own argument that reality produces sensations, sensations images, and that images can be accurately represented in words (especially nouns), the guarantee of the truth of *Leviathan* lies in the correspondence between its analysis and the reader's own experience of reality. Rather than being a work of philosophy (Hobbes has little but contempt for 'abstruse Philosophy' (p. 59)) *Leviathan* is put forward as a work of science in the traditional sense of *scientia civilis*.

Quentin Skinner has argued that Hobbes changed his mind, gave up his former distrust of deliberately elaborated language, and in *Leviathan*, despite misgivings, accepted 'that, if truth is to prevail, the findings of science will have to be empowered by the persuasive techniques associated with the art of rhetoric' (1996, p. 376). This analysis is limited by the fact that Skinner's conception of rhetoric consists of the figures of speech codified by the classical tradition (simile, metaphor, *diasyrmus*, *aestismus*, etc.). In contrast, the conception of rhetoric upheld in this present study would in principle open for inspection the whole field of the signifier deployed to bring about meaning. From this perspective it is evident: (1) that Hobbes' officially avowed purpose in using classical rhetoric is to subordinate language to meaning as a better means to an end; and (2) that at a deeper stratum the operation of the signifier has to be repressed for the Hobbesian universe to body forth.

The forty-six years separating *Leviathan* from *The Advancement of Learning* have banished Bacon's rhetorical repetitions and persistent citation of authorities so that, relative to its predecessor, the style of *Leviathan* aims to be a styleless style. In detail there is an aggressively colloquial vocabulary, which would present things in as many words, as well as an analytic organisation and subordination of themes in the order of exposition. But the main effect of transparency is brought about by syntactical means, by 'the order of words', which if rightly placed 'carries a light before it, whereby a man may foresee the length of his period [i.e. sentence], as a torch in the night shews a man the stops and unevenness in his way' (Hobbes 1908, 2, p. 69).

Yet no matter how discreetly the signifier is contained and effaced, the implied author cannot escape his or her own misrecognition. In *Leviathan*, as in so much of the English discursive tradition, self-deception covers itself with a strategy which supports a privileging of the empirical subject: the delusion that one is never deluded. Freud's distinction between pleasure principle and the reality principle (see 1973–86, 11, pp. 29–44) may clarify the issue. In its mental functioning the subject is driven by the desire for pleasure. In so far as its wishes are refused satisfaction, that principle becomes modified by the reality principle in obedience to which the subject aims for satisfaction via detours and deferrals. Though seeming to acknowledge the reality of the outside world, the reality principle is as much an effect of desire as the pleasure principle.

Hobbes's writing claims to stick without compunction to the reality principle. Developed as it is through a series of unemphatic propositions, general statements, arguments and conclusions, the predominant tone and manner of *Leviathan* are very much that of casual and brutal 'take it or leave it':

> Sometime a man desires to know the event of an action; and then he thinketh of some like action past, and the events thereafter one after another; supposing like events will follow like actions. As he that foresees what wil become of a Criminal, recons what he has seen follow on the like Crime before; having this order of thoughts, The Crime, the Officer, the Prison, the Judge, and the Gallowes. Which kind of thoughts, is called *Foresight.*
>
> (1991, p. 22)

The Hobbesian voice makes a show of its freedom from sentimentality and wish-fulfilment in a rhetoric which continuously awakens wish-fulfilment in order to reject it. Why otherwise choose to define foresight, which might have so many attractive exemplifications, exclusively – in this grim little narrative – as what enables you to avoid the gallows? For deflating of expectations a frequent trope he uses is sardonic redefinition in a 'that is to say' or an 'is nothing but'.

In *Leviathan* Hobbes has to hand a repertory of figures staged to prove his own realism, his anti-sentimental adherence to the reality principle. Always there are the schoolmen, given over entirely to the infantile pleasures of the signifier and 'canting' words 'that signifie nothing' (p. 35). There are books, if these are treated as authority when experience should be – those who trust 'onely to the authority of books' are like someone who has trusted a bad fencing master and gets killed as a result (p. 37). There is religion or superstition, a childish 'Feare of things invisible' which deceives itself by believing in the supernatural when there are such things 'onely in Man' (p. 75). And there are 'Women and Children' who are especially prone to weeping because instead of relying on themselves they rely on 'helps externall' (p. 43). All these figures are characterised by believing what they want to believe rather than knowing what is really there.

The ultimate self-deception is the belief that '*every private man is Judge of Good and Evill actions*' rather than the law. As one of 'the *Diseases* of a Common-Wealth' (p. 223), this calls up some of Hobbes's most violent denunciation so that he classifies inspiration or 'Private Spirit' (p. 55) under madness. As well he might, because that which most closely threatens his notion of the privileged and autonomous individual who has learned reality from experience is the individual who finds in their selfhood the source of all authority.

Whether writing of men who attribute wet-dreams to 'Succubae' (p. 80) or those ignorant of 'Sciences' as being 'like children, that having no thought of generation, are made believe by the women, that their brothers and sisters are not born, but found in the garden' (p. 36), Hobbes invites the reader to join him in his superiority over those who think what they do because it suits them, a superiority which opposes objectivity, detachment, an open-eyed assessment of reality to a subjective wish fulfilment which imagines reality to be as we'd like it. In such passages Hobbes may be 'trailing his coat'. After the Restoration Hobbes (in his eighties) was at the court of Charles II; Aubrey tells this story: 'The witts at Court were wont to bayte him. But he feared none of them, and would make his part good. The King would call him *the Beare*: Here comes the Beare to be bayted' (1972, p. 312).

Reading this as a comment not on *Leviathan*'s author but its writing I would take it as suggesting that Hobbes' appearance of impassivity acts as an ironic provocation, his 'take it or leave it' neutrality derives from an aggressive desire to be baited and so find a chance to convict others of the mawkishness they think they've given up. Why, a contemporary reader of *Leviathan* wondered, had Hobbes been so 'copious in jearing' at his opponents (Henry More, cited Skinner 1996, p. 425)?

However ironically understated (and irony is a central topic in English empiricism), *Leviathan*'s condemnation of its 'others' causes an excess which undoes its avowed intentions. If the text hopes to give the effect of a more or less transparent viewpoint on reality, its rhetoric shows it consists of writing. When its voice affirms its grasp of the reality principle against inward tendencies to self-deception, it reveals the pleasure to be found in denouncing the pleasure principle, the desire to deny desire. Its tone of confidently disabused masculinity speaks of an unease about sexual difference and femininity ('the women' as Hobbes says). Far from being idiosyncratic, such features in Hobbes's writing will turn out to be aspects of a recurring structure.

Locke's Englishness

Within the English tradition there is an important and continuing distinction between Tory and Whig, between figures who identify unequivocally with the gentry, with law and order, with 'King and Country', and who generally, in the name of a certain naked materialism, consider constitutionalism, rights and civility a genteel cover to the real struggle for power; and others who, conscious of an effortless superiority and fully confident of their parity with the rest of the gentry, can afford to regard them from an ironic distance characterised by a rationalism which ascribes greater substance to popular consent, civil order and the virtues of urbanity.

The English Civil War was fought between those who supported monarchy and those who supported Parliament but after 1660 a less violent conflict took place between those who found political sovereignty in established authority and those who looked for it in social consent. In 1679 the Whigs united with Dissenters to put a bill through Parliament excluding the king's Roman Catholic brother from succession; they were opposed by the Tories and the Church of England. In this crisis John Locke acted as political secretary to the Whig leader, Anthony Ashley Cooper, and subsequently, in his *Two Treatises of Government* (1690), defined foundationally liberal arguments in opposition to those of the aristocratic royalist, Robert Filmer. T.S. Eliot wrote, 'The Civil War is not ended; I question whether any serious civil war does end' (1957, p. 148): in England Tory and Whig are with us to this day (among twentieth-century Whigs I would name Bertrand Russell, Clement Attlee, Edward Thompson, Tony Benn, and, yes, Terry Eagleton).

Locke's writing in *An Essay Concerning Human Understanding* (1689) is both symptom and cause of the English empiricist tradition. Whether or not the *Essay* was 'the most widely read book apart from the Bible in eighteenth-century England' (Wood 1991, p. 140), its vocabulary ('things', 'sensation', 'reflection', 'definition of terms') has passed into wide currency in English, as have its tone and attitudes.

In Locke empiricism is extended and developed (though it is not certain that Locke read Hobbes very carefully). While Hobbes assumes bluntly that we have more or less direct experience of exterior reality, Locke stresses that the mind is directly and immediately acquainted only with ideas and these have a more indirect relation to reality. The moral distance between the two thinkers is well signalled if one compares the iron-fisted way Hobbes knocks down the belief put about by 'the women' that babies are 'found in the garden' with Locke's gentle and ironic phrasing of the same thought, that '*Sempronia* digged *Titus* out of the Parsley-Bed, (as they use to tell Children)' (II.28.19) (all references are to Locke 1975).

Reality

Locke shares with Hobbes a refusal to believe the soul is born with certain innate ideas or principles but strengthens this with a new grasp of cultural relativism (he refers from time to time to the bizarre but nevertheless comprehensible practices of the Americans, Native Americans that is, II.16.5) and shows a more sympathetic attention to the experiences of children.

As for Hobbes, so also for Locke, the world consists of self-defining particularities, including the individual subject, a consciousness isolated in its direct experience of what are termed 'ideas':

> The Senses at first let in particular *Ideas*, and furnish the yet empty Cabinet: And the Mind by degrees growing familiar with some of them, they are lodged in the Memory, and Names got to Them. Afterwards the Mind proceeding farther, abstracts them, and by Degrees learns the use of General Names. In this manner the Mind comes to be furnish'd with *Ideas* and Language, the Materials about which to exercise its discursive Faculty.
>
> (I.2.15)

All thoughts or mental representations (IV.21.4) Locke terms ideas, and proposes that they arise either from sensation, our '*Perceptions* of things' (II.1.3), or from reflection or introspection, our '*Perception of the Operations of our own Minds* within us' (II.1.4) (for difficulties on this distinction between percepts and concepts, see Lowe 1995 and Ayers 1991, 1, Chapter 5).

On this basis Locke goes on to discriminate between simple and complex ideas. Simple ideas come from sensation and reflection but the understanding 'has the Power to repeat, compare and unite them to an almost infinite Variety', making new 'complex *Ideas*' (II.2.2). Passive to simple ideas, the mind is active in fashioning complex ideas by compounding, comparing or abstracting simple ideas, 'put together by the Mind' (II.22.1). Sensation comes first, however, since it is involuntary, while reflection is subsequent, since it is voluntary.

Reality provokes sensation, and sensation in turn produces ideas which are not identical with objects in reality but a 'likeness' (II.8.7) due to the effects caused in us by the qualities of the objects. With this power to produce ideas in us, qualities come in two kinds. 'Real' primary qualities (such as bulk, density, motion) are able to produce ideas which resemble the objects with these qualities; 'imputed' secondary qualities (notably colour) also produce ideas in us though these ideas do not resemble the qualities of the objects which caused them (Locke presumes a colourless universe). Sensation produces simple ideas except for ideas of substance which, though complex, do correspond to reality (at least, that is the probability).

It follows that the mind does not know 'Things immediately' (that is, without mediation) but only 'the *Ideas* it has of them' (IV.4.3, 4). Locke says these are '*real Ideas*' because they have 'a Conformity with real Being, and Existence of Things' (II.30.1), that there is a 'steady correspondence' (II.30.2) between things and simple ideas of sensation. He wants some kind of guarantee for that correspondence but cannot invoke a position outside and looking on from which someone could assess and validate that correspondence. Locke argues for 'conformity between our *Ideas*' and 'the reality of Things' on the grounds that, since the mind cannot make simple ideas itself, they must be 'the product of Things operating on the Mind' (IV.4.3, 4), but now he is relying on psychology rather than the empirical, not reality but a conception of language and subjectivity.

Ideas and words

For Locke all 'Things, that exist' are particulars (III.3.1). A main way of constructing complex out of simple ideas is the process of abstraction in which '*Ideas* taken from particular Beings, become general Representatives of all of the same kind' (II.11.9). What happens is this:

> the same Colour being observed to day in Chalk or snow, which the Mind yesterday received from Milk, it considers that Appearance alone, makes it a representative of all of that kind; and having given it the name *Whiteness*, it by that sound

> signifies the same quality wheresoever to be imagin'd or met with; and thus Universals, whether *Ideas* or Terms, are made.
>
> (II.11.9)

As Geoff Bennington recalls (1987), in his story 'Funes the Memorious', Borges imagines a language in which naming particularities went at least as far as every leaf of every tree of every wood. Locke rules out any procedure such as this on pragmatic grounds as beyond 'humane Capacity' (III.3.2), so safeguarding his view that reality dictates simple ideas, all 'perfectly distinct' (II.2.1), which the mind combines in abstractions parallel to but separate from words.

Locke follows Hobbes in treating language as though it consisted essentially of nouns. What he would really like is for us to have access to an idea 'such as it is in the Speaker's Mind' (IV.4.9) but he knows that to have someone's thoughts 'laid open to the immediate view of another' (IV.21.4) would require telepathy. In default of that, he sees the use of words as being 'to stand as outward Marks of our internal *Ideas*' (II.11.9), so that, according to what becomes a familiar English tactic, words (the signifier) should be as far as possible transparent to meaning (the signified), mere 'outward' expression of an 'internal' thought, which thus may be 'conveyed' directly from one mind to another (III.1.2). Or almost directly.

On the topic of language the *Essay* displays a constant slippage between what people do and what they should do. With the arrival of the signifier into discussion, this slippage, like that of a worn clutch-plate, becomes loud and clear. Anticipating Saussure, Locke recognises that word and idea by nature are related only 'arbitrarily' (III.2.1) though brought together by custom and use. On the one hand, 'constant use' brings about such a connection between sounds and ideas that words 'almost as readily excite certain *Ideas*, as if the Objects themselves, which are apt to produce them, did actually affect the Senses' (III.2.6) (as if, that is, things determined ideas and ideas determined the words). On the other, because of the same 'familiar use from our Cradles' in which words and ideas become associated, it often happens that men '*set their Thoughts more on Words than Things*' (III.2.7). This turns them into parrots (because they epitomise signifier without signified meaning, Locke is very exercised about parrots, the *Essay* mentioning them at least five times: II.27.8, II.28.15, III.1.1, III.2.7, IV.8.7). The collective convention without which ideas could not be linked to words, ensures they can never be joined as Locke would wish.

At this point, like Bacon and Hobbes before him, hoping to seal off proper from improper usage, Locke launches a sustained attack on

'*Jargon*' (III.4.9 but see also II.1.19, II.13, 27, III.10.4). Since only linguistic convention links sound and idea, a worrying 'doubtfulness and uncertainty' enter signification, for a word may not excite in the addressee 'the same *Idea* which it stands for in the Mind of the Speaker' (III.9.4). Admitting this gap Locke at once tries to close it by castigating the '*Abuse of Words*', a disorder which includes men not 'taking pains' to attach words to 'clear and distinct *Ideas*' (III.10.2), 'contenting themselves with the same Words other People use' (III.10.4), applying old words to 'new and unusual Significations' (III.10.6). By this abuse (writes Locke, picking up Bacon's image of the spider) men weave a 'Web of perplexed Words' to procure for 'themselves the admiration of others, by unintelligible Terms' (III.10.8). In the worst case they can end up taking words '*for Things*' (III.10.14), and what can stop them?

Unable to establish a satisfactory foundation for discriminating between proper and improper use of language, Locke proceeds into the famous condemnation of rhetoric concluding Book III (10.34). He begins by accepting that in discourses designed for pleasure some verbal 'Ornaments' are acceptable, then continues:

> But yet, if we would speak of Things as they are, we must allow, that all the Art of Rhetorick, besides Order and Clearness, all the artificial and figurative application of Words Eloquence hath invented, are for nothing else but to insinuate wrong *Ideas*, move the Passions, and thereby mislead the Judgment; and so indeed are perfect cheat: And therefore however laudable or allowable Oratory may render them in Harangues and popular Addresses, they are certainly, in all Discourses that pretend to inform or instruct, wholly to be avoided.

That rhetoric is everywhere evidences 'how much Men love to deceive and be deceived', though, having spoken with such rhetorical force against rhetoric, Locke finds himself compelled to end with a revealing piece of gallantry: '*Eloquence*, like the fair Sex, has too prevailing Beauties in it, to suffer it self ever to be spoken Against. And 'tis in vain to find fault with those Arts of Deceiving, wherein Men find pleasure to be Deceived.'

'Thinking about philosophy', Derrida has hinted, is a way of 'avoiding women' (1992a, p. 101). Locke's reference to 'the fair Sex' leaps off the page because it is almost the only acknowledgement that sexual difference may excite erotic pleasure in over 700 pages politely but relentlessly cajoling the reader to be a man, learn from his own experience of reality and stand by that, clarify his ideas, define his terms, work hard, above all freely suspending judgement so as not to be seduced by desire and will into the collective defiles of the signifier. Locke's determination to close off meaning from rhetoric, language from the signifier, discloses that his own desire is to be free from desire, to stand above sexual difference, to be wholly self-sufficient. The passage shows that when Locke writes 'Men' he means it.

Noting that children first learn the names for simple ideas, '*White, Sweet, Milk, Sugar, Cat*' (III.9.9) and then those for complex ideas, Locke believes that it is hard to make complex ideas as clear and reliable as simple ideas, a difficulty compounded by the necessary disjunction between words and ideas. Failure to define terms is 'not seldom the occasion of great wrangling' (III.4.4) and yet, Locke speculates, all the great contests over complex ides such as '*Honour, Faith, Grace, Religion, Church* etc.' are 'only about the meaning of a Sound' (III.9.9). If men could specify complex ideas as firmly as their simple ideas, and observed a few simple rules about definition of terms and the use of clear language, then, Locke hopes, '*Morality*' would become as '*capable of Demonstration*' as 'Mathematicks' (III.11.16) and agreement would be universal. It's a big if.

Language matters so much to Locke because it undoes the conscious, undetermined, self-inspecting individuality he puts at the centre of human understanding. He prescribes a language in which nouns would correspond to things but describes a world in which that is impossible. Locke writes very suggestively '*Of the Association of* Ideas' linked merely by 'Chance or Custom' (II.33.5), and cites the example of a man who learned to dance with an old trunk in the room and couldn't dance afterwards unless a similar item were present (Freud mentions the association of 'the box' with feminine sexuality, 1973–86, 1, p. 189). The wrong connection of ideas of this kind will carry over into the connection of words with ideas. For language instances use, habit, practice as against reflection, the world which speaks us before we ever learn to speak as separate selves, a double danger then to the Lockeian self because it is both collective and home of the unconscious. Disparities between 'is' and 'ought' regarding language use in Locke's empiricism are to be recuperated by personal morality and right individual choice.

Subjectivity and morality

Quite as decisively as for Descartes, individual self-consciousness is Locke's own starting point: 'Every Man being conscious to himself, That he thinks' (II.1.1, see O'Connor 1952, pp. 35–6). The self is conscious of its perceptions, conscious of the operations of its own mind, and conscious of its own persisting identity which provides a space for this consciousness. Morality hopes to make good any interval between this absolute self and its others (language, collectivity, the unconscious).

The 'great difference' in the 'Notions of Mankind' ensues from the right and wrong uses they put their faculties to, abuses leading away from true knowledge being:

1 laziness;
2 willing enslavement to the opinions of others;
3 accepting things 'blindly' and on faith;
4 letting thoughts run 'loose'.

(I.4.22)

True knowledge, in contrast, '*depends upon the right use of those Powers Nature hath bestowed on us*' (I.4.22; also II.13.27).

To use his powers rightly the individual must above all guard against self-deception. Locke notes how quick a man is to spot and condemn extravagance 'in the Opinions, Reasonings, and Actions of other Men…though he be guilty of much greater Unreasonableness in his own Tenets and Conduct, which he never perceives, and will very hardly, if at all, be convinced of' (II.33.1). Free agency is founded in the subject's undetermined ability to direct attention, to 'remove his Contemplation from one *Idea* to another' (II.21.12.). Ideally, in self-consciousness the perspective of the individual and that of the Other coincide; in principle, access to this position of immunity from self-deception is *always open*.

What can go wrong arises from desire, desire being an '*uneasiness* of the Mind for want of some absent good' (II.21.31) which may determine the will. Nevertheless, everybody has the capacity to suspend desire, examine their own actions and choose good; everyone ultimately is absolutely responsible. Locke's view is staunch that 'the satisfaction of any particular *desire* can be suspended from determining the *will* to any subservient action, till we have maturely examin'd, whether the paricular apparent good, which we then desire, makes a part of our real Happiness, or be consistent or inconsistent with it (II.21.71).

In this respect desire and will count as external to the self, which is equated with the moment of the suspension of desire (recognisable as the more commonplace injunction 'to defer judgement'; see Dunn 1984, p. 60). It is in this undivided, fully self-conscious space or moment that personal identity inheres. Fully transcendental (despite disavowals, this very English notion of a subject, as Catherine Belsey neatly remarks, 'takes the place of God' (1985, p. 86).

Clearly the body changes over time – does the identity of the person? Setting aside traditional belief that identity was conferred by an immaterial soul, Locke considers personal memory to be constitutive of individual identity conceived as diachronic. Since memory fades and we lose details of our past selves, 'doubts are raised whether we are the same thinking thing' (II.27.10). But identity continues even if the substance of the body changes:

> For it being the same consciousness that makes a Man be himself to himself, *personal Identity* depends on that only, whether it be annexed only to one individual Substance, or can be continued in a succession of several Substances. For as far as any intelligent Being can repeat the *Idea* of any past action with the same consciousness it had of it at first, and with the same consciousness it has of any present Action; so far it is the same *personal self.* For it is by the consciousness it has of its present Thoughts and Actions, that it is a *self* to it *self* now, and so will be the same *self,* as far as the same consciousness can extend to Actions past and to come.
>
> (II.27.10)

On this showing, I am the same person if I can repeat a memory with the same consciousness of it now as I had of it then. Locke's very modern account of identity has been profoundly influential – identity, that is, which is constituted inwardly as 'the Identity of *consciousness*' (II.27.19) rather than on the basis of the continuity of the body or identity socially ascribed (passports, etc.). His theory relies on a number of assumptions – that his definition of first-person memory does not itself *presuppose* the very notion of identity it is meant to substantiate, that a past idea repeated is the same as it was the first time, that there is no problem in telling the difference between a memory and a fantasy ('the most delicate question in the whole domain of psychoanalysis', says Freud; 1973–86, 9, p. 344).

Locke sets out to derive a theory of knowledge from our experience of ourselves and of reality but does not achieve the guarantee he wants that there is a correspondence between reality and the subject's knowledge of it (as Richard Rorty argues, Locke tries to pass off a more or less accurate description of how we perceive as a theory of knowledge; see 1994, pp. 137–54). Locke then hopes to find certainty in the constitution of the subject itself but there, too, uncertainty emerges. The self-defining 'I', proved to be such by its freedom to shift contemplation, guard itself from self-deception and always be the same, begins to look more like an absence than a presence and point of origin. Alongside passages in which Locke affirms that there cannot be 'a more dangerous thing to rely on' than '*the Opinion of others*' (IV.15.6), others occur in which he queries whether there is an isolate, free, conscious identity capable of independent knowledge of both its world and itself: ''Tis past controversy, that we have in us something that thinks, our very Doubts about what it is, confirm the certainty of its being, though we must content our selves in the Ignorance of what kind of *being* it is' (IV.3.6).

Locke's rhetoric

What will define and support the Lockeian subject if it cannot support itself? It has to be a demarcation between the right and wrong use of language, on the one hand, a discourse of full meaning and perfect clarity in which the subject appears present to itself, partitioned off from wrong use which comes about whenever the signifier intrudes. Absolute clarity in ideas and appropriately denotative language may be striven for but are reluctant to emerge from entanglement with social custom and common use. Since complex ideas are put together 'by Men alone', differently in different cultures, and since the relation between words and ideas is conventional, in the end the criterion by which to separate proper and improper use can only be social convention, agreement enacted within a shared mode of discourse. The *Essay*'s own writing, then, far from being a purely externalised mark of Locke's internal ideas, becomes a crucial means to validate its claim to truth (Walker (1994) also recognises the importance of Locke's style but concentrates almost exclusively on his metaphors).

The *Essay* is written in a style of courteous demystification and self-deprecation integral to its avowed purpose, that is, to make philosophy, defined as '*nothing but the true Knowledge of Things*' capable of being '*brought into well-bred Company, and polite Conversation*' (as Locke says in the 'Epistle' at the beginning of *The Essay*; 1975, p. 10). While aggression in Hobbes is a sign of insecurity, Locke's easy manner displays the confidence of the text in the authority of its own discourse. Although it opens with a flattering letter to an Earl, it sees itself as addressed to a small group of equals, '*five or six Friends meeting at my Chamber, and discoursing*' (*Epistle to the Reader*, p. 7).

In fact Locke does not write, he speaks, and the effect of the text as informal speech rather than a written document recurs throughout – Locke frequently promises to 'return' to something, begs 'pardon' for his procedure, especially if it risks 'Obscurity' (III.6.43) or using a word in 'a different sence from its ordinary signification' (II.12.4), says something will be mentioned 'by the bye' (III.11.17), craves indulgence if he has been engaged in enquiries 'a little farther than, perhaps, I intended' (II.8.22) and asks leave 'to propose an extravagant conjecture' (II.22.13).

So Locke aims to practise what he advocates, demonstrating in his text:

1 that his concerns are shared and communicable, not abstruse, sectarian and merely personal;
2 that his inquiry is impartial and disinterested;
3 that he is entirely self-conscious and self-reflecting so that he *can see himself as others see him*, citing their view of him, for example, when he says 'I doubt not but my Reader, by this time, may be apt to think that I have been all this while only building a Castle in the Air; and be ready to say to me, To what purpose all this stir?' (IV.4.1).

Locke's writing aims to draw on and perpetuate a vocabulary easily mixing concrete and abstract words, a syntax apt to mark complex discriminations without sounding overfussy, and overall a tone which can move with relaxed confidence between ironic wit and difficult exposition. His style, enormously dependent upon irony, anticipates the fully realised urbanity of Pope. Although the *Essay* declares that rhetoric does nothing but 'insinuate wrong *Ideas*' when what we need is to 'speak of Things as they are', its arguments would become unthinkable apart from its very specific discourse. Rewritten in the mode of Hegel, the *Essay Concerning Human Understanding* would be as impossible as the *Phenomenology of Spirit* articulated according to the style, manner and discourse of Locke.

Rhetoric and class

In trying to prescribe a right use of language Locke proposes that the standard must be 'the *Ideas* of those, who are thought to use those Names in their most proper Significations' (II.32.12). Discussing resistance to the truth as he pronounces it, Locke reflects on the class status of his own discourse. Men's ignorance of truth, he says, comes from reliance on bad arguments, laziness, differences in intellectual ability, the lack of opportunity to think. He explains this last by saying that 'the greatest part of Mankind' are 'given up to Labour' so that 'their whole Time and Pains is laid out, to still the Croaking of their own Bellies, or the cries of their Children'. The passage tends to confirm the *Essay* as itself a special form of class discourse, one affording its reader a position as knowing, morally justified, masculine and a member of the gentry ('The general Maxims, we are discoursing of', Locke remarks, 'are not known to Children, *Ideots*, and a great part of Mankind'; I.2.27).

Rhetoric and the body

Within the context of this genteel conversation and modest, ironic tone, there appears a startling effect, in which the writing of the *Essay* is interrupted by a violent breaking in from outside, the sudden arrival of contingency and the body in pieces. 'Let a Cannon-bullet pass through a Room' (II.14.10), writes Locke without anticipation. To illustrate one complex idea he takes the example of 'the killing a Man's Father' (II.22.4), compares killing a sheep and killing a father (III.5.6), and notes that 'killing a Man with a Sword, or a Hatchet' are not looked on as distinct species of action (III.5.11). To show the persistence of individual identity, Locke says 'Cut off an hand…it's still same person' (II.27.11). He debates the rights of 'taking away his Sword from a Madman' (II.28.16) and illustrates the idea of individual liberty by pointing out that 'A Man standing on a cliff, is at liberty to leap twenty yeards downwards into the Sea…' (II.21.27) but points out that 'Likewise a Man falling into the Water (a Bridge breaking under him)' (II.21.9) does not instance a limitation on freedom.

Officially, these are *exempla*, whose content is marginal and trivial, a means to illustrate a thought. But why are they so highly charged and so consistent in import? One could argue that English empiricism, explicitly committed to individual experience of reality, embraces a strong awareness of the body. Yet the French rationalist tradition, tied in with the Catholic tradition, encompasses a far more generous and intimate sense of anus, mouth and genitals, their pleasures and their pains, than we find anywhere in Locke's Protestant austerity. And in any case, with Locke's empiricism, reality becomes progressively attenuated, appearing initially as sensation but soon recast into ideas discriminated between those the mind is passive to and those, the important ones, which it actively constructs.

An earlier instance may explain the effect. In Marlowe's play, Faustus, having sold his soul to the devil, tells Mephostophilis 'I think hell's a fable' and receives the wolfish reply, 'Ay, think so still, till experience change thy mind'. Hobbes enjoys exactly that same righteous pleasure in disabusing self-deception, and goes out of his way to find it. A much softer Locke draws on an equally moralised apprehension of reality when he replies with the deepest irony to someone who might argue that a dream could simulate reality, 'I believe he will allow a very manifest difference between dreaming of being in the Fire, and being actually in it' (IV.2.14). The same pleasure at watching experience destroy self-deception is expressed in Hobbes though Locke's version is more refined.

In Locke these textual eruptions by the body perform according to a strategy of projection, naming what is most feared and to that degree exorcising it, so as to leave consciousness more free. Such references are dropped in so that the body in pieces may be moralised, transformed by recuperation into a sardonic warning against wrong choice, self-deception and overweening personal expectation. In this rhetoric (which introduces the larger question of 'the English body'), awareness of the body is to be contained, and along with the body, sexual difference and desire.

Rhetoric between simple and complex

If it is a principle of empiricism that all true knowledge derives from the senses, surely that's that? How can there possibly be *arguments for* empiricism, and these arguments produced in textual form? This contradiction or aporia at the core of empiricism has been pointed out by Derrida with some scorn when in *Of Grammatology* he describes 'the opposition of philosophy and nonphilosophy' as

> another name for empiricism, for this incapability to sustain on one's own and to the limit the coherence of one's own discourse, for being produced as truth when the value of truth is shattered, for escaping the internal contradictions, etc. *The thought of this historical opposition between philosophy and empiricism is not simply empirical and it cannot be thus qualified without abuse and misunderstanding.*
>
> (1976, p. 162)

Elsewhere he refers to empiricism 'as the philosophical pretension to nonphilosophy' (1978, p. 152). The issue is a key to the main discursive operation and effect of Locke.

The vocabulary of the *Essay* circles interminably around the words 'obvious', 'evident', 'plain', 'clear' (as in 'clear that'). Again and again Locke turns from argument into what he calls an '*appeal* to Mens own unprejudiced *Experience*' (I.4.25):

> whether this be so, or no, I will not here determine, but appeal to every one's own Experience.
>
> (II.8.5)

> *What Perception is*, every one will know better by reflecting on what he does himself, when he sees, hears, feels, *etc.*
>
> (II.9.2)

> 'Tis evident to any one who will but observe what passes in his own Mind.
>
> (II.14.3)

> whether this be not so, I desire every one to observe in himself.
>
> (II.21.38)

> [we should] warily attend to the Motions of the mind, and observe what Course it usually takes.
>
> (II.32.7)

These appeals to common sense are both theoretically consistent with the empiricist project and necessary to it. To ground his position Locke needs the consensus called up by his casual discourse, with its assured poise and easy, incontrovertible tone ('this is so, isn't it?').

At this juncture, as commentators have noted, the bridge Locke is crossing threatens to break under him. For if all Locke's writing had to offer were urbanity laced with deictic invocations of reality, who would have heard of him? In fact there are two Lockes, one simple, one complex (to adapt his own terms). For example, Locke does refer to 'Things, as they are in themselves' (II.25.1) but a more scrupulous reading undermines this simplistic notion. Although it is qualified more carefully elsewhere, particularly in terms of the active powers of mind in constructing complex ideas, Locke can still repeat that '*Words…stand for nothing, but the* Ideas *in the Mind*' and that 'those *Ideas* are collected from the Things they are supposed to represent' (III.2.2). In this vein he can write that such is the connection between sounds and ideas that names heard 'almost as readily excite certain *Ideas*, as if the Objects themselves, which are apt to produce them, did actually affect the Senses' (III.2.6).

Another, more complex Locke partakes of the European philosophic tradition, yielding, as Peter Nidditch says, 'the most thorough and plausible formulation of empiricism' (Locke 1975, p. vii). Though Derrida's question might be whether *any* 'formulation of empiricism' really can be 'thorough and plausible', there is no doubt the *Essay* has won the position it holds because for much of the time it does sustain to the limit the coherence of its own discourse. On the other hand, the simple Locke aims to bring philosophy, defined with English bluntness as the true knowledge of things, '*into well-bred Company, and polite Conversation*'. If empiricism is right and we all have more or less direct knowledge of reality, then philosophy will amount to no more than friends having a chat and agreeing. Consistent with its theme, the *Essay* frequently does adopt this tone and manner but only at the cost of becoming a deeply fissured text, grafting together common-sense views with long sections of sustained, rational, philosophic analysis.

Trying to keep the *Essay* within the civil and disinterested discourse of the English gentry, five or six (male) friends discoursing together, has massive consequences for the English tradition. Locke's strand of everyday, colloquial discourse gives foundational authority and voice to a common-sense English view that things enter our heads as ideas where we turn them into words which, if we define our terms properly, are more or less the same as things. Such empiricist discourse, constantly retrieving attitudes from some half-forgotten precedent in Locke, continues to define limits for English culture.

4

AN EMPIRICIST TRADITION

> Wanda! Have you any idea what it's like to be *English*?
> (Archie Leach (John Cleese) in *A Fish Called Wanda,* 1989)

In his *Life of Johnson* James Boswell records how he and Johnson came out of church and stood talking for some time about 'Bishop Berkeley's ingenious sophistry to prove the non-existence of matter, and that every thing in the universe is merely ideal'. Johnson was clearly appalled at this threat to empirical reality. Boswell continues:

> I observed, that though we are satisfied his doctrine is not true, it is impossible to refute it. I shall never forget the alacrity with which Johnson answered, striking his foot with mighty force against a large stone, till he rebounded from it, 'I refute it *thus*'.
> (1945, p. 130)

Though Boswell is right to warn how hard it would be to refute Berkeley, and Johnson wrong to suppose an event refutes an argument, Johnson's boot has the full weight of Englishness behind it.

Some further examples, not from philosophic or scientific writing but from an area of discourse more everyday and certainly closer to the ideological heartlands of contemporary Englishness, literary criticism. In 1936 the American literary theorist, René Wellek, challenged F.R. Leavis to elaborate 'a theory' in defence of his assumptions about literature; Leavis refused to be drawn away from experienced particularity, replying only, 'My whole effort was to work in terms of concrete judgments and particular analysis. "This – doesn't it? – bears such a relation to that; this kind of thing – don't you find it so? – wears better than that", etc' (1937, p. 63).

In a way that makes it sound as natural as breathing, Richard

Hoggart in a recent review invoked the 'important principle' that you should 'not apply to the text, from outside, your predetermined theories, like an ideological waffle-iron' (*Times Literary Supplement*, 9 July 1993). A speech by Prince Charles calling for a return to moral basics demonstrated his grasp of commonplace empiricist discourse when he turned on those who, he said, tear literature apart to fit the 'abstruse theories of the day' (see *Guardian*, 5 May 1994).

These straws in a prevailing wind show how much in England it is a matter of course to call up a cluster of assumptions: reality is just there – watch, I'm going to kick it; forget theory, all that matters is concrete judgements and particular analysis; like Johnson's stone, the literary text is simply given, there to be experienced, an object inside a line which firmly marks off theory as outside.

The great oppositions

Across modern English history a set of attitudes and vague assumptions, a manner and idiom made up of habitual phrases and tropes, an informal empiricist discourse working at a deeper level than an explicit ideology (as Edward Thompson suggested), actively touch all kinds of texts far away from the philosophy-writer's desk and surface in places which include books of literary criticism, car enthusiast magazines, popular science journals, cooking recipes, football reports, television news, the House of Commons, the public house, the academy, the factory canteen, the board room, the laboratory. When he describes how everyone uses 'the *Words* they speak (with any meaning) all alike' (1975, III.2.3) Locke distinguishes, as he would, between 'the Knowing and the Ignorant', 'the Learned and the Unlearned', though, as was argued, he himself slides between an elaborated formal philosophic discourse and common-sense discussion. I shall explore this more casual empiricist discourse as functioning in a scenario with three terms, these governing the object, the means of representation, and the subject:

1 The object is assumed to exist in a reality which is supposedly pregiven. All you have to do is observe reality 'objectively', that is, without prejudgement or self-deception, and reality will yield knowledge of itself (the English seem to be obsessed with reality).
2 The means of representation by which the object is represented to the subject is presumed not to interfere – or to intervene only minimally – with the subject's access to reality. In principle, discourse is transparent so that the only problem for knowledge is, as it were, to go and look and see what things are *there*.

3 In an epistemological scenario, subject and object always correspond to each other. If, according to the empiricist conception, reality is thought of as simply autonomous, given, then reciprocally the English subject is envisaged not as the effect of a process of construction but as always already merely *there* as the subject of or for knowledge/experience. (A specially English version of morality inheres in this structure of subject, object, and knowledge.)

This is a short, introductory outline, and my enterprise in the rest of this book will be to test how far it can be run in analysing a discursive formation and its effects.

The English preoccupation with reality sits on the stone of Johnsonian 'common sense'. Whereas 'common' is pulled between a descriptive meaning (= general, ordinary) and a derogatory one (= vulgar), 'common sense' in English is almost always honorific. The *OED* gives meanings for the term corresponding to perception of the object, the faculties of the subject, and the discursive formation in which the two are brought into relation:

> (1) An 'internal' sense…centre of the five senses, in which the various impressions received were reduced to the unity of a common consciousness; (2) The endowment of rational intelligence possessed by rational beings; (3) The general sense, feeling, or judgment of mankind, or of a community.

In this account, sense is common in that it is immediately, objectively and impartially available to anyone whose sense – and senses – are not distorted by self-interest.

If philosophic empiricism in England is founded in an opposition between innate ideas and experience, then its country cousin, empiricist discourse, leaning on its philosophic partner, similarly defines itself against an adversarial discourse. A form of rationalism, claiming that correspondence between human rationality and the rationality of reality is innate, neatly fills a named role as antagonist for empiricist discourse, its disparaged other. Across history at different times a number of actors have taken this role, including scholasticism, Roman Catholicism, metaphysics, as well as rationalism itself; in England, especially in the past two decades, the part has been played by something referred to vaguely and disparagingly as 'theory'.

English empiricist discourse, I propose, maintains itself on the back of a binary opposition between the real and the apparent, an opposition reproduced and reworked in many directions, including:

objective/subjective
concrete/abstract
practice/theory

clear/obscure
fact/fiction
serious/silly

common sense/dogma
sincere/artificial
amateur/professional

hard/soft
truth/pleasure
right/wrong

Protestant/Catholic
English/French
home/foreign

centre/extreme
virility/effeminacy
masculine/feminine

Certain key oppositions – common sense/dogma, serious/silly – bear with them historical connotations derived from Protestant/Catholic, and so in one powerful strand of association, English/French, and so, also, home/foreign (both Linda Colley (1992) and David Simpson (1993) have drawn attention to how the experience of the decades before and after 1800 reinforced the opposition English/French with the oppositions Protestant/Catholic and common sense/dogma).

Although listed with the others, masculine/feminine actually requires a three-dimensional model since all the other oppositions tend to map on to and equate with masculine/feminine. Moralising the series, English empiricism frequently characterises masculinity as realistic, objective, clear, serious, sincere, and right because it cleaves unrelentingly to fact while femininity is relegated as subjective, obscure, silly, dogmatic, artificial, because it is prone to fantasy, self-deception and being wrong. That this association has often been made is not itself sufficient grounds for arguing that empiricism is always and everywhere by nature masculinist.

My purpose in this chapter is not to write a history but to suggest how we might understand a typical and representative structure. This structure is upheld by the process of an economy, a continuing disposition or deployment at once thematic and formal, which works to stabilise oppositions by promoting and denigrating, accentuating a centre by relegating margins. It operates both within the specificity of a given discourse (in so far as that can be separated out) and across particular discourses imbricated with each other in a discursive formation.

Milton and morality

The English subject is envisaged pre-eminently as a *moral* subject, self-conscious, responsible for choice, obliged to defer judgement. Empiricist discourse would promote this effect according to the following logic: to see and know reality as it is objectively constitutes the basis for right action; to allow desire and fantasy to interfere with your perception of reality leads to self-deception and thus to error.

A foundationally English text, Milton's *Paradise Lost*, first published 1667 (1958), is profoundly concerned with truth, a moral and spiritual truth which consists of knowing and then conforming to God's will. Further, as Stanley Fish has argued, the poem does not just make a general statement but rather as an act of reading, a performance, it provides a test for the reader who must positively resist rhetoric, 'the verbal equivalent of the fleshly lures that seek to enthral us', and cleave to that 'logic which comes from God and speaks to that part of us which retains his image' (1967, p. 61). For fallen mortals correct choice is problematic but for Adam and Eve it comes as a matter of clearly seeing what's right (at once true and good) and then cleaving to that. According to the gender asymmetry of the text, Eve falls because Satan's false rhetoric seduces her into thinking it is right to eat the apple, Adam falls because he chooses to:

> he scrupl'd not to eat
> Against his better knowledge, not deceav'd,
> But fondly overcome with Femal charm.
>
> (IX, ll. 997–9)

Yet Milton, the voice of the poem, cannot really believe that knowing truth as clearly as they do they could have done what they did:

> For still they knew, and ought to have still rememberd
> The high Injunction not to taste the Fruit.
>
> (X, ll. 12–13)

Like Locke, Milton thinks we can always suspend desire from determining the will and so is at pains to try to expel the threat it poses.

According to the ancient poets, Mulciber was thrown out of heaven by Jove and Book I (ll. 742 ff.) of *Paradise Lost* describes, lingeringly, how,

> from Morn
> To Noon he fell, from Noon to dewy Even,
> A Summers day

until this soft pagan story is cut off round the end of the line in a single brutal word:

> thus they [the pagan poets] relate
> Erring

The text evokes and enjoys Mulciber's floating skydive only to reject that delight as surely as Mulciber was thrown out of heaven. Pleasure is found in the denial of pleasure, the desire is to eradicate desire. Here perhaps we touch the English enjoyment of self-righteousness, that which has earned from 'our sweet enemy, France' the condemnation of 'perfide Albion', not because the English are any more economical with the truth but because they always justify it.

In the Milton passage one sees desire becoming separated from itself by an opposition which privileges truth over error, a realistic grasp of the facts over any self-deceiving wish for fantasy. Truth – so often 'hard' truth – is opposed to pleasure so that, in a peculiarly English inflection, the cognitive and the ethical overlap. Like morality, a matter of truth or falsehood for Milton as much as for Locke is a matter of *right* and *wrong*.

In the middle of the seventeenth century the Church of England was mainly given over to Calvinism. Marx describes how 'Cromwell and the English people borrowed speech, passions and illusions from the Old Testament for their bourgeois revolution' but adds that when the real aim of the gentry had been achieved, after 1660, 'Locke supplanted Habbakuk' (Marx and Engels 1950, 1, p. 226). He does, but the sense of regenerate and unregenerate does not vanish – rather, the extreme Protestant conception of self, choice and morality is transplanted into empiricist ethical discourse.

On 21 May 1988, speaking as a Christian, Margaret Thatcher addressed the General Assembly of the Church of Scotland (see 'The Sermon on The Mound', *Guardian*, 23 May 1988). If I had to summarise Christianity, as she did, I would fall back on loving one's neighbour as oneself and St Paul's assertion that 'we are members one of another' (Ephesians 4: 25). In Margaret Thatcher's view the first distinctive mark of Christianity was 'the fundamental right to choose between good and evil', its second, that we must use 'our power of thought and judgement' in exercising that choice, and the third lay in the fact that, like Jesus, we may face the 'terrible choice' of having to lay down our life. For the former British Prime Minister love has nothing to do with it since Christianity is specified by three things: choice, choice and choice. A Lockeian sense of moral responsibility supplants Christianity expressed in tones which would have caused little discomfort to Milton.

The example is representative, and worth taking further. 'It is not,' Lady Thatcher went on, 'the creation of wealth that is wrong, but love of money for its own sake', so ascribing to the Lockeian tradition that property and economic relations simply lie beyond moral discourse. Lockeian also was her view that though Christianity does not tell us what political institutions we should have, it is 'certain' that any set of social arrangements 'not founded on the acceptance of individual responsibility' must be wrong. However, this is not where it ends. Saying that the purpose of democracy is something higher than democracy, Margaret Thatcher closes with the words of a hymn:

> I vow to thee, my country, all earthly things above,
> Entire and whole and perfect, the service of my love.

(Written by Sir Cecil Spring-Rice, 'The Two Fatherlands' or 'I vow to thee, my country' is better known with the music by Gustav Holst). Thatcherism, the political programme which set the agenda in England for nearly two decades after 1979, contained its Whiggish enthusiasm for economic liberalism within an iron frame of Toryism.

Three versions of empiricist discourse

1 The 'transparent' style

It is over the question of language that the common-sense attitudes of empiricist discourse encroach hardest on the terrain of empiricist philosophy and a wider cultural pressure is felt most strongly. With urgent unanimity, Bacon, Hobbes and Locke castigate jargon and recommend the plain style, one in which, apparently, things have been turned into words so that words can deliver the equivalent of things and meaning pass from head to head: 'When a man upon the hearing of any Speech, hath those thoughts which the words of that Speech, and their connexion, were ordained and constituted to signifie; Then he is said to understand it' (Hobbes 1991, p. 30). The English empiricists write in the way they say people should.

To recall the seventeenth-century development of the plain style documents stylistic progress from Bacon to Hobbes and Hobbes to Locke. Bacon's overtly rhetorical constructions and frequent appeals to written authorities give way in Hobbes to reliance on a sense of authority vested in the argument itself, coupled with a colloquial, often forceful, directness in a style which serves that argument without appearing to intervene on its own account. Keeping some grip on the spoken feature, Locke adds an urbane self-control, self-reflection and wit enacting the confidence that the writer can see himself as others see him.

Although a necessary condition for this empiricist style is the development of a stable vocabulary unresponsive to the pull away from common use, its crucial feature is an exact and supple syntax able to distinguish between meanings equated through co-ordination and meanings hierarchised through subordination. From a knowledge of its past you may anticipate how the syntagmatic chain will unfold in the future, so that 'a man' may 'foresee the length of his period', as Hobbes says.

For example, in Locke:

> For it being the same consciousness that makes a Man be himself to himself, *personal Identity* depends on that only, whether it be annexed only to one individual Substance, or can be continued in a succession of several Substances. For as far as any intelligent Being can repeat the *Idea* of any past action with the same consciousness it had of it at first, and with the same consciousness it has of any present Action; so far it is the same *personal self*.
>
> (II.27.10)

From the previous subordinated conditional clause ('it being') the main clause of the first sentence ('*personal Identity* depends') effortlessly and without ambiguity picks out its object ('that only' = 'the same consciousness'), redefining it across two co-ordinated clauses ('whether'...'or') which mark a precisely weighted contrast ('be annexed' versus 'can be continued', 'individual' versus 'several Substances'). In the second sentence there are two co-ordinated clauses ('as far as'...'so far it is'), the first containing two co-ordinated phrases ('with'...'and with'), each containing a further co-ordination ('the same [as]...it had', 'the same [as]...it has'). Despite this complex embedding, which certainly demands to be read with care, the meaning is clear across the pronouns (though the thought may not be): in 'it had of it' the first 'it' = 'intelligent being' while the second 'it' = 'the *Idea*'.

If that is the English plain style in 1689, here it is in 1859 in Charles Darwin's *The Origin of Species*:

> Hence the inhabitants of one country, generally the smaller one, will often yield, as we see they do yield, to the inhabitants of another and generally larger country. For in the larger country there will have existed more individuals, and more diversified forms, and the competition will have been severer, and thus the stand of perfection will have been rendered higher. Natural selection will not necessarily produce absolute perfection; nor, as far as we can judge by our limited faculties, can absolute perfection be everywhere found.
>
> (1970, pp. 232–3)

Close analysis would be redundant. Syntax and the articulation of the meaning exhibit the same controlled linearity, making it easy for the reader to look back in order to move forward, the same sure-handed relay as in the Locke; or for that matter today:

> The Prime Minister yesterday denied any covert plans to extend the scope of VAT as Labour limbered up for an all-out assault on the Government's tax record in the final days before Thursday's European elections. With his future on the line if the results are as disastrous as the opinion polls are predicting, John Major attempted to defuse the row by accusing opponents of scare tactics. Mr Major dismissed suggestions that he will be overthrown if the Tories manage to hold fewer than 10 of the 85 British seats in the European Parliament.
>
> (BELEAGUERED PM DENIES PLANS FOR FOOD TAX, *Guardian*, 6 June 1994)

Within the less formal journalist mode, always tending towards shorter sentences and familiar metaphors ('limbered up' for an assault, 'defuse' a row), those sentences, picked casually from this morning's newspaper, conform to the tradition.

Whether representing the logic of an argument or concrete description, general reflection or a situation in reality, this is the main form of English empiricist discourse, the 'objective' or 'transparent' or styleless style – which is neither objective nor transparent nor styleless. It would translate the givenness of the English real into discourse without rhetoric or with a minimum of appropriate rhetoric, transform matter into ideas, deliver things in words.

2(a) Classic irony

Effacing its own textuality and point of view in favour of perceived reality, such objective discourse breeds irony. By suppressing explicit notice of the addresser's position, it opens a gap between intention and meaning, subjective attitude and object rendered, which encourages the reader to ask: who is making this seemingly impartial statement and why?

Linda Hutcheon begins her book on contemporary forms of Canadian national culture by recalling an article in a Canadian journal that asked its reader, on the model of 'as American as…', to fill in a phrase around 'as Canadian as…'. It answered its own question by saying the most Canadian of replies would be 'as Canadian as possible under the circumstances'. Hutcheon comments: 'The self-deprecating irony that underlies such a response has been considered typical of the inhabitants of Canada' (1991, p. 1). Although irony is not exclusive to the English discursive tradition, attending as it does on empiricist attitudes, irony is pervasive.

Since it involves a play of words or ideas, irony is strictly one form of the joke. At the level of theory, irony is a large issue (see Booth 1961; Muecke 1982; Barthes 1975; Fish 1989), one whose complexities I shall by-pass to reach its most persistent form in English discourse, classic irony. Irony can be distinguished from sarcasm. Whereas irony is conventionally defined as 'saying one thing to mean another' (Hutcheon 1994, p. 11) and so relies on a contrast between 'apparent' and 'real' meaning, sarcasm is an extreme form of irony in which the apparent meaning is opposite to the real one. If it's pouring with rain and I say, 'Not a very nice day', that's irony, but if I exclaim, 'Another lovely day!', that's sarcasm.

Literary tradition has generated a number of interesting ways to apply the concept of irony. These include: dramatic irony (in which, for example, the reader knows something about the situation of a character in a narrative which the character does not know); romantic irony, as when the text of a romantic lyric acts to question or undercut the status of its own *persona* and assertion; 'Flaubertian' irony, an irony 'impregnated with uncertainty' (Barthes 1975, p. 140), which may occur if a reader, moved sympathetically by part of a text, comes to doubt whether the passage consists of anything more than writing; postmodern irony, a particular form of contemporary writing in which (in default of Grand Narratives able to disambiguate response) every assertion becomes open to ironic reading from someone's point of view.

Classic irony would avert these intricacies. It seeks to be an indirect means to refer to reality by inviting its reader to discard the offered significance as either understated (*litotes*) or overstated (*hyperbole*), and go straight to the 'real' meaning. But, the invitation, being linguistic, is subject to interpretation and so always liable to misinterpretation. When Locke writes of someone who argued that a dream could simulate reality, 'I believe he will allow a very manifest difference between dreaming of being in the Fire, and being actually in it' (IV.2.14), his apparent circumspection ('I believe he will allow') really means 'I know for certain he will experience' (doesn't it?). But when he interrupts his discussion of individual freedom by saying, 'Likewise a Man falling into the Water (a Bridge breaking under him) has not herein liberty, is not a free Agent' (II.21.9), a reader may wonder whether this is just literal statement or ironic understatement (*of course* unforeseeable accidents to the body do in fact limit freedom). However signalled by markers, by unusual or deviant phrasing ('I believe he will allow'), even classic irony depends upon context, upon the reader's appreciation of what is usual and normal, both discursively and ideologically.

Classic irony, if it succeeds, produces the effect of referring to reality almost as surely as does transparent discourse. But it is not equivalent to direct statement because the interpreter has to respond to both meanings, 'apparent' and 'real', and irony is the effect of both (so argues Hutcheon 1994, p. 12). All texts can be misread but irony especially opens this door. Classic irony, I suggest, is prepared to take this risk because of the generous pay-off resulting from indirect statement.

In the first place such irony affirms a sense of collective identity by excluding an other, discriminating insiders from outsiders, those party to the irony from those stuck with a literal reading (Pope and Swift were delighted – or ironically claimed to be delighted – by reports that some people had read *Gulliver's Travels* literally, as a true record). The knowing reader is granted a pleasurable position of shared superiority to whatever or whoever is the target or object of the reference. Irony is able to call up meanings and values without explicitly naming them, so creating a feeling of consensus, and this is particularly attractive to an empiricist culture which believes truth resides in collective experience of reality rather than anything one can say about it. And again, aspiring to discriminate confidently between apparent and actual meaning, irony promises control over the play of language, to keep the signifier in place.

For these reasons, even when there may be little other point to it, in an English context there is always some advantage in using irony. On the

29 April 1994, when polls gave Labour a 23 per cent lead over the Tories, Michael Howard, then Conservative Home Secretary, was asked on television for his response and replied, 'no one is pretending that the Government is at a high point of popularity'. His meaning was, 'we all know the Government is unpopular', but his ironic circumlocution, pretending to quote someone who thought they showed the government at a high point of popularity, achieved a tone of authority not otherwise possible.

English empiricist discourse is saturated with irony through and through, and although it frequently dramatises the privilege of the gentry, its use is certainly not confined to them (with terrible irony soldiers shut inside the British tanks during the 1944 Normandy campaign referred to their machines – so demonstrably inferior to the opposition – as 'Ronsons', the name of a cheap cigarette lighter).

2(b) Irony in Pope, Rawnsley and Littlejohn

Alexander Pope's justly renowned satirical portrait of Joseph Addison was published in 1735 in 'Epistle to Dr Arbuthnot', ll. 193–214:

> Peace to all such! but were there One whose fires
> True Genius kindles, and fair Fame inspires,
> Blest with each Talent and each art to please,
> And born to write, converse, and live with ease:
> Shou'd such a man, too fond to rule alone,
> Bear, like the *Turk*, no brother near the throne,
> View him with scornful, yet with jealous eyes,
> And hate for Arts that caus'd himself to rise;
> Damn with faint praise, assent with civil leer,
> And without sneering, teach the rest to sneer;
> Willing to wound, and yet afraid to strike,
> Just hint a fault, and hesitate dislike;
> Alike reserv'd to blame, or to commend,
> A tim'rous foe, and a suspicious friend,
> Dreading ev'n fools, by Flatterers besieg'd,
> And so obliging that he ne'er oblig'd;
> Like *Cato*, give his little Senate laws,
> And sit attentive to his own applause;
> While Wits and Templers ev'ry sentence raise,
> And wonder with a foolish face of praise.
> Who but must laugh, if such a man there be?
> Who would not weep, if *Atticus* were he?
>
> (1965, p. 604)

It would be hard to miss the main irony here, that the sustained use of the conditional ('were', 'shou'd', 'if') must be set aside as a mask behind which the real meaning emerges: there is indeed such a man and Atticus is Addison.

Addison's fault is exposed as self-deceit according to an implicit moral opposition between self-deception and objective empirical knowledge – he imagines himself fair and impartial when in fact he is insecurely egotistical. His failure lies in not seeing himself as the Other sees him. The portrait does not need to moralise explicitly because morality is felt to inhere in the viewpoint of the Other and whether the individual can or cannot internalise that viewpoint.

The rhetoric of the text would confirm its judgement; its irony solicits the reader to join a club of those knowingly superior to a familiar but excluded other, Addison, and that position of metalinguistic exteriority is strengthened when Addison's own tone of voice, his own ironically indirect judgements, is cited. The condemnation founds its authority in its claim to enact the voice of the Other, introducing a disinterested verdict on what Addison is really like (of course, as a number of critics have pointed out with reference to the portrait, if Pope does not persuade a reader that he speaks from the impersonal point of view of the Other, the judgement fails).

Allied as it is to transparency, classic irony forms a continuing strand in the empiricist inheritance This is a contemporary example, part of Andrew Rawnsley's 'Sketch' from the *Guardian* on the State Opening of Parliament (7 May 1992):

> NOBS IN FINERY USHER IN CLASSLESS SOCIETY
> The Lord Chancellor was trying to walk backwards without tripping over the Rouge Dragon Pursuivant, animated playing cards were blowing trumpets, Black Rod was getting the door slammed in his face like a Jehovah's Witness, and Her Majesty was straining to convince the nation that she really was looking forward to a visit from the president of Portugal.
>
> By the grace of God and the electoral system, the Queen presided over the State Opening of Parliament, the seemingly centuries-old ceremony which traditionally ushers in another five years of Conservative government.
>
> As Beaumont Herald Extraordinary, Gold Stick in Waiting, The Keeper of the Gilded Bidet and the rest of the cast of Iolanthe did their stuff before an audience of dukes, earls, marquesses and viscounts, Her Majesty outlined her government's plans to create a modern, open and classless society.

> It did not cause the slightest tremor of apprehension among the glorification of hierarchy assembled in the House of Lords. They thought they already understood what John Major meant when he talked about letting wealth cascade down the generations. Most of it was cascading down the diamond encrusted cleavages of peeresses.

Irony asks us to distinguish apparent from real, here masquerade from the body: the Lord Chancellor tries not to trip over his dress, Black Rod has the door slammed in his face, Her Majesty was 'straining' her voice to sound sincere. The Queen's power is apparently named via the zeugma between 'the grace of God' and 'the electoral system' but the irony points the reader from what it says to the knowledge that sovereignty rests with Parliament rather than the monarchy. Ironic also is the straight-faced allusion to ancient ceremony ushering in more Conservative government (it doesn't) and how the Keeper of the Gilded Bidet will create a modern, classless society (he won't).

Developing from these ironies Rawnsley's text draws on a thematic opposition between fact and fiction when it equates the apparent with textuality known to be textuality: 'animated playing cards' refers the scene to *Alice in Wonderland*, 'Iolanthe' matches it to comic opera. And the dismissive reference to 'a Jehovah's Witness' summons up the opposition between common sense and dogma.

Irony, but irony to what purpose? In empiricist fashion the text refers to a reality by showing discrepancy between the apparent and the real (almost the apparel and the real). If the 'Sketch' had a consistent social commitment the irony would add up, resulting in satire. But this irony remains merely personal, goes nowhere except to call a reader to join in the writer's superior awareness of what's 'really' going on behind the facade of a traditional English ritual.

Rawnsley's gentrified irony can be set alongside an extract from the notorious Richard Littlejohn, writing in the tabloid, the *Sun*, on 9 November 1992 (since this is scathing about Saint Diana of the Pont de l'Alma let me apologise in advance to all the true believers):

> PUT A SOCK IN IT, DIANA
>
> In the overall scheme of things it makes little difference whether Di is sharing a bed with Prince Charles or the Harlem Globetrotters. Mind you, she might not look so miserable if she was snuggling up to the Harlem Globetrotters for an evening....Why do they persist with this farcical marriage? Say what you like about Fergie, but she did have the bottle to get

> out. I have always preferred Sarah to Diana. She never made any bones about being a gold-digging bimbo....Diana has come to believe her own publicity. She really does think she is a cross between Jerry Hall and Mother Teresa. Give me Jerry Hall any day. At least she has a bit of conversation. And I can live without miracles. It was always an unlikely match. Imagine you are a 19-year-old Sloane Ranger with a half-decent boat race and a figure out of a Slim-Fast commercial. You have the option of going out with a few randy racing drivers of your own age or an old man who looks like Biffo the Bear and talks to trees. Who would you choose? Be honest. Diana made a career decision. She made her own bed and now she doesn't want to lie in it.

Unlike Pope or Rawnsley, Littlejohn is writing in the genre of popular journalism, tending to shorter sentences and a spoken rather than written model, in a text full of jokes and matey colloquialisms with a touch of Cockney ('boat race' for face). It is a comic version of classic irony nevertheless: 'in the overall scheme of things it makes little difference' really means it makes no difference; 'she might not look so miserable' in bed with several large African-Americans means she would be a lot happier.

What seems and what is: Diana's calculating hypocrisy is contrasted with Sarah's frank self-seeking, supernaturalism and dogma (Mother Teresa's 'miracles') is rejected in favour of common sense (Jerry Hall). Littlejohn assumes that under a genteel surface we all act out of the same real and knowable motives ('Diana made a career decision'). His lampoon does not admit that its own assumed voice of common sense, its outspoken honesty, is a rhetorical effect, but this itself may read ironically as a mask: he says it like this, without hesitation or apology, but we know from his very exuberance he is really being irreverently polemic.

Littlejohn and Rawnsley illustrate irony in two different class registers. Rawnsley eschews Littlejohn's plain speech in favour of urbanity, educated reference, elaborated vocabulary, complex sentence structure. Both texts, however, deploy the real/apparent opposition and appeal to an empiricist notion of reality. Whereas Littlejohn's claim to blunt honesty denies his own rhetoric, Rawnsley does not try to conceal his, as when he likens the idea of wealth cascading down to diamonds cascading down cleavages. No doubt, such rhetorical display is to be recuperated as personal expression. If Littlejohn shares with Hobbes an aggressively anti-sentimental belief in basic motives, Rawnsley's knowing tone recalls classic English Whiggery.

Irony, like transparent discourse, would refer to reality; it ascribes to a disinterested acknowledgement of truth, the point of view of the Other, particularly if it follows its own easy tendency to make visible the self-deception individuals succumb to if they fail to see themselves as others do. Classic irony has a special effectivity if it is directed back against the speaker's own self, as when Locke writes, 'I doubt not but my Reader, by this time, may be apt to think that I have been all this while only building a Castle in the Air' (IV.4.1), or when Pope in the same 'Epistle to Dr Arbuthnot' (ll. 125–6) asks the rhetorical question:

> Why did I write? what sin to me unknown
> Dipt me in Ink, my Parents', or my own?
> (1965, p. 602)

By naming his poetic vocation as a black sin and asking whether it was the fault of his parents or of himself, Pope himself consciously reflects a point of view, a possible point of view, from within the Other, as though he sees himself seeing himself (Lacan discusses the fantasy that '*I see myself seeing myself*', 1977b, p. 80). When a speaker uses irony to denigrate themself this yields the English tradition of mock-modesty and ironic self-deprecation. In Evelyn Waugh's *Brideshead Revisited* Sebastian at one point says about his sister, 'I love her. She's so like me'. His friend Charles asks how she is like him, and Sebastian replies, 'In looks...and the way she talks. I wouldn't love anyone with a character like mine' (1951, p. 76).

Modesty of this kind is not simple. The gesture apparently directed against the self also draws attention to the self, in fact to the self viewed in a favourable light, as capable of self-criticism. And while the tradition of self-deprecation allows the English to criticise themselves, the same license is not extended to foreigners.

Irony, rooted as it is in rejection of the apparent in favour of the real, goes a long way to explain one of the distinguishing features of English discourse compared to some European counterparts: its overwhelming preference for *informality*. This may seem attractive but its less attractive side appears in the tone of indifference and casual cruelty always so ready to hand for the English gentry – as when Sir George Young, former Housing Minister, referred to beggars in London as 'the sort of people you step on when you come out of the opera' (see YOUNG DEFENDS BEGGING ATTACK, *Guardian*, 29 June 1991).

3 Romantic empiricist discourse

For Locke knowledge derives either passively from sensation (corresponding to reality) or from reflection (in which the mind is active in combining, comparing and abstraction). In a Lockeian spirit Pope asks in *Essay on Man* (I, l. 18), 'What can we reason, but from what we know?' (*Poems*, p. 504), expecting the answer, 'Nothing', believing that what lies outside knowledge and reason can only be problematic if not actually dangerous. It is exactly this domain outside that Romanticism in England claims for itself, willing therefore to repudiate Lockeian empiricism root and branch. William Blake, notably, is explicit in attacking Locke (see Frye 1947, especially Chapter 1, 'The Case against Locke').

Against Locke's denial of innate ideas Blake in his 'Annotations to Reynolds' exclaims, 'Innate Ideas are in Every Man, Born with him' (1966, p. 459). While Locke's empiricism accords a priority to reality, Blake's view is that 'Mental Things are alone Real' (p. 617); Locke says ideas are general and Blake asks angrily, 'What is General Nature? is there Such a Thing?', adding, 'Strictly Speaking All Knowledge is Particular' (p. 459). And when Locke writes of the sun, 'What is it, but an aggregate of those several simple *Ideas*, Bright, Hot, Roundish, having a constant regular motion, at a certain distance from us?' (II.23.6) Blake in 'A Vision of the Last Judgement' cries out:

> 'What', it will be Question'd, 'When the Sun rises, do you not see a round disk of fire somewhat like a Guinea?' O no, no, I see an Innumerable company of the Heavenly host crying 'Holy, Holy, Holy is the Lord God Almighty'.
>
> (p. 617)

Blake certainly has the rhetorical edge here.

Yet perhaps Locke's complacent empiricism and Blake's enthusiasm are disputes across shared ground. Read to the letter, Locke as much as Blake believed we had no direct access to reality but only mental ideas of it. When Locke privileges the individual as consciously responsible, Blake thinks this is the voice of the Devil; but still Blake, in very different terms, asserts the experience of the individual self as an absolute. Romanticism inevitably partakes of the empiricist discourse it would reject, and Blake might be seen as a kind of wild-eyed English Kantian who, in the name of an imaginatively creative rather than passive subject, insists it is *only* within humanly constructed categories that the individual experiences reality (as will be suggested, Blake's writing remains specially problematic for the mainstream English tradition).

Although poetry is a different kind of discourse from philosophic empiricism, English poetry is a home for empiricist attitudes, particularly in the Romantic period. It is a commonplace of literary criticism that late eighteenth-century descriptive poetry (influenced in part by the way Locke had left the subject confident of the ideas in their head but uncertain how they derived from reality) dramatises a vague and shadowy sense of how mind relates to perceived reality. In contrast, the four major Romantic poets (Blake again an exception), though staking out different epistemological positions, 'all face the central need to find a significant relationship between subjective and objective worlds' (Wasserman 1964, p. 33). That quest holds them firmly on the terrain of the empiricist enterprise.

It is only fair to note that Blake scribbled savage marginal comments ('Annotations to *The Excursion*'; 1966, p. 784) against the self-satisfaction of the writer I shall take to exemplify this Romantic empiricism: William Wordsworth. The very fact that the individual mind experiences reality, as though nakedly and for the first time, becomes in Wordsworth's poetry a cause for joy. In *The Prelude* (I, ll. 336–9), recalling a time when he went rock-climbing as a boy, he exclaims :

> While on the perilous ridge I hung alone,
> With what strange utterance did the loud dry wind
> Blow through my ear! the sky seems not a sky
> Of earth – and with what motion moved the clouds!
>
> (1979, p. 47)

The wonder is that it is *there* – for him.

In a typical and well-known example, 'The Solitary Reaper' (1807), Wordsworth enacts in poetry the experience of a passing traveller, implicitly male (the I of the poem), observing, himself unseen, a Scots woman at work in a field and singing while she works. The poem is phrased in the present tense, as though it were happening now:

> Behold her, single in the field,
> Yon solitary Highland Lass!
> Reaping and singing by herself;
> Stop here, or gently pass!
> Alone she cuts and binds the grain,
> And sings a melancholy strain;
> O listen! for the Vale profound
> Is overflowing with the sound.

No Nightingale did ever chaunt
More welcome notes to weary bands
Of travellers in some shady haunt,
Among the Arabian sands:
A voice so thrilling ne'er was heard
In spring-time from the Cuckoo-bird,
Breaking the silence of the seas
Among the farthest Hebrides.

Will no one tell me what she sings? –
Perhaps the plaintive numbers flow
For old, unhappy, far-off things,
And battles long ago:
Or is it some more humble lay,
Familiar matter of today?
Some natural sorrow, loss, or pain,
That has been, and may be again?

Whate'er the theme, the Maiden sang
As if her song could have no ending;
I saw her singing at her work,
And o'er her sickle bending:–
I listened, motionless and still;
And, as I mounted up the hill,
The music in my heart I bore,
Long after it was heard no more.

(1952–9, 3, p. 77)

Struck by the woman's figure and song, the speaker is at first at a loss in the face of this alien object, made especially other to him by her gender, self-absorption and foreign tongue. Speculatively, he compares her singing to a nightingale in the desert and the first cuckoo of spring in gloomy northern islands; he wonders whether her theme may not be some universal and eternal human statement of 'sorrow, loss, or pain'. Through his creative reflection, the original sensation of an object ('Behold her') is made over into a subjective possession:

And as I mounted up the hill,
The music in my heart I bore,
Long after it was heard no more.

Afterwards, as the poem moves into the past tense, the woman remains there in her own externality, 'singing at her work', but she has becomes part of his experience, a personal memory in his developing identity.

What tends to confirm the connection of this example to empiricist discourse is its refusal to acknowledge its own means of representation. The poem treats the speaker's reflections as entirely his own, not owing anything to convention as mediation between object and subject. Comparison of human song to a nightingale is orthodox but its conventionality is to be cancelled by placing the bird not in the usual Greek wood but in an Arabian oasis; the reference to the cuckoo seeks to evade poetic commonplace, its idiosyncratic strangeness reinforced by the geographical location ('the silence of the seas'). Yet without nearly a century of fascination with noble primitiveness as represented in ballad and the song of the people, the poem would never have come to be written. Its effort is to push awareness of this history of representation to the margins, to present the woman as 'Individuall and Singular' (in Hobbes's phrase) and the speaker correspondingly as a free-standing self with direct access to this particular, given object.

Experience is assumed to be personal and to take place apart from forms of social construction, including linguistic forms. Wordsworth denounced rhetoric as fiercely as Hobbes or Locke (though for different reasons) and declared he would write in a language which directly renders meaning. What counts in the poem is the bare empiricist scenario of subject, active verb and object: 'I saw her'.

While the impersonal tone and manner of Pope's exposure of Addison's self-deception profess to speak from the point of view of the Other, the Romantic text adheres, typically, to an alternative deployment of self and Other. In 'The Solitary Reaper' the speaker sees her but also wants to see himself seeing her, be conscious of himself in the act of perceiving her. That position is implied by the address to himself, as though to another, to 'Behold her' and 'Stop here' (he stops) and sustained in his conjectures about what it is he is perceiving. Entirely in accord with the Romantic programme, the speaker hopes his self-consciousness will internalise the point of view of the Other, guarding him against self-deception and guaranteeing the uncontaminated authenticity of his experience.

The strategy must fail, since a subject's internalisation of the Other cannot be finally separated from misrecognition. In Pope's poem the claim to an objective assessment of Addison is tainted by personal interest, in Wordsworth's the speaker's assertion of authentic experience misrecognises how far he *appropriates* the woman to his own unacknowledged desire – appropriations which include: eroticisation of her otherness; the pleasures of the specular male gaze; aestheticisation of someone else's sweated labour; humanist universalisation of particularity and region; identification with an idealised position as 'lover of the people' (disavowing these, Wordsworth's *persona* speaks as though he had no gendered body, no unconscious).

The central misrecognition or self-deception, however, is the speaker's unswerving confidence that he has really experienced an object directly, personally and for himself. English Romantic poetry rejoins the tradition of empiricist discourse it may think it challenges. Appealing to the idea of an experience beyond all argument or poetic persuasiveness, Wordsworth says of one of his most famous poems, 'A Reader who has not a vivid recollection of these feelings having existed in his mind cannot understand that poem' (1952–9, 5, 464). Reality is given, the individual subject is given, and the first is available to the second outside socially constructed representation, through language which is, in principle, transparent to meaning. How very Lockeian! How very English!

This account of the 'transparent' style, classic irony and Romantic empiricism does not exhaust the strategies of empiricist discourse but may suggest important versions and variations of it. What might be alternative forms of discourse? In asking this it is best to avoid a binary model of dominance and opposition, and to think rather of overlapping fields between margin and centre. Are alternatives in fact imbricated with empiricist discourse and dependent upon it? I have two candidates in mind, and both lie on the far side of irony.

Alternatives: English silly discourse

Among the binary oppositions which strive to maintain the Western tradition Derrida includes 'seriousness/play' (1981, p. 85). For the English tradition more appropriate terms would be 'serious/silly'. Just as the repressive rationalism of France breeds a counter-discourse of extremity, violence and irrationalism, from de Sade to Rimbaud to Lautréamont to the Surrealists, so the English preoccupation with fact generates its converse in a special kind of consciously playful, seemingly harmless but excessive fictionalising and white magic (both the founding fathers, Hobbes and Locke, admit the pleasures of fancy so long as they are contained in subordination to fact).

Landmarks of silliness are Mercutio's speech on Queen Mab, *Midsummer Night's Dream*, the sylphs in Pope's *The Rape of the Lock*, much (not all) Romantic supernaturalising, Lewis Carroll, Edward Lear, strange now unread books such as Kipling's *Puck of Pook's Hill*, the extraordinary English Edwardian tradition of children's literature

(*Peter Pan*, *The Wind in the Willows*). 'What were we trying to achieve?', Terry Jones asks himself of *Monty Python's Flying Circus*, and answers in a word: 'Silliness' (SOMETHING COMPLETELY DIFFERENT, *Guardian*, 10 August 1996). Such discourse occupies the space assigned to it by certain denigrated terms in the Great Oppositions: as well as being fictional it will be obscure, artificial, soft, pleasurable, feminine (as well as effeminate), and wrong. Its dependence on serious discourse is evidenced in the degree to which it openly foregrounds a transgressive awareness that it qualifies for all of these adjectives. My example is from *Alice in Wonderland*.

After falling down the rabbit-hole at the beginning of her adventures Alice finds a small cake labelled 'EAT ME', and when she eats it, finds herself getting bigger and bigger:

> 'Curiouser and curiouser!' cried Alice (she was so much surprised, that for the moment she quite forgot how to speak good English); 'now I'm opening out like the largest telescope that ever was! Goodbye, feet! (for when she looked down at her feet, they seemed to be almost out of sight they were getting so far off). 'Oh, my poor little feet, I wonder who will put on your shoes and stockings for you now, dears? I'm sure *I* shan't be able! I shall be a great deal too far off to trouble myself about you: you must manage the best way you can – but I must be kind to them,' thought Alice, 'or perhaps they won't walk the way I want to go! Let me see: I'll give them a new pair of boots every Christmas.'
>
> And she went on planning to herself how she would manage it. 'They must go by the carrier,' she thought; 'and how funny it'll seem, sending presents to one's own feet! And how odd the directions will look!
>
> Alice's Right Foot, Esq.
> Hearthrug,
> near the Fender,
> (with Alice's love).
>
> Oh dear, what nonsense I'm talking!'
>
> (1952, pp. 9–10)

It would take some time to unpack even the major implications of this passage of comic wit, especially in its context (Alice has just recalled boxing her own ears and wondering if she was really 'two people').

I would note first of all the distortion of common-sense empirical fact (the body is the body) into fantastic shape (literally, within this narrative). This is accompanied by an unusual play around logic and rationality (Alice 'went on planning'). If she is so much larger, will her head lose contact with her feet? If she (and where is 'she'?) is so distant from her feet, will she have to treat them as an other, like siblings or cousins, perhaps, who have grown up and moved away but remain intimate (these 'dears' will be sent new boots at Christmas)? What pushes this fancy towards the edges of Englishness is the way it is sustained, into the second paragraph, envisaging the necessity (reasonable given the circumstances) to send them new boots 'by the carrier' and on into the details of how the label on the package would have to be (affectionately) addressed. All this reasoning is based on a fallacy, for if she is 'opening out' like a telescope, then her arms will be in proportion, and the problem of their reaching her feet will not arise (as Carroll's drawing of Alice, despite its Magritte-like phallic head and neck, makes clear).

Far from seeking to be transparent to meaning, the language calls attention to itself, not only because Alice's complacent tone is wildly inappropriate (if this were a real situation) and but also through parody (the discourses of family affiliation and label-addressing) and effects of explicit self-reference. When Alice says 'curiouser and curiouser', the text remarks her failure 'to speak good English' ('curiouser', though a deviation from common use, is a grammatically regular formation from 'curious' and the coinage has passed into currency but see discussion by Jean-Jacques Lecercle; 1994, p. 53). And the whole soliloquy concludes with Alice reflecting on it, 'Oh dear, what nonsense I'm talking!'.

For all its avowed nonsense, this little text hides serious concerns. Besides the anxieties of a growing adolescent there is the question of personal identity and the mind/body relation. In wondering how large she can get without losing touch with herself Alice undertakes a kind of Lockeian inquiry into personal identity (how much of a person's body can you cut off before they cease to be themselves?). Her words split the supposed unity of the traditional subject by treating her self-awareness and her body as if they were two identities ('Goodbye, feet!').

But of course all of this is a joke, deliberate absurdity, pleasurable and playful exaggeration and impossibility, fantasy known to be fantasy when seen from the point of view of common sense, and this is invoked by the passage's *awareness* of its own excess ('what nonsense I'm talking'). But 'nonsense', as Lecercle acutely remarks, is a 'true product of the venerable tradition of British empiricism' (1994, p. 200). English silly discourse recognises the norm of empiricist discourse by departing from it, though a departure that may easily carry it to a troubling extreme (here, two troubling extremes, Alice's feet).

Alternatives: satire

Because the trope does not explicitly state its real meaning ('no one is pretending that the Government is at a high point of popularity') but invites the reader to infer this from their own common-sense understanding of a real situation, classic irony is always evasive, whether in Pope or Andrew Rawnsley. There is a surprisingly widespread use in English of a simplistic irony which seeks to rule something out of court by nothing, by the mere act of referring to it ironically.

A jokey column in the *TLS* (3 May 1991), written by someone known only as 'D.S.', discussed *The Hysterical Male: New Feminist Theory* edited by Arthur and Marilouise Kroker. The comment – it was not a formal review – included the following passage:

> It would be a brave man who would claim to understand just what it is that is getting the Krokers' goat so. But, broadly, they seem to be saying that, as men lose their grip on things, they are becoming hysterical and imitating women (disappropriating women of the privileged ontology of the Other). For, far from women still being tormented by penis-envy, it is now clear that male sexuality is but a distorted, partial version of female sexuality. 'Why not the penis now as a sign of the mutant clitoris, as a postmodern clitoris under the sign of abuse value? No longer the clitoris as a minimalist penis, but the postmodern penis as a runaway outlaw clit – like Pinnochio's nose?' Why not indeed? Many have long suspected it to be the case. It is good to have the matter out in the open at last.

The last three sentences, apparently welcoming the book, are undoubtedly ironic but the irony is so clumsy and so vague that the only meaning it refers to is a common-sense judgement that this book is nonsense, just not worth considering (the text also, to my ear, speaks of the writer's own hysterical insecurities, but that's another matter). Claiming superiority to its object simply by enclosing it in irony, such usage dismisses the book without in any way confronting its arguments, citing its own discourse ('disappropriating women of the privileged ontology of the Other') in the confidence that this alone is enough to demonstrate the book is silly (according to that opposition).

Irony points to the reality behind appearance. But irony sustained risks accumulating into an alternative interpretation of the reality referred to. It becomes satire. Satire has many uses but one strand develops, first, from the political satire of John Dryden after the Restoration, into the satire on manners written especially by Pope. In the English tradition satire is often joined with parody and the extended adoption of a *persona* and associated style. From the 1790s and the formation of the London Corresponding Society parodic satire is co-opted (though not exclusively) for a radical position, often deployed after 1830 in the unstamped press and *The Poor Man's Guardian* or, notably, in the Chartist 'Autobiography' of John James Bezer (see Louvre 1988). Such parody too often lapses into a merely facetious, inverted account of what 'they' are up to but at its best can be used to turn the proclaimed values of the gentry against their own actions.

Here is Terry Jones again, writing about the shooting by the British secret police of three alleged members of the IRA in Gibraltar in 1988, so it is alleged, after they had surrendered:

> The Rule of Law must be upheld. That's what the Prime Minister has said, and who would dare to gainsay her? Whatever the cost to the fabric of our society, the 'Rule of Law' is, as Mrs Thatcher says, 'inviolate'. Of course, we ought to be quite clear what she means by the 'Rule of Law'.
>
> If, for example, some people jump out of a car, gun down three other people in the public streets and then jump back into the car and disappear, then that is the 'Rule of Law'.
>
> If ministers then tell the House of Commons tall stories about what happened – claiming there was a bomb, when there was no bomb, and that the three dead people were armed, when they were not armed – then that is the 'Rule of Law'.
>
> Furthermore, if ministers and their apologists state on TV that the three dead people were behaving suspiciously and looked as if they were about to draw weapons, then that too is the 'Rule of Law'.
>
> (WHEN RULE OF LAW MEANS RULE OF GOVERNMENT, *Guardian*, 11 May 1988)

These emphatic yet banal repetitions of 'that is the "Rule of Law"' parody the Thatcher government's own constant asseverations, building into satire and coherent critique of what is referred to – when men gun down people in the streets or ministers lie to the House of Commons that is definitely *not* the rule of law (further on Jones drops the mask of satire and states explicitly: 'the "Rule of Law" means the "Rule of

Government" – and not just any government, but *this* government'). Representing a mode of discourse more common in other national cultures, this text strays far from the centre of English empiricist discourse with its more comfortable ironies (is it coincidence that this was Jones's last piece in the otherwise impeccably ironic *Guardian*?). Aggressive, divisive, interested (in the sense that it has a consistent and committed viewpoint), writing like this constantly reappears in the English radical inheritance.

The defining limits of empiricist discourse can be seen by looking at two modes, silly and satiric discourse, which run at a tangent to its centre. This account prompts the reflection that the work of William Blake, which notoriously resists recuperation into familiar notions of Englishness, *combines* silliness and satire in a style at once uncompromisingly gnomic and visionary.

There are other alternative forms besides those I've singled out, especially in the high cultural tradition. These would include the English tradition of Neoplatonism from the seventeenth century, and later, English Hegelianism and idealism (in the writing of F.H. Bradley, for instance). Following Keats, Tennyson wrote poetry of such unalloyed sensuality and eroticism that it kicks against the received inheritance, as in this 'Song' from 'The Princess':

> Now sleeps the crimson petal, now the white;
> Nor waves the cypress in the palace walk;
> Nor winks the gold fin in the porphyry font.
> The fire-fly wakens; waken thou with me.
>
> (1969, p. 834)

The English Marxist tradition, as it had to to be Marxist, set its face against empiricism (though arguably neither Raymond Williams nor Edward Thompson properly extricated themselves from the grip of the prevailing discourse; see Eagleton 1976).

One could debate in each case how far the intervention remains predicated on the empiricist norm by transgressing it or actively seeking to be its other. This chapter has advanced a speculative outline: for illustration of the degree to which the empiricist tradition has penetrated English discourse I shall turn in the following pages to exclusively contemporary examples. But first one particular manoeuvre in empiricist discourse needs mention.

Terminal closure

'Whether this be so, or no, I will not here determine, but appeal to every one's own Experience' (Locke, *Essay* II.8.5): with this kind of colloquial gesture beyond discourse to experience and reality the English tradition initiates a trope which may be called 'terminal closure'. A contemporary literary critic, for example, polemicising against 'theory', asks, 'Who, after all, ever chose a meal, or a husband or a wife – all instances after all of exercising critical judgement – by first establishing agreed criteria?' (*The Certainty of Literature* by George Watson, cited Pascoe 1990, p. 351). English conversation is pestered with this verbal gesture in phrases such as 'after all', 'when all is said and done', 'at the end of the day', 'it's a fact', 'in actual fact', 'as a matter of fact', 'no doubt about it'. Many uses of 'actually' , 'really', 'exactly' and (that footballer's favourite) 'obviously' are instances of terminal closure.

In 1682, when controversy over religious denomination and biblical interpretation was still intense, Dryden published a poem entitled *Religio Laici*, a layman's religion. After refuting deism by citing the fact of original sin, *Religio Laici* opposes both the 'Papist' view that the Bible means what tradition and clergy say, and the sectarian (Dissenting) position that the Bible means what the individual takes it to mean, Dryden steers a middle way towards the Church of England because it accommodates individual freedom within a traditional body ('When in doubt', remarks Raymond Williams, 'the English imagine a pendulum'; 1961, p. 69). After rehearsing both sides of the argument in detail, Dryden's poem falls back on an apology for the 'Treasure' of the Bible via what I have called the Great Oppositions, defending the centre (the Anglican Church) against extremes, appealing to clarity over obscurity, endorsing practice as against theory, preferring common sense to dogma, all in urbane heroic couplets:

> What then remains, but, waving each Extreme,
> The Tides of Ignorance, and Pride to stem?
> Neither so rich a Treasure to forgo;
> Nor proudly seek beyond our pow'r to know:
> The things we *must* believe, are *few*, and *plain*:
> But since men *will* believe more than they *need*;
> And every man will make *himself* a Creed:
> In doubtfull questions 'tis the safest way
> To learn what unsuspected Ancients say…
> And, after hearing what our Church can say,
> If still our Reason runs another way,

> That private Reason 'tis more Just to curb,
> Than by Disputes the publick Peace disturb.
> For points obscure are of small use to learn:
> But *Common quiet* is *Mankind's concern.*
> (ll.427–36, 445–50; 1962, p. 293)

In a tone of weary yet satisfied finality the concluding passage points decisively away from appearance to the self-evidently real, regarded equally as a matter of truth and consensus. English empiricist discourse has few better monuments.

This and the preceding chapter aimed to outline some of the main features of the English tradition as it was established in the seventeenth century and at certain crucial junctures after that. The next four chapters will test for empiricist discourse in some key examples from present-day writing, in each case looking to see how far the organising structures from the 'founding moment' resurface in contemporary forms.

Part III

ENGLISHNESS TODAY

5

THE DISCOURSE OF LITERARY JOURNALISM

> It is the business of criticism not only to keep watch over the vagaries of philosophy, but do the duty of police in the whole world of thought.
>
> (T.H. Huxley 1879, p. 58)

The rise of a nation-state is accompanied by the development of an identifiable national culture. Increasingly from the beginning of the nineteenth century such national culture has been defined in terms of a canon of the national literature, the particularity of a national identity thus laying claim to a place within the proclaimed universality of art. Political struggle was needed to establish the canon of English literature, and its nature and ideological consequences have been well documented (Baldick 1983; Doyle 1989). From many sources which might serve to instance this power play I choose the words of Helen Gardner when she writes that, since literature confers 'the sense of national identity' (1982, p. 45), English literature shows 'the virtues inherent in "The British way of life"' (p. 46).

The English cultural situation today

What English literature shows, however, is subject to interpretation, and this chapter addresses not English literature but some of the discourses in which it is construed. In England literary criticism has come to be entrusted with a peculiar mission in establishing, reproducing and nurturing Englishness; the empiricism of English culture has been mirrored and reinforced in the empiricism of the criticism which has interpreted its literary canon. That situation, though, has recently become open to change, for reasons partly to do with a social history (see Gross 1969).

If one considers the careers of some earlier English 'men of letters' – Desmond MacCarthy (1877–1952), John Middleton Murray (1889–1957), Cyril Connolly (1903–74) or George Orwell (who died in 1950) – it is evident that for them there was an easy exchange of ideas, creative writing and criticism between the three points of a triangle formed by higher journalism, publishing and the universities. That shared literary and critical culture, which lasted well on into the 1930s, has since broken down. In England since 1945 a yawning split has opened up between the academy and higher journalism, that London circle around which thoughts and personnel revolve easily between the broadsheet newspapers, what remain of the weekly periodicals (*New Statesman*, *The Spectator*), BBC2 slots such as *The Late Show* (now defunct) and discussion programmes on Channel 4. This schism has been bad for both sides, encouraging academics to mount further up the spiral staircase of their ivory tower, pushing London literary culture ever deeper into the gloomy recesses of indigenous empiricism.

F.R. Leavis was a pivotal figure here. He waged a lifelong crusade against the *Times Literary Supplement*, London reviewers and (latterly) British Council literature pamphlets, his role being thus 'to mediate the establishment of a new, professionally chartered discourse on literature in the national culture' (Mulhern 1979, p. 318). Leavis' seriousness and professionalism made way for a generation of university-based critics in the 1950s, John Bayley, Donald Davie, Richard Hoggart and Raymond Williams, as Bernard Bergonzi points out (1990). This marked the start of a further degree of separation between journalism and the academy, which was pressed to a new extreme when theoretical approaches to literature – at first, semiotics and Marxism – began to penetrate English universities after 1968.

Theory at the margin of criticism

My aim is to demonstrate that contemporary literary criticism in its crucial form as London literary journalism – typically, in most but not all cases – works with a version of empiricist discourse. An immediate obstacle in the path of this endeavour lies in the very assumptions and procedures of empiricist discourse, its willingness to invoke reality as self-evident and step aside from any explicit theoretical discussion (as mentioned before, Leavis would admit only that his method combined the deictic with an appeal to consensus, 'This – doesn't it? – bears such a relation to that'). Left to itself, empiricist discourse is not going to say what it is.

In recent years, however, criticism has been forced out of concealment and into a more open defence of itself by the arrival of an adversarial discourse, theory (aka critical theory, deconstruction, post-structuralism). At the interface, where criticism comes up against theory, its own assumptions begin to be exposed. For example, in the following.

James Wood, formerly the *Guardian* newspaper's chief literary critic, registers defensively the impact of theory in an article, LITERATURE ITS OWN BEST THEORY?:

> We need to move away from morality, and back to language. A new criticism would do well to ground itself in Walter Benjamin's dictum (from *One Way Street*) that 'Criticism should speak the language of artists'. From this everything flows. Such a criticism would be aware that literature is its own best theory. It would let, as it were, literature interpret itself.
>
> (*TLS*, 7 June 1991)

In this view, the literary text is given as a kind of empirical object and its interpretation is determined by the work itself (the difficulty of annealing the gap between object and subject, text and reader, forces Wood into the nervous disclaimer of 'as it were'). If the object is to be perfectly represented for the experiencing subject, discourse must be, in principle, transparent: in Wood's account this is achieved when the 'language' of criticism becomes 'the language of artists' (there is certain sleight of hand hidden underneath the word 'language' here, for literature and criticism may equally be in the same *language* though not in the same *discourse*).

Theory would deny that the text interprets itself and affirm reading as a positive act. To disable this view Wood undertakes two moves, in the first, excluding theory on the basis of an empiricist opposition between the real and the apparent: 'Prematurely obsolescent, our age attracts a rust of theory (the creeping stain of pseudo-analysis, the blisters of jargon).'

Like rust on iron, stain on (perhaps) wood, or a blister on skin, theory is rendered as a surface effect which leaves the reality beneath unaffected. What still remains of theory is to be explained away in move two: 'So theory is suspended between an explanatory zeal, a rage to uncover, to reveal, and a fetishising of incoherence that attaches a *moral* significance (such undecidability is either "good" or "bad") to something which has to do with style.'

On this showing, whether busy 'fetishising' or overcome with 'zeal', practitioners of theory are subject to self-deceiving desire in contrast to the objectivity of the true critic, who lets the text interpret itself. To achieve this clear-sighted attitude, Wood adds, you need to approach the work with 'a sense of proper humility'.

The article merits close reading. In a short space it professes its trust in the three defining features of empiricist discourse: the literary object is pregiven, yielding knowledge of itself to experience (as it were); the critical subject is similarly autonomous and pregiven, able to experience the text objectively (so long as he or she resists the subjectivity of desire); and language, not interposing significantly between object and subject, text and reader, is essentially transparent (or can be).

Contemporary literary journalism

Reality

Theory would contend that a knowledge of reality is always constructed in and through language: in response, criticism has conjured up a stark opposition – if you suppose knowledge of reality takes place in and through language, then you believe in words not reality. Persistent in literary journalism, this imposed either/or reveals the classic empiricist conception of reality as that to which there can be naked and direct access apart from language and systems of representation:

> intellectuals have been worried about whether language refers to anything 'real', or is just a system of empty signs. With the advent of…'deconstruction', this anxiety has redoubled.
>
> (John Carey, *Sunday Times*, 21 May 1989)

> It follows, so this thought goes [i.e. 'postmodernist thinking'] that reality does not really exist, or exists only as a text exists, since reality, like a text is just a vast system of arbitrary signs failing to refer to any pre-existing reality.
>
> (James Wood, *Guardian*, 27 February 1992)

> French linguistic philosophers…argued that language could never reflect or describe external reality, only create it.
>
> (Peter Jones, *The Times*, 25 May 1996)

If theory says only words exist and reality does not, then theorists will inevitably become impaled on the assumed opposition between the apparent and the real so that they are themselves rendered as fakes, impostors, an appearance masquerading as reality: 'Lacan's crackpot theories…this extraordinary charlatan' (Raymond Tallis, *THES*,

31 October 1997) (a charlatan is an 'empty pretender to knowledge or skill', the word deriving from the Italian *ciarlare*, to gossip or chatter). 'Derrida's motive is perhaps little more than exhibitionism' (Robert Grant, *TLS*, 14 November 1997).

A book by Bricmont and Sokal entered a careful and detailed criticism of French writers, including Lacan, Kristeva and Deleuze, for misappropriating and misusing certain scientific and mathematical ideas. This was reported by saying: 'American Alan Sokal and Belgian Jean Bricmont have dared to say what no one else would: modern French philosophy is simply a load of old tosh' (Jon Henley, *Guardian*, 1 October 1997). The last phrase was taken out to be used as a headline A LOAD OF OLD TOSH.

An adjunct to the idea that we have to choose between reality and discourse is the traditional English assumption that reality itself extorts from us a moral attitude. The disappearance or vanishing or wishing away of reality associated with these 'French philosophers' removes obligation and opens the door to an amorality which seems especially to promise sexual licence.

> There are those...who have taken the path of deconstruction, for whom life is a text, an endless chain of signifiers where everything is play and anything goes.
>
> (Paul Gordon, *TLS*, 16 September 1994)

> if you follow deconstruction to its logical conclusion, then nothing means anything any more, there are no values and further discussion becomes impossible.
>
> (David Mills, *Sunday Times*, 27 April 1997)

In another critic 'the steely onward march of the structuralists, post-structuralists and deconstructionists' is said to have led to this situation: '*Il n'y a rien dehors du texte* declaimed Derrida – if all the world were text and all its men and women mere signifiers, anybody was up for grabs' (Elizabeth Young, *Sunday Times*, 26 June 1994).

What Derrida actually writes is '*Il n'y a pas de hors-texte*' (1976, p. 158), but this has been re-imagined into a version whose consequences appear almost orgiastic (we will come across again this belief that only a tight grip on reality holds us back from unbridled sensuality).

In this structure of ideas the opposition 'English/French' overlaps with 'truth/pleasure' and 'common sense/dogma' (not to mention 'right/wrong'): 'The new doctrinal texts [i.e 'Cultural Studies, Media Studies'], arcane and largely post-Parisian, make no claim to standards, and delight in postmodern permissiveness' (Malcolm Bradbury, *Sunday Times*, 9 July 1995). A similar fantasy is at work when one critic comments (a little wistfully, I think), 'Play, for post-structuralist writers such as Jacques Derrida, thus replaces verification as the scholars's primary task' (Charles King, *TLS*, 15 March 1996).

If reality in general – an empiricist notion of reality – is put in doubt by this 'steely onward march', then so, crucially, is the fixed identity presumed to be given in the literary text, and that fixity has to be defended:

> This notion of the vacant or ever-spongy text is logically impossible, since if Shakespeare is a black hole, then so is Dickens or Eliot; clearly, these writers do not represent identical black holes; *something* intrinsic to these black holes gives them differing qualities.
>
> (James Wood, *TLS*, 23 April 1993)

This '*something* intrinsic' insisted on as the work of the canonical author is thought of in empiricist terms. I will end this particular group of citations with one which, though journalistic, is in fact from television criticism and which takes what is 'intrinsic' to the text to be reality itself. A review of *A History of British Art* on BBC2 affirms: 'Holbein did not draw attention to his own artifice; when you look at Titian up close you see brush strokes; at close quarters with Holbein, you see flesh' (Stuart Jeffries, *Guardian*, 29 April 1996). Here, the difference between reality and representation is so completely effaced that on inspection a painting turns out to consist of bodily tissue (not Titian, perhaps, but Damien Hirst?).

Language

Few would deny that the vocabulary and manner of theory are often philosophically demanding and at the same time deliberately playful, always liable to incur the oppositions 'seriousness/play' on this side of the Channel (not to mention 'English/French'). The anxiety excited by the mere idea of jargon can be measured by the apologetic gestures made in this next citation, from a discussion of media and politics:

> I hate to use pseudo-academic jargon, but since I've made this bit up myself I'm willing to dare. It is the totality of the media experience – that means all newspapers and TV and radio stations – which affects people's views and, by extension, their voting decision.
>
> (Roy Greenslade, *Guardian*, 24 March 1997)

The little word 'totality', not entirely unfamiliar since the time of Hegel, can only be risked if off-set with blokeish informality ('I've made this bit up myself').

The ferocity, assurance and consistency with which literary journalism denounces theory for its 'jargon' exposes its own trust that language by nature communicates meaning with the ease of light passing through a pane of glass:

> [Modern literary criticism is] written in difficult and apparently pretentious dialects.
>
> (Frank Kermode, *Guardian*, 10 October 1991)

> the quasi-scientific, jargon-laden offerings of British Eng.lit. since it discovered European systems of analysis.
>
> (Hugh Hebert, *Guardian*, 18 March 1991)

> the jargon of semiological analysis.
>
> (Tom Shone, *Sunday Times*, 20 June 1993)

> the impenetrable jargon of postmodernism.
>
> (Nial Ferguson, *Sunday Times*, 19 October 1997)

> Derrida's inordinate polemical scripts are the written counterpart of his lecturing style, an advanced case of logorrhea.
>
> (Claude Rawson, *LRB*, 25 April 1991)

> The expansionist designs of the theorists are nowhere more apparent than in their terminology. To make sense (where possible) of what they are saying, you have to submit to a new language....Some of this jargon serves a justifiable purpose: every discipline needs its specialised vocabulary. But...you can't in fact travel very far in this particular territory without encountering unmistakable specimens of deliberate obscurity, wild generalisations and high-sounding guff.
>
> (John Gross, *TLS*, 15 November 1991)

This last does make some concession to the necessity for precise terminology while the others dismiss jargon with something of the full, Lockeian afflatus.

Postmodern textual practice and the more abstract insights of theory have definite affinities. The empiricism of literary journalism bares itself once again in some confrontations with the postmodern novel.

One journalistic commentator dismisses the way 'the contemporary novel experiments, potentially disastrously, with the narrative tradition': '[failing to rise] to the grandeur of Tolstoy and Flaubert…we play post-modern games that seem designed to cover our embarrassment at the fact of having to do something as simple as tell a story' (Bryan Appleyard, *Sunday Times*, 21 December 1997). If you think Flaubert did something simple like telling stories I suppose you could equally believe telling a story was simple, a matter of life rather than art.

One postmodern text is reviewed as:

> a dazzling linguistic pastiche [with its] cleverness too obviously on show, [leaving the reader uncertain whether some] authorial heart-on-sleeve stuff…isn't just another of the novel's clever devices; [but] it falls down in denying its reader any real focus of human attention.
>
> (Jonathan Coe, review of Julian Barnes, *A History of The World in 10 and a Half Chapters*, *Guardian*, 23 June 1989)

This calls into play the opposition between the real and the apparent across several classic English binary oppositions:

fact/fiction
serious/silly
sincere/artificial
amateur/professional

So, 'real focus' and 'human attention' line up on the left, with 'linguistic pastiche', 'cleverness' and 'clever devices' firmly denigrated as forms of textuality on the right.

A similar deployment underpins another review of a postmodern novel (one set in the film world, *Silver Light* by David Thomson) 'Unfortunately, amid all the subject allusions and self-conscious time-shifting of the narrative, he [the author] hasn't managed to breathe much life into them [his characters]…he has an unreliable grasp of how real feelings work' (Robert Sandall, *Sunday Times*, 24 June 1990). Here the positions are filled by 'life' and 'real feelings' on one side with 'allusions', 'self-conscious time-shifting' and 'narrative' on the other.

Yet a third review of a postmodern novel develops the binaries in its own terms: 'At every turn we are dutifully reminded of the artificiality of the fictional process.…This literary trickiness…is inimical to the imagination; [but sometimes the characters do] become fully animated and memorable [in] a gripping narrative' (Elizabeth Young, review of Alasdair Gray, *Poor Things*, *Guardian*, 3 September 1992).

Neglecting the fact that all novels are text and only text, the distinction made between linguistic display and real life, 'literary trickiness' and 'fully animated' characters, wishes that art could be a pure, unmediated experience, beyond language – not painting but flesh, as it were. And these assumptions can as easily be brought to bear on a novel which is only tenuously post-modern so that Ian McEwan's *Enduring Love* is criticised because its characters do not have 'much more life' than in a thriller, are 'efficient fictional containers, but not people' (James Wood, *Guardian*, 4 September 1997). For literary journalism the life of the subject depends on the death of the signifier.

The subject

Such apprehensive reactions to the postmodern novel, organising themselves around notions of 'the real' and 'the human', point towards a conception of the subject as free-standing, itself self-sufficient and unconstructed as the literary object experienced more or less directly. After attacking 'cultural materialists' and 'post-structuralists/deconstructionists' who appear to attack Shakespeare in the name of theory, one writer asserts: 'Those who love Shakespeare (like I do) [*sic*] are apt to become inarticulate in his defence, to talk about beauty and truth, and to start quoting, rather hazily, great lines from the plays like hammy actor-managers' (James Wood, *Guardian*, 13 October 1994).

Quoting the lines, 'And take upon us the mystery of things,/As if we were God's spies' to illustrate how ineffable is such beauty, he continues: 'It is difficult to watch King Lear in a theatre and not hear people crying at this moment in the play.' Literature becomes the vehicle for absolute experience registered in an unpremeditated response which is beyond expression. Its value (to recall a Lockeian phrase, II.14.3) is 'evident to any one who will but observe what passes in his own mind'.

Theory intervenes in this immediate response, turning the amateur into a kind of professional, replacing sincere feeling with artificiality. Before theory, 'A self-respecting undergraduate simply picked up his native literature as he went along' (Edward Pearce, citing with approval John Gross 1969, *Guardian*, 25 September 1991); now theorists 'insist on the priority of theory over literature', as John Gross himself writes (*TLS*, 15 November 1991) (to be fair, Gross does make the concession that 'every discipline needs its specialised vocabulary'):

> criticism and bogus theory have displaced our direct encounter with works of art.
> (John Carey, citing with approval George Steiner's *Real Presences*, *Sunday Times*, 21 May 1989)

> Theory is offered, not as an adjunct to the reading of books, but as a replacement of that process.
> (Claude Rawson, *LRB*, 25 April 1991)

> [in literary study] theory has foolishly been allowed to dominate pedagogy.
> (Alastair Fowler, *TLS*, 29 November 1996)

On the basis of the crucial opposition between 'objective' and 'subjective' an ethical dimension is opened up, a domain for a certain kind of subjectivity: the worthiness and rightfulness of those capable of a direct and spontaneous encounter with art and literature are contrasted with the error of those who let theory interpose itself.

Wilful perversion by 'bogus' theory is explained as a form of self-deception. As noted already, in this structuring of ideas reality is knowable, certain and stern, but its imperatives can be eluded by those who are 'silly' rather than 'serious', who desert 'truth' in their search for 'pleasure'. These are the ones who desire play, a world in which 'anything goes', for whom all men and women are 'up for grabs'. At the same time – and in complete contradiction to this imagined hedonism – submission to theory is seen as constituting mere passive acquiescence to higher authority.

Literary journalism seeks out for condemnation 'doctrinaire critics' (Frank Kermode, *Guardian*, 10 October 1991) who would rule by 'decree' (Desmond Christy, *Guardian*, 22 October 1991). It is said to be this 'theory' which 'decreed that authors should not be regarded as the originators of their works' (John Carey, *Sunday Times*, 7 August 1994) supported by those who find sanction for themselves in 'the new doctrinal texts' (Malcolm Bradbury, *Sunday Times*, 9 July 1995). Surely this composite attack on figures pictured as simultaneously sybaritic and authoritarian reactivates that old English opposition, 'Protestant'/'Catholic'?

Individual freedom and responsibility, in contrast, exhibit themselves in an encounter with literature which is first-hand. Hence discussion of response – and theory's supposed denial of response – invokes a sense of value:

> A prerequisite of some at least of the new-paradigm programmes

> is simply an indifference to literature, an ignorance of what it is to read it, even a denial that it genuinely exists.
>
> (Frank Kermode, *Guardian*, 10 October 1991)

> Deconstruction [is] indifferent to literature, except as a launching-pad for its own cerebral arabesques.
>
> (John Carey, *Sunday Times*, 21 May 1989)

This latter accuses 'deconstruction' of narcissistic playfulness in a phrase which neatly combines pedantry with self-indulgence, 'cerebral arabesques'. Again:

> Broadly speaking, the new regime disallows questions of literary value. Since all value is contingent, there is no absolute way of defending a preference for one book over another.
>
> (Frank Kermode, *Guardian*, 10 October 1991)

> the idea [in 'Structuralism, Post-structuralism, Deconstruction and the rest'] is that nothing is valuable in itself.
>
> (Hugh Hebert, *Guardian*, 18 March 1991)

Just as in the claim that either you believe in a given, empirical reality or you live in 'a vast system of arbitrary signs', 'an endless chain of signifiers', so here another uncompromising either/or is imposed: either literature has absolute value or it has no value at all. What is at stake, I would guess, is not literature so much as the transcendental conception of subjectivity its reading is thought to exercise, enact and justify.

Reality, language, subjectivity: structured together, the empiricist prescriptions of literary journalism are sometimes epitomised together.

> Theory denied that language was a medium by which humans could communicate; it decreed that authors should not be regarded as the originators of their works; it rejected the idea of people as free agents with individual inner selves.
>
> (John Carey, *Sunday Times*, 7 August 1994)

> Language, by deconstructive decree, is alien from human purposes, a stranger to human wishes and wills. As a doctrine this is pernicious to the precise extent that it acquiesces in the curtailment of human freedom, for that is what is at stake in our ability to shape words for our own purposes.
>
> (Desmond Christy, *Guardian*, 22 October 1991)

It's all there: communication is direct, experience unmediated, the self is self-originating and a 'free agent'. In a recent lecture Prince Charles took up a position on the side of empiricist criticism, castigating those said to tear literature apart to fit the 'abstruse theories of the day', preferring instead George Eliot's *Middlemarch* on the grounds that it is a 'wonderful story of human nature' (see *Guardian*, 5 May 1994).

And irony, of course...

Literary journalism is replete with examples of irony and I shall restrict myself to three. Reviewing *Vested Interests* by Marjorie Garber, a Harvard professor, the critic summarises its argument, that transvestism challenges 'vested interests' (the pun is Garber's though the name is her own), adding '(among others, presumably, those of Harvard professors with tenure)' (Liam Hudson, *TLS*, 28 May 1993). The real meaning is that the theorist, deceived by zealous fervour, fails to recognise how her arguments impinge on her own interests. We (those who get the irony) are invited to see the theorist as she cannot see herself.

Under the headline, HAS THE FRENCH FEMINIST PHILOSOPHER HÉLÈNE CIXOUS GOT ANYTHING COMPREHENSIBLE TO SAY?, a reviewer discusses a book by Cixous which contains some autobiographical writing. There is a brief and vague summary of the notion of *écriture féminine* (details of why Cixous might consider transparent, linear writing as masculinist are omitted). The article insists:

> There is a fascinating story to be told....One yearns for a straightforward, coherent, narrative history of her life – no doubt a desire which is the last thrashings of the phallus, the sad dreams of the Anti-Other in papaperson (*sic*).
>
> (Stuart Jeffries, *Guardian*, 29 October 1997)

At exactly the point at which the context threatens a rather obvious rebuff to this yearning for a straightforward history, the text wards off the threat by itself introducing the idea but in the form of ironic citation.

One more example. After reviewing two books (Fred Inglis, *Cultural Studies* and Andrew Milner, *Contemporary Cultural Theory*) with plenty of irony and urbanity, a critic in the *TLS* concludes by putting the following paragraph in quotation marks:

> 'Irony is a textual strategy legitimated by the discursive norms of the dominant metropolitan culture. the cultural contradictions of market-sensitive capitalism are evident in all such

> attempts to contain challenges to establish categories without having seriously to engage with the destabilising power of genuinely oppositional analysis. In these circumstances, urbanity is the reviewing classes' equivalent of turning water-cannons on strikers. The *TLS* cannot in fact carry a serious and adequate discussion of cultural studies without calling its own existence and rationale into question.' Discuss.
>
> (Stefan Collini, *TLS*, 27 May 1994)

This is irony at degree zero, tending towards undecidability. For one, audience citation alone is enough to expose the phoney and self-important politicising of cultural studies to the gaze of the Other (while demonstrating the writer's own mastery of both his own and the alien culture). For another, this paragraph is bang on target and has to be read straight: 'irony', is a 'textual strategy' which *does* attempt 'to contain' etc., and criticism in the present-day *TLS cannot* carry a serious discussion of cultural studies (or theory) without calling its own 'existence and rationale into question'. At this point consensus on what constitutes reality and its interpretation has broken down so that irony is impossible – all the writer dare claim in the way of metadiscursive dominance is a lame parody of an examination rubric: 'Discuss'.

That double reading suggests how separated and incommensurate the academy and 'the dominant metropolitan culture' have now become. Undeterred, though in a damaging isolation from a more public forum, the analysis of literary and other texts according to various explicitly theoretical perspectives expands daily through the academy, exploring with another audience and another consensus the themes empiricist criticism represses. Meanwhile, committed to the text as unconstructed given, language as transparent and the self as freely autonomous, London literary journalism goes round the much the same circle it has retraced since at least 1945. As one journalist summed up the current situation, 'Britain did not become part of the deconstructionist empire: its traditions and arrogantly self-confident institutions are powerful enough to exclude ideas from abroad – good or bad' (Desmond Christy, *Guardian*, 22 October 1991).

Empiricist content/empiricist style

In England the empiricist style and attitudes in critical discourse, both in journalism and the academy, were not seriously challenged until the late 1970s. At that juncture empiricist criticism ran up against an alterity in the form of a revitalised Marxist literary criticism (Althusserian tendency), laced with semiology. Like the first meeting of Pilgrims and Native Americans, that encounter is instructive, not only because once again it drives from cover the hidden assumptions of empiricism but because it exposes a number of cultural problems. I shall explore these through close reading of one text, hoping to justify its treatment as exemplary by using it to explore two issues: how does an empiricist style of discourse operate in depth (in metaphor and tone)? Is there really an alternative to it in England today (a question flagged at the end of Chapter 1)?

On 20 May 1977 the *TLS* published LITERATURE AS SYMPTOM, a long review by John Casey of Terry Eagleton's work of 1976, *Criticism and Ideology: A Study in Marxist Literary Theory*. When it attacks Eagleton for 'a knowingness based upon carefully selected facts', one may suppose that Casey's text implicitly appeals to the possibility of an object able itself to select what facts would be appropriate for its interpretation, so providing knowledge and not just a knowledge effect ('knowingness'): an object conceived in terms of empiricist reality therefore. And when Casey complains that 'the most influential contemporary theories in England, deriving from Marxism and semiotics, all subordinate reading to interpretation' he shows he subscribes to the view that reading gives direct access to the meaning of the literary text while interpretation is a separate and subordinate activity.

Casey's allegiance to empiricist discourse informs the details of his writing. Thus a term from Leavis ('sincerity') is discussed on the assumption that to see is to know:

> *At first sight* 'sincerity', for example, *looks like* a value imposed from the outside, but when *we examine* the connections that Leavis establishes between the 'sincerity' of a poem and the precision or concreteness of the language in which a feeling is 'realised', *we see* that this is not the case throughout [my italics].

Metaphors rendering knowledge as vision recur throughout the text: 'sight', 'insight', 'view' (nouns), 'see', 'look', 'recognise', 'seem', 'face' (a problem), 'hide' (a fact). Visible through what is conceived as a limpid and unmediated Newtonian space, the meaning of reality is assumed to be contained in reality itself.

Belief that language by nature opens directly on to that reality is upheld by Casey's dismissal of Eagleton's own textuality as simply too manifest, too obviously written; his writing is various referred to as consisting of 'grey slabs' of prose, a 'mimicry of Stalinist rhetoric', 'the language of liturgical Marxism', a 'liturgical language' which is referred to as 'positively Tridentine'. The Council of Trent of 1545–63, we may recall, fixed Roman Catholic doctrine and practice for the Counter-Reformation – perfect confirmation of my argument that in the English discursive formation the classic oppositions (especially in the form 'clear/obscure' and 'common sense/dogma') bear with them a historical resonance derived from 'Protestant/Catholic'.

Eagleton can be 'convicted of an entire lack of a sense of humour purely on the basis of his style' says Casey, whose own text exhibits little in the way of sense of humour except in the form of irony. Mentioning a statement by Eagleton on the nature of language, Casey refers to 'the large amount of work done by bourgeois philosophers in an attempt to produce a theory of language that will be a little more refined than this': 'refined' and 'a little more' understate the ironic meaning while 'bourgeois philosophers', citing the language of his opponent, positions him as object for his own metalanguage. Having noted that the book acknowledges a debt to the Oxford Critical Collective, the review comments: 'It is after all doubtful whether even the Oxford Critical Collective regularly responds with aesthetic pleasure to a re-telling of the tale of the Luddites.' Here the real meaning is something like 'the Luddites are childishly uninteresting like a fairy tale', the implication being that those who pretend to find them interesting are hypocritically self-deceived.

A particular application of irony adapts phrases from canonical literature for present purposes. When Casey writes with reference to language of 'an infinite variety of sentences', he assumes familiarity with Shakespeare's description of Cleopatra; 'The theme is familiar, though the notes are forced' recalls 'The sound is forc'd, the notes are few!' from Blake's 'To the Muses'; and the syntax, 'if there is any author who…Mr. Eagleton is he' picks up the classic instance of classic irony, Pope's Atticus. These references are neither innocent nor neutral, and are not indicated as allusions by the use of quotation marks – it is up to readers to take them on board. If they do, the review captures some of the reflected authority of the English literary canon while the reader is afforded pleasurable identification with a knowing elite who are on easy terms with great literature.

Empiricist metaphor, empiricist tone?

Now suppose you wished to cleanse your text by writing at a distance from English empiricist critical discourse, then so far, on the evidence of Casey's example, the principle would be clear: avoid classic irony, avoid knowing citations. There are other forms of language in the review –

metaphor, cliché and colloquialism – which appear more neutral, much more a matter of pure style. Even these, however, turn out to have a complicity with empiricist discourse.

Casey's metaphors conjure up a whole world. In the first place they invoke an individual body which is 'nurtured' and can experience 'helplessness', 'impotence', 'immersion' (in a problematic), as well as 'feelings of claustrophobia' and the force of gravity as when Eagleton 'falls' (into simplicities), until finally it is 'set to rest' (like certain problems). Its imagined head may be bald (as in an assertion). This body inhabits a world in which terrain is measured: a 'literary map' is redrawn, a tradition 'traced', 'boundaries' remain 'undefined', a theory 'encompasses' literature. On this land edifices are constructed – a 'gap' is bridged (between material conditions and experience), a story is 'recast' into 'grey slabs' (of concrete?) – and there are gardens (presumably) in which one might 'uproot the flower of beauty' and in which flying creatures are 'hovering nervously' (a mind, that is, uncertain of its argument). All this activity takes place within a market economy: Shakespeare is dealt with, attention paid (twice), a 'debt' acknowledged, a method 'credited' with an achievement and an ideology regarded as 'clearly bankrupt'. A complexity is said to be 'rich', as is the possibility of a 'subtle Marxian aesthetic'. And law is part of this economy since at one point practical criticism is 'accused' while at another it 'entails' a philosophy of mind.

The metaphors Casey's text reproduces with a certain innocence reveal an origin in the past three centuries of English life, particularly as seen from the point of view of the gentry. From the complete range of metaphoric sources one might draw upon, which would include astronomy, geometry, physiology (very much the metaphoric repository for, say, John Donne), Casey's selection concentrates upon everyday life as experienced by the individual. These seemingly natural as distinct from far-fetched metaphors – rising, falling, crossing, bridging, mapping, uprooting, planting, and so on – are in fact naturalised, constructed by a certain discursive history. They are, one might say, Lockeian metaphors (and we will find them again).

So, if you wanted to step right outside the empiricist style, you would have to keep your metaphors under constant review ('step outside'? 'keep under review'?). You might try to do without them altogether, like writing a book without using the letter e. But the desired move from metaphorical to literal, from concrete imagery to rigorously enforced abstraction, would not be easy. Casey is very relaxed about using a lot of abstract terms in ready-made combinations: for him attacks are increasing, concern continuing, influence enormous, problems fundamental, references desultory, coincidences happy and assertions confident (when not bald). These, again, arrive loaded with connotations from their discursive history – Locke, Addison, the Johnsonian periodic style, Jane Austen.

A more scrupulous use of abstraction might avoid the inherited associations of these adjective/noun pairings. But any attempt to escape metaphor and concrete language altogether would face an inherent difficulty. The opposition between metaphorical and literal cannot be upheld since all abstract terms bear with them some concrete significance, sedimented, as Derrida remarks, 'in the entangling of their roots' (1982, p. 253). Even the phrase 'The ball is in front of the rock', admirably literal as it appears, hides a secret metaphor, as Lakoff and Johnson explain: 'Some things, like people and cars, have inherent fronts and backs, but others, like trees, do not…the rock has received a front-back orientation, as if it had a front that faced you. This is not universal' (1980, p. 42). No discourse in Modern English can escape such essentially abstract words as 'account', 'value', 'interesting', 'to offer' yet each of these harbours some kind of metaphor.

Casey's review works with frequent colloquialisms: 'well aware of' 'easily the best', 'pretty similar to', 'cannot…however hard he tries'. Generally kept out of high serious discourse in French, German and Italian cultures, the use of such idiom in a literary review is peculiarly English and has several effects (one of these being to let a professional academic sound like a literary journalist).

If philosophy is defined as '*nothing but the true Knowledge of Things*' capable of being '*brought into well-bred Company, and polite Conversation*' (Locke 'Epistle', in 1975, p. 10), then the function of this idiom from the everyday is empiricist, to demonstrate rhetorically that knowledge of reality is obvious and not a matter of elaboration or contrivance. Certain usages in Casey's text I would want to name as terminal closure: 'simply', 'purely', 'after all'.

Colloquialism has more than one effect. Casual, approximative assertions ('more or less', 'some sort of', 'perhaps') exhibit gentlemanly poise, a refusal to be fussy or formal about mere detail, an assurance that knowledge of reality is readily available and commonly shared (hence the tone informing Casey's phrasing of 'We might notice' and 'One finds oneself protesting'). Yet such colloquialism is not always what it might appear – real, careless spontaneity – for it also consists of the qualifications of a scholar. In these idiomatic expressions philosophy masquerades as common sense, another instance, then, of irony.

The 1977 textual encounter between Casey and Eagleton was symbolic. At that time a number of radical writers, impelled by the precedent of Althusser, were determined to break with the English empiricist manner. Certainly one might try to ditch classic irony and stick to the more radical mode of satire (though satire might not necessarily be appropriate for the topic of discourse). But flight from metaphor into abstraction, even if it were strictly possible, would not necessarily elude the connotations of the English tradition, which has its own repertoire of abstractions. And the refusal of colloquialism, for all its dubious complicity, does risk frightening off even what is now left of a wider audience.

In 1976 Arnold Kettle attacked what he called '"theoretical" writing' (which he instanced in the work of Terry Eagleton) on the grounds of its 'incomprehensibility' and for being 'hopelessly undemocratic'. In a disarming footnote he reflects:

> I'm aware that the idiom I adopt myself isn't beyond criticism or outside the struggle. It's an idiom that any sectarian will be quick to categorise as 'bourgeois'. I'm aware of this but think the advantages of being fairly widely comprehensible in a given social situation greatly outweigh the disadvantages.
>
> (p. 5)

Kettle was right. His own writing (like Casey's) does inhabit an 'idiom' which is only too evidently that of the English empiricist tradition. A sectarian might indeed call it 'bourgeois' but would surely be wrong to think that anything in the English proletarian tradition offers a firm and distinct alternative to it. The high theoretical mode did try to make a radical break. It failed – not because it was necessarily 'incomprehensible' or even 'undemocratic' (there is nothing very democratic about Casey's knowing ironies) but because it simply could not naturalise itself into English, the weight of the inherited discourse being too great. A text (including this one) must inhabit a given discourse since, as Derrida says, 'one always inhabits, and all the more when one does not suspect it' (1976, p. 24).

That it did not actually establish itself is not a final verdict on 'theoretical writing'. Like the gap which the arrival of 'theory' opened at the edge of journalistic criticism, its effect has been to unsettle the inherited discourse, to begin to make it visible as such.

6

THE DISCOURSE OF HISTORY-WRITING

Since the second half of the nineteenth century history has become increasingly the refuge of all those 'sane' men who excel at finding the simple in the complex and the familiar in the strange.

(Hayden White 1978, p. 50)

The desire of the historian

Constantly reaffirmed, the belief of most contemporary English writers of history is that through sustained, painstaking and disinterested effort they may work their way towards a knowledge of the truth about the historical past. Yet temporality ensures that the past, even if it is the past as yesterday, only exists for us in its *traces*. In this respect history-writing has a similar ontological status to cinema. Film presents objects, figures, landscapes, cities and the bric-a-brac of everyday life with a breath-taking actuality not possible from any other means of representation (the three dimensions of space but also *movement*) but only on condition that those very objects, figures, etc. are placed somewhere else, 'made present' on the screen 'in the mode of absence' (Metz 1975, p. 48); history-writing is able to present a world of people, events and structures resembling our own in the most extraordinary complexity and detail, a non-fictional world, but only on condition that it is absent.

Lack constitutes desire. Of the self-ascribed task of the modern historian to present facts from the past in the form of a narrative, Hayden White asks, 'What wish is enacted, what desire is gratified, by the fantasy that real events are properly represented when they can be shown to display the formal coherency of a story?' (1987, p. 4).

One answer is proposed by Michel de Certeau. Drawing on the psychoanalysis of Lacan and the semiology of Christian Metz, de Certeau affirms that 'the figure of the past keeps its primary value of representing *what is lacking*' (1988, p. 85) because the very attempt to understand a historical other on our terms marks its actual distance from us. Thus:

> A gap is folded into the scientific coherence of a present time, and how could this be, effectively, unless through something that can be objectified, the past, whose function is to indicate alterity? Even if ethnology has partially relieved history in this task of a staging of the other in present time...the past is first of all the means of *representing a difference*. The historical operation consists in classifying the given according to a present law that is distinguished from its 'other' (the past), in assuming a distance in respect to an acquired situation.
>
> (p. 85)

Our ancestors are different or were different, another people, another culture, an alterity which resists every reduction. History-writing, in summoning up these others, cannot escape a certain 'exoticism', as de Certeau proposes; neither can it elude a desire for knowledge. Inevitably, the historian's narrative expresses a drive to master the otherness of a past, the drive Freud terms *Bemächtigungstrieb*.

Nietzsche gives another answer to White's question, that the desire of the historian is to produce 'a past from which one would wish to have descended' (cited White 1987, p. 149). What is this desire to bring together the *disjecta membra* of the dead and breathe our life into them if not a rite of the dead, a 'Nekuia', which finds its Western archetype in Homer when Odysseus calls up the spirits of his forebears, giving them blood now so they may empower his future? Since every human society has practised a form of ancestor-worship, even the most dry, abstract and seemingly objective history written today desires to establish a narrative coherence between the past and a possible future, one able to confer an identity on the present.

Contemporary English history and 'postmodernism'

Such considerations are a million miles away from the thoughts of most contemporary English history-writers, whose conscious conviction that they are exclusively or mainly engaged in essentially objective fact-finding and truth-telling confirms how deeply they are caught up in a version of empiricist discourse. Recently, that island complacency has been unsettled a little, some of its hidden assumptions brought to light, through an encounter with post-structuralist theory and what has been christened 'the linguistic turn', 'the semiotic challenge' or simply 'postmodernism'. It began when Lawrence Stone attacked postmodernism and 'the linguistic turn' in 1991 in *Past and Present* (the debate which followed took place mostly there and in *Social History* so that although not all the participants were English the site of the discussion was).

A useful preliminary in thinking about what's at stake is to pick up some of the terms in which for their part historians have foreseen the encounter, a perception which is not separable from some lively and revealing fantasies (since opponents of postmodernism invest a great deal in the opposition objective/subjective it is not unfair to ask after possible subjectivism in their own viewpoint). In this, for example:

> Historians, for the most part, have not yet directly confronted the issues raised by post-structuralism and postmodernism. They have tended to avoid the opening forays, dismissing them as philosophical tracts of interest to soft-headed theoreticians rather than the real practitioners of the profession.
>
> (Patterson 1989, p. 86)

These 'tracts' no doubt stand for dogma, in opposition to common sense. And what gender, one might ask, is being imputed to 'soft-headed theoreticians'? Again:

> Historians are by no means helpless in these polemics. Critical theorists strike them as belletristic triflers who would rather posture about history than actually read a work of history, much less set foot in an archive. They see theorists as seduced by rhetoric rather than devoted to a sober search for truth, as given to obscurantism not lucidity.
>
> (King 1991, p. 171)

To read 'actually' is set over against belletrism, trifling and posturing, and, indeed, in the classic Lockeian trope, being 'seduced by rhetoric'. And, again, what is the sex of those who are being seduced? Could it be the same as that of the 'soft-headed theoreticians'?

This is how a sustained passage imagines the experience of 'historians who adopt semiotic procedures': they 'find themselves suddenly released into a free-floating open space.…They can thrill to the experience of weightlessness…take the higher ground where universes of meaning clash.…Instead of painstakingly documenting the past, they can imaginatively reinvent it' (Samuel 1992, p. 233).

Real historians are opposed to these as earth to air:

> Historians, by contrast, at least according to their own lights, cleave to the worm's eye view. They are notoriously preoccupied with, indeed as critics allege, obsessed by detail, making a crab-like progress from point to point. In their ideal persona, they are sceptics, never happier than when puncturing generalisations, exploding fallacies, or multiplying exceptions to the rule.
>
> (p. 232)

Through these vivid metaphors the contrast between 'semiotic' and serious historians is staged on the grounds of sexuality and pleasure. If, as Freud notes, 'flying dreams are dreams of erection' (1973–86, 4, p. 518), then the facile aerobatics of 'the deconstructionists' lack the substantial phallic power ascribed to the down-to-earth historian, a worm or crab, who steadily penetrates 'from point to point'. Although 'painstaking' and apparently immune to pleasure, these – so the language suggests – do find pleasure in 'puncturing', 'exploding' and 'multiplying', the victim of their aggressive power being exactly the kind of 'generalisations' and 'fallacies' enjoyed so casually by the high-flying followers of deconstruction. This is an example of the historian's Hobbesian satisfaction in imposing the reality principle on self-deception which appears surrendered to the pleasure principle.

Each extract proclaims its allegiance to the left-hand side of the classic empiricist oppositions, opting for practice, clarity, fact, common sense, hardness, truth and virility as against theory, obscurity, fiction, dogma, softness, pleasure, and, yes, effeminacy (not to mention real against apparent, right against wrong).

The view that post-structuralism or 'the linguistic turn' turns everything into text seems to yield a deeply attractive image. The unexamined Englishness of the historians' debate over 'postmodernism' is displayed in their hands-in-the-air empiricist horror at the very thought of the disappearance of reality into textuality. If there is no reality (of the kind the historian wishes for), chaos is come again:

> social life is essentially a play of discursive behaviour, the interaction and combination of artificial, disembodied signs in unstable relationships to one another, cut off from any purchase on a world exterior to language.…the imaginary is real and the real imaginary.
>
> (Spiegel 1990, pp. 62, 68)

> Texts thus become a mere hall of mirrors reflecting nothing but each other, and throwing no light upon the 'truth', which does not exist.
>
> (Stone 1991, p. 217)

> Meaning is in the eye of the beholder, and it is filtered through invisible grids. There is no 'objective' reality which can be apprehended independently of images of it.
>
> (Samuel 1991, p. 102)

> My only objection is when they ['postmodernists'] declare that truth is unknowable, but that there is no reality out there which is anything but (*sic*) a subjective creation of the historian; in other words that it is language that creates meaning which in turn creates our image of the real. This destroys the difference between fact and fiction.
>
> (Stone 1992, p. 193)

> [If] there is *no* reality beyond language and discourse – for example, no economy, no society, no cultural or political systems and structures, but only economic, social, cultural and political discourses....Reality would become the narrow cul-de-sac of language, and *nothing more.*
>
> (Kirk 1994, p. 226)

Not all these passages are equivalent in detail but they are the same in that for these writers 'postmodernism' is charged with anxiety and desire. A fear is evident that the death of reality might instigate some kind of transcendental loss. At the same time this loss is covertly desired as escape from obligation, a view implicit in the next passage:

> In history, it ['postmodernism'] is a denial of the fixity of the past, of the reality of the past apart from what the historian chooses to make of it, and thus of any objective truth about the past. Post-modernist history, one might say, recognises no reality principle, only the pleasure principle – history at the pleasure of the historian.
>
> (Himmelfarb 1992, p. 12)

If there were no reality, then the life of the history-writer could be entirely given over to pleasure (we've come across this manoeuvre already in English literary journalism).

Historians generally do concede that in principle history-writing is, to some degree, an effect of writing. But such gestures contain an element of denegation for they do not prevent these writers from making resounding and traditionally empiricist affirmations:

> What the traditional historian sees as an event that actually occurred in the past, the post-modernist sees as a 'text' that exists only in the present.
>
> (Himmelfarb 1992, p. 13)

> We want to know what actually happened.
>
> (Samuel 1992, p. 245)

> Surely we can see real events occurring behind people's backs…?
>
> (Eley and Nield 1995, p. 61)

The 'actual' of what 'actually' happened or the 'real' of what occurred involves an empiricist epistemology with a fairly untroubled confidence that accounts of the historical past can be discriminated once and for all between the apparent and the real, as does the would-be scientific force of the 'clearly *demonstrated*' in the following: 'as a result of many years of hard theoretical and empirical labour, historians and others have clearly *demonstrated* that socio-economic, political and cultural systems and processes have emerged and changed over time' (Kirk 1994, p. 238, italics original).

Another historian aims to resist the semiotic challenge by showing that a text 'can only be understood in the light of a social and political context wholly absent from the body of the text itself' (Spiegel 1990, p. 83) and insists vehemently 'that context is not simply another text' (p. 85). Surely this 'context' she calls on must be derived from another text or set of texts, unless we assume it is somehow pregiven outside narrative and interpretation?

Historical thinking along these lines is committed to an opposition between the textual and reality which is fundamentally empiricist. In a crippling alternative it assumes:

1 *either* texts do not refer to reality (as the 'linguistic turn' is supposed to claim), in which case they can refer only to other texts (this idea opens on to the pleasures of the labyrinth fantasy, texts as a 'hall of mirrors', reflecting only each other in an 'empty' world 'cut off' from reality from which there is 'no exit');

2 *or* texts do refer to reality, in which case it is assumed that their textuality, their materiality as texts, does not or does not in any significant way interfere with the transparency of the access they afford to historical reality.

You do not have to put your head into the noose of this false option in which each side presumes the other (another manoeuvre already seen in literary journalism). I want to develop briefly some arguments to show that the opposition (*either* discourse and only discourse *or* reality and only reality) ensues from a thoroughly empiricist belief that reality – in this instance, historical reality – is given in such a form that it only takes dedicated hard work to learn the truth about it.

The epistemological question

Far from being novel topics, epistemological questions have been part of the discussion of history-writing for some time. Twenty-five years ago, for example, in an essay, 'The Discourse of History', Roland Barthes pointed out that history-writing generally thought of a meaning (signified) as if it were a copy of a referent (reality) and on this basis presented a meaning as if it were 'the real itself' (Barthes 1981, p. 18). Few would disagree that reality is real and discourse is discourse: in dispute is the question of correspondence or adequacy between discourse and reality, realists taking the view that correspondence between discourse and reality can be demonstrated while anti-realists doubt that possibility.

Realism is untenable because there is no way to establish the validity of such correspondence, however defined. Someone might try to put forward criteria by which adequate or inadequate correspondence might be assessed. But in that gesture the question immediately arises as to the validity of these criteria; further criteria are needed to validate these, and so on in infinite regression. Once you step on to this escalator you cannot get off: as Jean-François Lyotard puts it succinctly, 'what proof is there that my proof is true?' (1984, p. 24).

Anti-realism fares no better. To deny that discourse corresponds to reality *at all* is to take a position of radical scepticism. It is impossible to refute this position and it is impossible to confirm it. The epistemological demand for a way of refuting sceptical anti-realism, as Richard Rorty explains, is a quest 'for some transcendental standpoint outside our present set of representations from which we can inspect the relations between those representations and their object' (1994, p. 293). To refute anti-realism requires access to an exterior point from which you could judge the relation between discourse and reality.

When, following Nietzsche, Martin Heidegger in *Being and Time* reaches the issue of realism versus anti-realism he cannot decide at first which least incurs his sympathy (1962, pp. 63–148). His reason is that human beings are (always already) thrown into the middle of Being, contingent on a world we have not and could never choose. So for us there is simply no *position* available from which to inspect the possible correspondence or non-correspondence between our discourse and reality. God could do it, but we cannot because we are inside, part of the process we want to judge. Realism and anti-realism mirror each other for both presuppose a point at which Knowing might stand outside Being. No such point exists.

This discussion reflects back on historians and the either/or they want to impose on the 'linguistic term' in their certainty that kinds of writing about history can be discriminated into radically opposed categories. One compartment contains texts which reflect nothing but other texts, and which, even if they do attempt to refer to historical reality, remain trapped inside their own textuality. Another is reserved for proper works of history which show 'what actually happened' and which, escaping their own textuality, refer to something outside themselves. But the categories cannot be validly opposed to each other in this fashion for the same reason that you can neither confirm realism nor refute anti-realism: no one is in a position to demarcate reality from textuality and so draw a decisive line between what is inside and what outside the text.

Jacques Derrida, notoriously, has become associated with the claim, '*il n'y a pas de hors-texte*' (1976, p. 158). It is hard to know what a world would be like in which the sign was absolutely free, life consisted simply of an unconstrained play of discourses, and textuality was determined only by textuality. But we do not even have to speculate about this because if Derrida is read carefully, as Dominick LaCapra acutely remarks, it is clearly his view that 'there is no inside-the-text either' (1989, p. 157). We are not in a position to decide fundamentally where the text ends and reality begins, where the door shuts on what is inside the text (and therefore inseparable from fiction) and what is outside the text (and therefore a matter of fact). If we discard the claim that reality provides knowledge of itself, more or less directly, then fiction and fact, what's inside and outside the text, arrive together, a package deal.

If this is the case, one must wonder how English historians reach their stern demand that texts either refer to other texts or refer to reality. The answer can only be that they are victims of an empiricist belief that historical reality exists somehow 'in itself', in knowable form outside discourse. Some general points about the integration of facts, discourse and narrative in historical writing may confirm this.

Historical facts and historical narrative

'At Stalybridge Wakes in 1850, a vendor of gingerbread, as the result of some petty dispute, was deliberately kicked to death by an angry mob': as we know in Manchester, Stalybridge can be a rough place, though this was not E.H. Carr's concern in *What is History?* when he mentioned this fact (1964, p 12). His point is that whether a fact gains currency in history-writing depends upon whether 'the thesis or interpretation in support of which' this incident is cited becomes 'accepted by other historians as valid and significant' (p. 12). Carr's hapless vendor of gingerbread might be victim of 'an angry mob' or, in another account, 'the incensed proletariat'. He could figure in many histories, a history of Cheshire or nineteenth-century crowd behaviour, a history of leisure activities or food adulteration, and so on. In each history the 'same' item of information takes on different force and significance depending on the particular kind of historical interpretation it is expected to threaten or uphold.

Carr's argument that the value and meaning of a historical fact are established on the grounds of interpretation rather than the other way round in no way calls in question the reality of the past events historians aim to represent, as Hayden White explains:

> The events have to be taken as given; they are certainly not constructed by the historian. It is quite otherwise with 'facts'. They are constructed: in the documents attesting to the occurrence of events, by interested parties commenting on the events or the documents, and by historians interested in giving a *true* account of what *really* happened in the past and distinguishing it from what may *appear* to have happened. It is the 'facts' that are unstable, subject to revision and further interpretation, and even dismissable as illusions on sufficient grounds.
>
> (1995, pp. 238–9)

White might not be able to draw a line between 'events' and 'facts' quite as easily as his opposition between 'not constructed' and 'constructed' would suggest. This does not weaken his main point that historical facts cannot be separated from interpretation, a view which exposes candidly the empiricism of those White glances at ironically as 'historians interested in giving a *true* account of what *really* happened in the past'.

Facts are constructed; and in modern history-writing they must also be construed into a coherent narrative. Again, it is Hayden White who makes the argument with a cogent instance, citing a passage from the *Annals of Saint Gall*:

> 709. Hard winter. Duke Gottfried died.
> 710. Hard year and deficient in crops.
> 711.
> 712. Flood everywhere.
> 713.
> 714. Pippin, mayor of the palace, died.
> 715.
> 716.
> 717.
> 718. Charles devastated the Saxon with great destruction.
> 719.
> 720. Charles fought against the Saxons.
> 721. Theudo drove the Saracens out of Aquitaine.
> 722. Great crops.
> 723.
> 724.
> 725. Saracens came for the first time.
> 726.
> 727.
> 728.
> 729.
> 730.
> 731. Blessed Bede, the presbyter, died.
> 732. Charles fought against the Saracens at Poitiers on Saturday.
> 733.
> 734.
>
> (White 1987, pp. 6–7)

None of the annalist's facts are seriously in dispute (though, notably, the Battle of Tours of 732 is not mentioned while Poitiers is). Following Croce's modern view that 'Where there is no narrative, there is no history' (cited White 1987, p. 28), White's argument is that history-writing draws on facts referring to the past so as to construct a narrative in the present. It does this, as Roland Barthes shows in his account of narrative, through a double move, first making the facts over into a consecutive story by imposing what Barthes terms the proairetic code, and then transforming the story into a narrative proper by means of the hermeneutic code, that which not merely links events causally but sets up in the reader's mind questions which are later answered, a sense therefore of the total meaning and significance of the causally related events.

These arguments – that what counts as a historical fact cannot be separated from the discursive purposes for which it is adduced and that modern history-writing must work with a narrative which can never be free from rhetorical and discursive construction – have the effect of throwing into startling prominence the empiricist view of some English history-writers that fact and historical interpretation can be positively and finally discriminated (like 'objective' and 'subjective'). Moreover, empiricist historical discourse, assured that it is telling the truth and nothing but the truth, is more liable to the 'return of the repressed', in acts of rationalisation and unacknowledged prejudgement. Belief that you are objective and therefore untouched by subjective feeling may well render you more subject to desire.

From these general considerations I want to go on, with an example, to demonstrate in detail how the empiricism of an English historical text works, as well as to suggest how its avowed objectivity masks subjective investment. My concerns will be narrative, the object of historical knowledge, the means of representation, the kind of subject this way of representing knowledge assumes.

Romancing the stone

Though it would be difficult to choose some classic piece of history-writing that every English historian will identify with, I hope my example will be taken as reasonably representative. It has to be short, not a book, because I shall submit it to a close reading. 'The Inflation of Honours 1558–1641' by Lawrence Stone was published in 1958, and can now be seen from a safe distance.

Narrative

Narrative, as an overtly rhetorical device, is an embarrassment to the empiricist historian, and 'The Inflation of Honours' works hard to pretend it is not a narrative. It does tell a story, all the same, in six sections, including an introduction. Between 1558 and 1641 titles were increasingly sold to finance state expenditure: in the order of exposition this narrative is repeated at four levels, concerning the College of Arms (pp. 47–8), Knights (pp. 48–52), Baronets (pp. 52–5), Peers (p. 55 ff.), leading into a conclusion (pp. 59–65). At one point 'The Inflation of Honours' claims its story is the same as that narrated by royalists who, during the long years of the Interregnum, looked back over the previous half-century and agreed with Gervase Holles that 'that way of merchandise...was one cause (and not the least) of [the] misfortunes...of our last martered King' (cited Stone, p. 60). Here the move is to fasten the narrative on to another narrative, so that the narrativisation can be passed off as a matter of consensus and common sense.

That 'The Inflation of Honours' inescapably does have a narrative can be appreciated by comparing its narrative with some others. It could easily be told as a fairy story, for instance:

> Kings and queens are always short of money, but then, isn't everybody? Once upon a time there was a mean old queen who was short of money so she started letting people call themselves 'Lord Jim' and 'Sir John' if they gave her money. She was followed by a rather foolish king, whose name was James, and he did the same. His son Charles was even more foolish, and when he came to the throne he did just the same again. Well, children, in the end people got pretty sick of all this, but that's another story.

The sequel is much more interesting, and Shakespeare wrote at least two versions of it. *Hamlet* shows how a representative of the gentry, Hamlet, rises out of the prevailing corruption of a Jacobean court; though he is too entrammelled with the past to survive himself, his dying word heralds the domination of a new order represented by Fortinbras (admittedly, a rather sinister and uncertain figure). But Brecht noted, Shakespeare more often 'takes a tragic view of the decline of feudalism' (1965, p. 59), and in *King Lear* he gives a very different reading of the inflation of honours, showing great sympathy with a man who foolishly retains the name and title of monarch while divesting himself of its powers.

In marked contrast to this tragic version, Stone's Whig narrative conducts us from the bad old days of absolutism, via the rise of the gentry towards their triumph in the society we now have. Although tinged with irony at human folly, it is essentially a comic narrative, culminating in a happy ending: us. It conforms to the familiar Enlightenment story of demystification, a narrative of the defeat of a kind of supernaturalism and the triumph of reason, the overthrow of Catholic superstition by Protestant common sense.

The object

Sidelining as far as possible its own act of narrativisation, 'The Inflation of Honours' avoids a sense of the diachronic in favour of the synchronic. The text opens with a sociological generalisation, 'Perhaps the most immediately obvious feature of a society dependent upon monarchy is the existence of titles of honour' (Stone 1958, p. 45), and in its final paragraph, closes by asserting another atemporal principle said to govern social operations:

> The inflation of honours between 1558 and 1642 is proof of the truth of what has been described as 'Tawney's Law': that the greater the wealth and the more even its distribution in a given society, the emptier become titles of personal distinction, but the more they multiply.
>
> (p. 65)

In between, the text relies on this synchronic conception of the social formation as a self-defining, self-regulating object.

It is a 'system' (p. 45 [three times], p. 58, p. 60) with a 'function' (p. 45 [twice]) working through 'forces' (p. 45) whose main effect is to cause 'pressure' (seven times altogether, pp. 45, 46, 50, 51, 56, 57, 63). The energy source for the motor of this society is simple and obvious: people are 'socially ambitious' and driven by the desire for 'solid material advantages' (p. 62); this exerts 'pressure' which can cause 'strain' (p. 45) unless its force is controlled and directed to useful public ends. For 'The Inflation of Honours' society is a machine. What sort of machine is implicit in the following sentence: 'By 1600 the wheels of government were ceasing to turn without the sweet oil of bribes and gratuities at every revolution' (p. 46). Metaphors elsewhere – 'floodgates' (p. 50), something being 'dammed up' (p. 56) or 'swept away in the tide' (p. 59) – suggest that society is a water-mill. This system, what the text refers to at one point as 'established socio-economic fact' (p. 64), is equated with the reality the text represents (this is one of the ways the text contrives to convince a reader that it is telling the full and complete truth about a past which is correspondingly full and complete).

Given the existence of this system, 'The Inflation of Honours' is supplied with an empiricist ethic (to recognise reality objectively is right, to act out of subjective motives is wrong). Thus, knowing how the social machine works, a good ruler acts to maintain 'balance' (p. 45) and preserve 'stability' (p. 47) while a bad ruler will let the social pressure rise dangerously by failing to 'recognise an established socio-economic fact' (p. 49). Elizabeth is wrong because personal reasons cloud her judgement, her 'parsimony' (p. 63), just as James errs in the opposite direction, through 'prodigality' (p. 49).

It is not hard to think of all kinds of reasons why you might want a title in the seventeenth century – to make yourself more sexually attractive, to please your father, because you fancy yourself in ermine, because you see it as your religious duty to serve the anointed monarch. Today each of these might be seen as a different expression of desire – sexual drive, Oedipal submission, narcissism, obedience to the superego. 'The Inflation of Honours' upholds its notion of society as a machine driven by a single power source by deploying what might be called 'the Hobbesian reduction'.

The potentially various and contradictory desires of title-seekers are reduced to a single form, 'the socially ambitious' (p. 48), consistent with the idea of society as motivated by desire for power in the form of material advantage. What cannot be thus plausibly explained, the text tries to exclude by counting it as unreal. The system of honours is one of 'fundamental artificiality' (p. 45); people who seek titles are the kind who have 'forged' their genealogy and trust in 'make-believe' (p. 45). So the desire for 'solid material advantages' is real, a wish for any other form of pleasure is merely apparent.

The habitual English equation of objective/subjective with real/apparent functions at a number of levels in this essay, at each of which a false exterior is discarded so an essential inside may be retained. Thus:

1 Between 1558 and 1641 people were engaged in either recognising reality (the functioning of the water-mill driving society) or indulging in fantasy, 'make-believe'.
2 What these people were really doing can thus be contrasted with what they thought they were doing.
3 Since we as readers can thus discriminate real from apparent motives by assessing them in relation to reality of the social engine, 'The Inflation of Honours' refers to a reality to which we may have direct access.

Means of representation

A claim that textuality and narrative in 'The Inflation of Honours' are as good as transparent is repeated in a consistent vocabulary: something is 'obvious', 'immediately obvious', 'all too obvious', 'obvious enough' (pp. 63, 45, 46, 59); or something is 'clear', 'clear enough' (twice), 'comes out very clearly' (pp. 50, 51, 57, 55); or something is 'evident', appears 'evidently', there is 'clear evidence' for it (pp. 55, 59, 56); it is 'difficult to see' what else someone could have done, there 'can be no doubt' of something, a 'theoretical position' can be immediately contrasted with what happens 'in fact' (pp. 46, 60, 52).

Discourses other than history-writing make use of a distinction between text and footnote but in history-writing such as 'The Inflation of Honours' the distinction bears a special effect for it is worked out as a hierarchic contrast between metalanguage and object language. Thus, one discourse becomes itself the object of inspection by another discourse posing itself outside the object language and capable of knowing it as it cannot know itself (see MacCabe 1985).

In Stone's text facts as accumulated from 'primary sources' are largely consigned to footnotes. So the words 'these Marks of Honour, called Arms, are now by most people grown of little esteem', cited in the text (p. 48), is referred by number, superscript (7) to the footnote, superscript (7) 'W. Dugdale, *The Antient Usage in Bearing…Arms*, 1682, preface' (p. 65). Footnotes shorthand an object language which does not properly understand itself but whose real meaning as well as its own failure to understand itself is to be fully explained in the text, the metalanguage. While the discourse of 'the facts', the object language, is marked as manifestly textual (no one now says or writes things like 'are now by most people grown of little esteem'), the text or commentary, through contrast, can pass itself off as unwritten, having no textual force at all.

'The Inflation of Honours' is written in the English objective style, consistent in tone, evenly varied in sentence form and sentence length, seemingly obvious in choice of vocabulary – in a word, unremarkable, a style which invites its style to be overlooked. Since Stone's represented world is supposed to be just there, the representation of it may be offered as weightless. The aim is to provide the reader with a perfectly clear window through which to watch unobserved these Elizabethan–Jacobean people and see exactly what they are doing.

The denial of desire

With reference to an anthropologist's presentation of primitive people Derrida argues that 'The mere presence of a spectator…is a violation' (1976, p. 113). Because they are exposed to our voyeuristic gaze, Stone's seventeenth-century folk appear very much as 'natives' do in colonialist discourse: they are charming, amusing, naive, slightly sinister, occasionally unintentionally acute. Though their behaviour is exotically and pleasurably other, their motives turn out to be reassuringly similar to ours, readily described in a sardonic and demystificatory twentieth-century mercantilist vocabulary. Obliged by 'financial necessity' Charles takes a 'major policy decision' (p. 51); titles are 'put on the market', prepared for 'auction', knightage drifts into an 'inflationary condition' (p. 52); at one point there is a problem over 'the sale price of baronetcies, owing to the excess of supply over demand' (p. 53) but generally titles are sold 'for cash' (p. 56) because they promise 'social status' (p. 59). Following the logic of English empiricist morality, the text assumes that it is only wish-fulfilment which could delude these people about what they were really doing, selling titles for cash. Underneath they partake with us in a common humanity.

In this respect 'The Inflation of Honours' transforms difference into the same and reduces alterity to the familiar. Its overall procedure expresses a drive to master the otherness of a past, to make over into presence the lack posed by these traces of the other. Presenting itself simply as a transcription of the 'immediately obvious', confident it can decisively separate apparent and real, trusting it can communicate truth without subjective interference, Stone's text reveals a desire to be rid of desire.

This effect is well characterised as denial. Denial (*Verneinung*) combines 'sour grapes' with 'the dog in the manger' as though to say: 'I don't want what I can't have and so you can't have it either.' It emerges in the way 'The Inflation of Honours' decries fantasy as indulgent self-deception while asserting its own engagement with the Other as objective and clear-sighted, a detachment in fact subverted by the manner with which pleasure is addressed. A tone of irritated contempt becomes unmistakable when the desire for a title is dismissed as an expression of 'fundamental artificiality' (p. 45), and, later, the honours system is spurned as 'a romantic and increasingly unrealistic wish' (p. 55). A long section begins by describing how 'an indolent king' had to finance 'his day to day pleasures', how George Villiers sold titles to provide these, and concludes with the fierce satisfaction that all of this 'was put to an end by Felton's knife' (pp. 57–8). The text is tempted into imaginary identification with the pleasures of the Court but denies them as self-deceptive and unreal; thinking it refuses pleasure for itself, it enjoys refusing it to others. The great precedent for this is Hobbes.

Apparent/real, subjective/objective, self-deception/truth: another feature deeply buried in Stone's text gives insight into the historian's empiricism, for these oppositions are all joined together by a metaphorical contrast between the solid and the liquid. On the one hand, there are 'solid material advantages' (p. 62) and 'stability' (p. 47), on the other, a constant deliquescence. Besides the 'oil of bribes' (p. 46) there is 'fluidity' (p. 45), 'flow' (p. 45, p. 46), open 'floodgates' (p. 50), a 'flood' (p. 54), a 'spate' (p. 55) which gets 'dammed up' (p. 56), a 'tide' (p. 59) which sweeps things away (one remembers all that 'pressure'). And there is constant anxiety about a 'breach' (p. 55, p. 56), a 'gap' (p. 52) or 'cleavage' (p. 61) opening up in the solid so that fluid leaks through it.

Except for an allusion to 'fluidity' (p. 45) to mean social change, in every case material interest is equated with the solid, titles with fluidity, and a gap is what appears in the difference between the two. In sum, the solid is uncreated, substantial, self-identical, undivided, true, essential, extra-discursive, real and, I would hazard, masculine. Fluidity is forged, make-believe, duplicitous, ambivalent, fictitious, unnecessary, textual, unreal, and, I guess, feminine. In this hysterical fantasy the solid seeks but always fails to exclude flow from itself.

Possibly these speculations tempt Felton's knife. But they find support in Derrida's argument that the Western tradition has relied on an opposition between a masculinised logocentrism which thinks of itself as solid and self-present and the flow of textuality whose excess threatens all the boundaries logocentrism claims for itself (see 1981). In a text such as 'The Inflation of Honours' this more general organisation of ideas is put in the service of a hard-line empiricism.

History-writing and empiricism

Far from proving that Stone's text is untypical, this metaphorical opposition conforms to and confirms the general feelings among contemporary English historians as these come out in their denunciations (cited earlier) of the threat from 'the linguistic turn'. Contrast between 'soft-headed theoreticians' likely to be 'seduced by rhetoric' and the undeceived historian who is 'never happier than when puncturing generalisations' imagines an opposition between soft and hard, flying and penetrating, flow and solidity, between those who have surrendered to pleasure and those who have not. Yet the dispassionate objectivity of empiricist history-writing is driven by its own unacknowledged passion – to stamp on sentimentality and wish-fulfilment. Anyone who seems unwilling to submit to the hard discipline of facts, preferring instead to play with their own fantasies, is savaged with an intensity which shows that the demand for discipline, mastery and certainty is not itself free from desire.

'The Inflation of Honours' typifies the empiricism of contemporary English history-writing in its conception of its historical object as a kind of given, in its deployment of the 'plain style' of the English gentry, and in its constant presumption that it is to be read by an autonomous individual situated in a position of disinterested exteriority. For all this a price has to be paid – not just that it increasingly looks provincial but that this very English tradition blocks alternatives. Reluctant to admit that historical facts, narrativisation and the *writing* of history are each, in different ways, acts of construction, it precludes admission of the situatedness of the historian.

Contemporary history-writing was developed essentially in the Victorian period with a mode of discourse very like that of the nineteenth-century realist novel. A way forward might be for English history-writing to take on board some of the principles, insights and techniques associated with Modernist fiction, to move away from George Eliot and become a bit more like James Joyce.

There are, however, strong indications that this will not happen or will not happen soon. In 1994 an eminent and authoritative English historian, Keith Thomas, reviewed *Telling the Truth about History* by three Americans (Joyce Appleby, Lynn Hunt, Margaret Jacob) which apparently sees off the challenge of 'the linguistic turn' (*Guardian*, 6 September 1994). Not unexpectedly, the view of 'the deconstructionists' is said to be that 'language is wholly unstable' so that 'meanings cannot be represented'. In contrast, the book's authors are praised because they 'nevertheless think it is possible to establish some correspondence between the past and the historian's account of it'.

Moving to quarantine the English historian from this debate, the reviewer comments that 'some British readers may even wonder what all the fuss is about' (the colloquialism 'fuss' is symptomatic, suggesting commotion in excess of what is appropriate to reality). The review concludes:

> For the most part, British historians remain a stolidly untheoretical lot; and many of them have yet to experience the epistemological doubts which have afflicted their American colleagues. Neither has the challenge of multiculturalism and the ethnic minorities so far provoked much of a response from the writers of the nation's history. But cultural lag does not last forever and when we too are plunged into internecine battle about the possibility of any objective history we shall be grateful for this fine book's account of both the disease and the remedy.

It is accepted that in the end 'the linguistic turn' will reach English historians, no matter how stolid. When it does it will come as an affliction, arising not from any inherent intellectual difficulty but rather because an American-style multiculturalism will challenge the integrity of the national culture and those who write its history. But in any case, according to this reviewer, there is no need to worry. Since the book establishes a correspondence between discourse and reality, disease and remedy occur together, keeping empiricism safe for English historians.

7

ENGLISH TRAGEDY, ENGLISH COMEDY

Winston woke up with the word 'Shakespeare' on his lips.

(George Orwell 1983, p. 28)

English tragedy

The rhetoric of pathos

Tragedy presents loss but its audience experiences an affirmation. Though pain, suffering, even death is represented within the tragic text, the means of representation, through its formal measure and control, can provide the reader with a sense of uplift and mastery (see Freud 1973–86, 11, pp. 286–7).

Even without extended narrative, a tragic rhetoric of pathos results if misfortune is stated in a regulated tone, avoiding excess, as it is in the well-known passage from *Paradise Lost* in which Milton alludes to his own blindness:

Thus with the Year
Seasons return, but not to mee returns
Day, or the sweet approach of Ev'n or Morn,
Or sight of vernal bloom, or Summers Rose,
Or flocks, or herds, or human face divine.

(III: 40–44)

An apparently neutral phrasing contrasts the natural cycle with his situation ('not to mee') understating the implied meaning ('light does not return to my eyes when it should'). And the tone is carefully ordered to play off normal intonation against the imposed line endings, producing a rhythm slowed by monosyllables ('Rose', 'flocks', 'herds') but leading into the unanticipated climax of 'human face divine'. Later in the

English poetic tradition Wordsworth recalls the Miltonic precedent in *The Prelude*:

> The days gone by
> Return upon me almost from the dawn
> Of life: the hiding places of man's power
> Open; I would approach them, but they close.
> I see by glimpses now; when age comes on,
> May scarcely see at all.
>
> (XII: 272 ff.)

While Milton regrets his lack of physical sight and, with it, full pleasure in the external world and human company, Wordsworth mourns the passing of spiritual insight and the certainty of his own importance.

The rhetoric of pathos, an effect in which (to put it technically) the act of enunciation (*énonciation*) would make good loss stated in the statement or enounced (*énoncé*), recurs throughout European literature. But it is specially suited to English discourse with its preference for transparency over rhetoric, objective statement over subjective excess. In Wordsworth's poetry Coleridge found a certain '*matter-of-factness*' and considered it a fault (1907, 2, p. 101): English plain statement, however, promotes the rhetoric of pathos (stiff upper lip, quivering lower lip, as the cliché says), frequently expressing itself in indirection and ironic understatement ('Seasons return, but not to mee returns'). In the English formation the rhetoric of pathos is adapted especially for statements of personal loss, including loss of the personal itself. Locke at one point says individuals know that they are something but can't be sure what: ''Tis past controversy, that we have in us something that thinks, our very Doubts about what it is, confirm the certainty of its being, though we must content our selves in the Ignorance of what kind of *Being* it is' (IV.3.6). This is marked by an 'elegiac' tone, as Catherine Belsey points out (1985, p. 84), a dignified rhetoric of pathos.

The last Englishman

A formal effect, then, may seek to recuperate a stated loss. In contemporary English writing such pathos is generally deployed around the notion of the autonomous individual. Here is this structure, at once thematic and rhetorical, in a popular novel. In John le Carré's novel, *The Spy who Came in from the Cold*, first published in 1963, Alec Leamas, a secret service agent, is sent on a mission of betrayal to East Germany only to discover that he has himself already been betrayed by George

Smiley and his superiors in London; together with the woman he loves he tries to escape over the Berlin Wall. The novel ends as follows:

> Then they fired – single rounds, three or four and he felt her shudder. Her thin arms slipped from his hands. He heard a voice in English from the Western side of the wall:
>
> 'Jump, Alec! Jump, man!'
>
> Now everyone was shouting, English, French and German mixed; he heard Smiley's voice from quite close:
>
> 'The girl, where's the girl?'
>
> Shielding his eyes he looked down at the foot of the wall and at last he managed to see her, lying still. For a moment he hesitated, then quite slowly he climbed back down the same rungs, until he was standing beside her. She was dead; her face was turned away, her black hair drawn across her cheek as if to protect her from the rain.
>
> They seemed to hesitate before firing again; someone shouted an order, and still no one fired. Finally they shot him, two or three shots. He stood glaring round him like a blinded bull in the arena. As he fell, Leamas saw a small car smashed between great lorries, and the children waving cheerfully through the window.
>
> (1964, pp. 239–40)

Despite the dramatic events, the style is neutral and descriptive, only small touches pointing up the intended pathos – her hair in the rain, the hesitation before firing, his stance like a bull in the *corrida*, his memory (mentioned at an earlier point in the novel) of children killed by aerial attack during the war). Leamas' act of deliberate suicide affirms a dimension of individual heroism, just as the tone of pathos seeks to make good the loss described.

Asked what he believes in, Leamas says, 'I believe an eleven bus will take me to Hammersmith. I don't believe it's driven by Father Christmas' (p. 36). His empiricism supplemented by the Chandleresque detective tradition, Leamas asserts his privacy and individuality against the state, the novel implying that the English secret police are as bad as their Communist opponents. The motifs of the individual pitched against totalitarianism, interrogation by state machine, and the tragic defeat of the hero, all these derive from what is probably the greatest and certainly most famous English novel of the twentieth century.

Nineteen Eighty-Four

Published by Secker and Warburg in 1949, *Nineteen Eighty-Four* has since sold over 15 million copies round the world. In a recent poll of 25,000 people it was named as the second most popular book of the century after *Lord of the Rings* (see '100 books that made a century', *Guardian*, 20 January 1997). More than any other post-war English novel the book has come to pervade general consciousness so that '1984', 'proles', 'doublethink' and 'Big Brother is watching you' have become commonplaces. *Nineteen Eighty-Four* can be seen as a Lockeian novel in that it takes a tragic view of the destruction of its Lockeian hero.

Against the constant sliding reinscription of factual truth seen as necessary to the power structure of totalitarianism, *Nineteen Eighty-Four* poses explicitly 'the empirical method of thought, on which all the scientific achievements of the past were founded' (p. 157), though the rest of the novel makes it clear that what is meant is not merely an empirical method but a form of empiricism which assumes facts are simply given and interpret themselves. Winston Smith's explicit opposition to Big Brother is articulated in these terms. In 1973 he came across a document proving that *The Times* newspaper has lied:

> this was concrete evidence; it was a fragment of the abolished past, like a fossil bone which turns up in the wrong stratum and destroys a geological theory. It was enough to blow the Party to atoms, if in some way it could have been published to the world and its significance made known.
>
> (p. 66)

So, in the final struggle with O'Brien in which Smith is forced to deny the evidence of his senses (is O'Brien holding up four fingers or five?), against O'Brien's claim that 'Nothing exists except through human consciousness', Smith holds on to the idea of an empirical reality which is given and self-evidential: 'But the rocks are full of the bones of extinct animals' (p. 213).

For both Orwell and for Winston Smith this reality is, in principle, available transparently through discourse. In his essay 'Politics and the English Language' (1968, 4, pp. 172–40) Orwell mobilises a series of Lockeian oppositions to maintain the language of personal experience, sincerity, and the concrete, against jargon, prefabricated phrasing and abstraction, above all insisting that a word is chosen for its meaning, not its verbal felicity. *Nineteen Eighty-Four* embodies this same desire to eradicate the signifier, equating jargon with corrupt power and juxtaposing

'Newspeak' with its own would-be transparent narrative discourse (a topic to which I will come back).

'I am conscious of my identity' (p. 209) Winston Smith proclaims against O'Brien. In what many would call the most moving passages of the novel we follow while Smith, materially aided by the diary he has just opened, shuffles through 'the interminable restless monologue' running inside his head (p. 10). He wants to assemble dreams and memories – his mother, his sister, the Golden Country – into a narrative account of who he is, trusting in the Lockeian belief that if he 'can repeat the *Idea*' of a past action 'with the same consciousness' he had of it then and 'with the same consciousness' he has of present action, this proves he is 'the same *personal self*' (II.27.10). Through reflection Smith wins through to the certainty that in the society of 1984 'Nothing was your own except the few cubic centimetres inside your skull' (p. 25).

The novel presents it as tragic that Winston Smith's new-born inner self is washed away by torture and replaced with something – someone – else. We witness, in the words of one critic, 'the hopeless struggle of a man to retain his grasp on empirical reality and so on his own individuality' (Sandison 1986, p. 171). The reader is invited to think of what happens to Smith as an unspeakably atrocious perversion so that the more or less objective narrative of his heroic self-discovery, love affair and brain-washing takes on tragic significance: 'Two gin-scented tears trickled down the sides of his nose. But it was all right, everything was all right, the struggle was finished. He had won the victory over himself. He loved Big Brother' (pp. 239–40).

Pathos in *Nineteen Eighty-Four* attaches to the idea of the loss of autonomous individuality, not the hero's death (as with Leamas) but worse, the dissolution of his selfhood.

Realism and Modernism

Simply to give in to that effect of pathos, however, is not quite the end of the story, for that would disregard the very problematic status of *Nineteen Eighty-Four* as a text and its exemplary position in the twentieth-century English novel. *Nineteen Eighty-Four* faces the reader with a harsh opposition – either the absolute self of Winston Smith or the absolute tyranny of Ingsoc and Big Brother – and by that very harshness it tends to encourage a reader to unsettle the opposition. There are two ways in particular to go about this, and both point up the awkwardness contemporary English culture feels when faced with the great international cultural movement of the century, Modernism.

One is to consider how the novel actually consists of several different kinds of writing. There is Smith's narrative, Emmanuel Goldstein's 'Theory and Practice of Oligarchical Collectivism', the Appendix on 'The Principles of Newspeak'; Smith's narrative itself includes slogans, chunks of Newspeak from the Ministry of Truth, as well as the song of the prole (p. 113), and extracts from his diary. Intended to dominate and integrate these is the third-person omniscient narrative (critics of the novel, who have a lot to say about the other kinds of textuality in the novel rarely comment at all on this writing). Conversational, confidential, using short, generally concrete sentences, the narrative conforms exactly to the clear and straightforward journalistic style Orwell advocates. For example:

> The barman swished two half-litres of dark-brown beer into thick glasses which he had rinsed in a bucket under the counter. Beer was the only drink you could get in prole pubs. The proles were supposed not to drink gin, though in practice they could get hold of it easily enough.
>
> (p. 74)

This aims to be writing degree zero, a styleless style effacing itself before the directly experienced reality – beer glasses, bucket, beer, gin and proles – it mirrors so perfectly.

This is a style in a certain discourse for it consists of writing in the English transparent mode – familiarity might let it pass as invisible except that it appears in a text which foregrounds its own textuality. In consequence the metalinguistic claims of the main narrative are put in question: if it originates in the present, how can it have access to 1984? If it derives from 1984, how come it is not written in Newspeak? A similar effect is achieved thematically, for the more that Winston Smith insists on the absolute priority of truth and facts, the more he reminds us that he is a character in a fiction masquerading as fact.

Much of the charge of *Nineteen Eighty-Four* comes from its engagement with powerful contemporary discourses, so powerful, I suggest, that they undermine the avowed project of the text. The intellectual position O'Brien advances is devastated because events show it is upheld by torture and massive injustice. But suppose it were otherwise, suppose O'Brien's views were not discredited simply by what he does, then we might begin to realise he puts forward some of the main tenets of Modernism.

It is arguable that Modernism: (1) treats knowledge of reality as a variable construction inseparable from interest and desire; (2) recognises the materiality and inescapable partiality of all forms of discourse; (3) considers human subjectivity as effect rather than point of origin. For

O'Brien 'Nothing exists except through human consciou (he adopts another and more dubious position when h exists in the human mind, and nowhere else', p. 200); fo (such as Newspeak) profoundly shape if not actually con think about things; human nature is something 'we create' (p. O'Brien is a Foucauldian *avant la lettre*.

Winston Smith opposes O'Brien and Ingsoc as 'the last man' (p. 217). Orwell's novel struggles to hold in place the empiricist transparency of its realist narrative against the other discourses of the text (science fiction, political theory); it works hard to privilege Winston Smith and the personal consciousness he incarnates against a rendering of a culture and society that would make them impossible (and for which O'Brien is the speaker). The tension of *Nineteen Eighty-Four* is that it tries to sustain a traditional realist character in a Modernist world – it is as though Winston Smith fell out of a novel by George Eliot and woke up in the pages of Kafka: 'It was a bright cold day in April, and the clocks were striking thirteen' (p. 5).

What makes Orwell's novel of 1949 such a major and typical intervention within English culture is that it dramatises such a stark alternative. It tries hard to expel Modernism but it tries too hard, for the strain – the way that whole moral weight of the novel is stacked against O'Brien – becomes symptomatic of the actual uncertainty it feels about a traditional English individual and traditional empiricism. Readers may feel swept away with the pathos of Winston Smith's defeat. Or they may feel the text has manipulated them as relentlessly as any example of Newspeak.

The English sense of humour?

> the whimsical originality of the English.
>
> (Hegel 1956, p. 421)

To judge from the English newspapers there is firm agreement on two things: to be properly English you must have a sense of humour; but comedy (wit, humour, joking) is absolutely beyond analysis and understanding and should remain so. Discovery of a sense of humour, however belated, may restore a politician's reputation, as in the election for leadership fought between John Major and John Redwood in 1995. Matthew Norman in the *Guardian* (6 July 1995) commented:

> God be merciful, a sense of humour has suddenly emerged as the deadliest weapon in the political armoury. Mr Major's

> Wildean brilliance at Question Time was credited with igniting his recovery, while Mr Redwood's supporters vaunted the comedic genius he confirmed at a press conference, with 'I can reveal that everyone will vote for...someone called John!!'.

In this is writing with a hint of Restoration roguery ('God be merciful') the irony implying that neither Major's 'Wildean brilliance' nor Redwood's sally were as funny as some supporters thought does not obscure the assumption that it is a moral necessity for people like these to demonstrate a sense of humour.

Jokes are often used by men to exchange the idea of a woman among themselves, so excluding women and affirming the male bond. But it would be wrong to conclude that women do not share in jokes and laughter (see Gray 1994). Julie Burchill ends a discussion of a worthy but apparently over-serious 'woman's picture' by saying: 'I rarely felt so much in need of some cheap thrills, or even a laugh. Old English proverb: when going to find yourself, it is always wise not to lose your sense of humour' (*Sunday Times*, 28 November 1993). In the same gesture she claims both Englishness and a sense of humour.

Beyond analysis?

The English today have acquired a reputation for their sense of humour which has spread to the rest of Europe: 'Sabina Kolvey, who translated Fawlty Towers and Blackadder for German television, says the British are the jokers of Europe: "You do it better than anybody else"' (*Sunday Times*, 25 August 1996). And the English do seem to keep going on about a sense of humour, so much so that Gilbert Adair has remarked: 'The joke is to the British what the philosophical concept, let's say, is to the French, and we thus take our comedians a lot more seriously than our philosophers' (*Sunday Times*, 22 January 1995). A 'sense of humour' is felt to be very close to the heartlands of Englishness, and this is implied by any number of jokes about the humourlessness of other nationalities. In the 1941 English film, *Pimpernel Smith*, the Gestapo chief, General von Graum, reads extracts from Lewis Carroll, Edward Lear, and *Punch* to his assistants; they do not laugh; he concludes that the English have no sense of humour. In contemporary journalism a sense of humour is conceived as ineffable, rightly and necessarily defying analysis:

> Let us not get too much into the dreary business of analysing comedy.
>
> (Jonathan Margolis, *Sunday Times*, 9 October 1994)

> Why do we find jokes funny? The explanation would cause heavy frost to form over the heaving shoulders of the laughing policeman himself.
>
> (Stuart Wavell, *Sunday Times*, 9 July 1995)

> Nothing kills comedy faster than reading more into it than is there.
>
> (Hugh Hebert, *Guardian*, 26 June 1995)

> Dissecting TV comedy is like painting the Golden Gate bridge – you don't know when to stop, you wish you'd never started and you suddenly discover you've lost your sense of humour.
>
> (Adam Sweeting, *Guardian*, 10 March 1996)

In one respect these observations are accurate. The joke depends upon a play of words or ideas which present a meaning *indirectly*: if the joke is paraphrased, this play disappears and so does the joke effect. But more is at stake for English journalists than this feature, as is implied by the following account of two men who have written a book on television:

> the academic analysing a joke is the unreadable in pursuit of the unteachable...Neal and Krutnik wheel a joke into an operating theatre, carve it up, tinker around and lay out its viscera for inspection; we can now peer at the joke's corpse, confident in the knowledge of how it worked. We might nevertheless feel that one needed only to know *that* it worked...a book about comedy that leaves one completely depressed.
>
> (Anthony Quinn, *Sunday Times*, 8 July 1990)

This expresses disappointment at losing a joke by analysing it but it also reproduces a traditional English opposition between theory and practice: there is no need to understand how a joke works, all that matters is 'to know *that* it worked'.

A last example, from a review of a television discussion of popular comedy:

> One of the most joyful figures involved was The Professor, a bloke with a beard, who explained it all for us. 'In the last 15

> years,' said the professor, 'the British national character has become sour, spiteful, prurient and coarse. People looking at these shows see a gentler, nicer, decent kind of Englishness.' (Discuss coarsely)
>
> 'You can locate it in a concept of Englishness. Sir Ernest Barker isolated six qualities of Englishness, all of which applied to their work. Social cohesion, eccentricity, amateurism, a sense of voluntary service, the gentlemanly code and an eternal boyishness.'
>
> At which point June Whitfield materialised like a substantial fairy, 'I think the main thing is they are a good laugh,' she said.
>
> (*Guardian*, 19 April 1995)

This again refuses to countenance serious discussion of comedy. But while it is making its point through narrative, citing the intellectual ('a bloke with a beard') with his lecture on Englishness and comedy (complete with exam question) and then ending, in a joke of its own, with the deflating 'common sense' of June Whitfield, another feature about the English sense of humour emerges. The comic can be invoked not just to defy theory but because its mere presence can perform an act of terminal closure; the idea of 'a good laugh' can be drawn on with confidence as a way to stop discussion. English national culture, profoundly secular as it is, seems to treat only two things as genuinely transcendental – cricket and its own sense of humour.

Beyond a joke?

Humour in English culture has a similar place to literature but if we run humour past the classic oppositions, it is shown to be caught in a more contradictory dynamic. With

> concrete/abstract
> practice/theory
> common sense/dogma

joking appears as a positive, pricking the bubble of self-deceived theorising in the name of concrete practice and common sense (it can also signal sincerity against the artificial and the spirited amateur versus the professional). But humour as readily figures in the negative, weighing in on the wrong side of the crucial oppositions

> serious/silly
> truth/pleasure

(and probably also fact/fiction). Humour is also going to take on a specific resonance in different situations as it becomes superimposed on the oppositions virility/effeminacy and masculine/feminine.

It is a principle of linguistics that where there is an effect there is a system, where there is a meaning there is an organisation of the signifier which produces it. This suggests that we should be able to hazard some definition of the seemingly indescribable 'English sense of humour'. That it exists in a perceptible form is suggested by the way French writers recognise it immediately when they come across it. *Pariscope*, the weekly publication listing entertainment in the city (*'une semaine de Paris'*) in its brief notices refers to *4 mariages et 1 enterrement* as *'délicieuse et very British'* (English original) while Monty Python's *La vie de Brian* is said to contain *'un humeur très britannique'* (15–21 February 1995, p. 91, p. 99).

I will risk the hypothesis that the English sense of humour is defined mainly by three things: the use of irony; the exposure of self-deception; a tendency towards fantasy and excess. All of these features appear in other national cultures, are indeed part of humour in general. I would claim that this cluster of features is more condensed in the English tradition than elsewhere, and that irony, exposure of self-deception and the pleasures of fantasy can all be related back to a tradition of empiricism.

There are two possible strategies for testing this proposal. One would be a comprehensive survey of English comic writing starting from Shakespeare (read alongside Elizabethan books of riddles and jokes) and running through a whole series of names, including Dryden, Congreve, Wycherley, Pope, Sheridan, Sterne, Byron, Lewis Carroll, Wilde, Shaw, Noel Coward and P.G. Wodehouse to 'Monty Python' and the television political puppet cartoon, *Spitting Image* (English comic writing owes at least four of these names to people born or brought up in Ireland). I am not going to do that; instead I will take one reasonably typical text and examine it in depth, looking at most of the jokes and comic situations and asking how far they repeat aspects of a *structure*. For confirmation I will then turn briefly to the English tradition of caricature and cartoon. My question will be: is the English sense of humour empiricist?

Small World

Published in 1984, shortlisted for the Booker Prize, David Lodge's *Small World* has so far sold 400,000 copies world-wide and been dramatised on British television. A sequel to *Changing Places* (in which the American academic Morris Zapp exchanged jobs – and, temporarily, wives – with his English colleague, Philip Swallow), *Small World* is set in the world of international literary conferences and follows three main narratives: Persse McGarrigle tries to find the beautiful Angelica Pabst; Philip Swallow tries to divorce his wife Hilary and marry someone else; several literature professors compete for a Unesco chair which carries a $100,000 p.a. salary and no duties (it is 'a conceptual chair').

In theme the novel commits itself to a particular definition of Englishness, for, variously, it is:

1 *Anti-foreigner*. Little xenophobic references are secreted across the text, including Italians who 'scream and weep' (p. 69), a stereotype German (Siegfried von Turpitz), a comic Japanese (Akira Sakazaki) who cannot understand English slang, and 'a steaming Slav' (Lodge 1985, p. 197). England is a place where there is 'a general sense of nature well under the thumb of culture' (p. 101) (at least in the mind of a Turkish lecturer recalling his time in Hull). When 'Big Ben strikes nine o'clock' and 'other clocks, in other parts of the world, strike ten, eleven, four, seven, two' (p. 113), England is surreptitiously presumed as norm and centre.
2 *Anti-feminist*. There are two main feminists in the novel, Fulvia Morgana and Désirée Zapp; both behave badly, and so, according to the usual English moral assumption, their characters discredit their views.
3 *Anti-modernity*. Although to some degree the novel celebrates modernity ('jet travel, direct-dialling telephones and the Xerox machine, p. 43), its general tendency is to disparage 'our' civilisation 'of lightweight luggage, of permanent disjunctions' (p. 271) in comparison with some vaguely apprehended notion of fixity and permanence.

The novel is positively pro-empiricist and *anti-theory*, underwriting, as Terry Eagleton says, 'the old English empiricist prejudice that ideas are one thing and life another' (1988, p. 102). For example, at one point Morris Zapp reads a passage from Hazlitt which is undeniably empiricist: '*I have no positive inferences to make, nor any novelties to bring forward, and I have only to defend a common sense feeling against the refinement of false philosophy*' (p. 110).

False philosophy or false because philosophy? Zapp's response is to sigh and shake his head. Later, when he gives a lecture he takes the anti-empiricist position that all meaning is indeterminate, and feels he has 'offended the natives' (p. 29), the English audience that is. But the native tradition strikes back, and *Small World* makes it clear that Hazlitt is right and Zapp is wrong. The empiricist project of *Small World* is to confront

Zapp with a given brute reality which defies all theory, that is, the possibility of his own death. At the end Zapp is forced to concede that 'death is the one concept you can't deconstruct' (p. 328). Refuted by comic means as surely as O'Brien in *Nineteen Eighty-Four* is condemned via pathos, Zapp gets zapped.

Empirical reality and materialist motivation

Small World exaggerates and parodies its characters and narratives, drawing on some elaborate coincidences together with a light dusting of romance (see Holmes 1990). But the core material of the novel is solidly represented as an empirical everyday reality available to individual experience. Like the fact of Zapp's death, this all-enveloping real is beyond appearance, criticism or reflection – it is just *there*.

In the first place this reality is corporeal, and *Small World* emphasises the situation of the empirical body in space and time. This is expressed more than once in the connection between eating and excreting, the text tracking food and drink as it passes from an aircraft's refrigerated cabinets through microwave ovens and the 'bellies' of the passengers into the plane's 'septic tanks' (p. 88). Based in this bodily materialism *Small World* reflects a sense that everyone is impelled by sexual instinct or ambition or both (there's a similar crude materialism in Hobbes). 'What we really lust for is power', says Zapp battling to become 'the highest paid Professor of English in the world' (p. 59), as also do Philip Swallow, Michel Tardieu, von Turpitz and Fulvia Morgana.

Only Persse McGarrigle, Irish, a poet, and a virgin (until p. 325), who is saving himself for marriage (or was until p. 325), is exempt from ambition and lust, and this qualifies him as the book's hero. He is also remarkably free from self-deception and constantly works to control his own fantasies, to recognise that something he wants to see is, as he says, 'a mirage produced by his own desire' (p. 200). He is full of self-deprecating irony – as when he explains how he got his lectureship at university: 'They really meant to interview another fellow called McGarrigle – some high-flying prize scholar from Trinity. But the letter was addressed to me – someone slipped up in the Registry – and they were too embarrassed to retract the invitation' (p. 15). Persse is privileged within the narrative because he can present himself as others might see him.

Contingency, the body, the other

In *Small World* individual characters run up against reality in basically three forms (though the categories overlap): chance; the body; other people. These introduce a discrepancy between individual will and what goes against it, and this discrepancy is comically exposed for the reader. Here are some instances of the comic effect of chance:

1 Persse McGarrigle listens in a radio studio while the novelist, Ronald Frobisher, is interviewed from Australia by Rodney Wainwright; someone forgets to close down the line so they overhear as Wainwright at the other end continues to chat with his producer; at first the joke tells against Wainwright who is talking about naked women but then it is turned against Frobisher – Wainwright, thinking he's off-air, starts being very rude about Frobisher's writing (pp. 177–8).
2 Angelica tells McGarrigle to come to her room secretly so he can watch her undress; he hides himself in the wardrobe but it is Robin Dempsey who enters and undresses, sniffing 'himself under both armpits' ('it was not the spectacle Persse had been looking forward to'); when Persse coughs, Dempsey thinks it is Angelica, who has come to see *him* (pp. 54–5).

Reality is also represented by the body, which refuses to submit to the wishes and hopes of the individual. Two examples:

1 After a drunken lunch with his secretary, Felix Skinner takes her back to the office and down to the storeroom in the basement; they make love leaning over some boxes but at the moment of climax these topple and they fall 'together in a heap of crushed cardboard and spilled books' – books on Hazlitt by Philip Swallow which Skinner has forgotten to send for review (pp. 160–1).
2 Philip Swallow is invited to Turkey to give a lecture on Hazlitt but he forgets to take toilet paper with him; Turkey turns out to be prone to power cuts; Swallow goes out for a meal and eats some strange food; later, suffering from diarrhoea, he wakes up but finds it's dark because there's a power cut; he makes his way to the lavatory and uses as toilet paper some material from his briefcase: 'When the lights came on of their own accord he found he was up to page five of his lecture on "The Legacy of Hazlitt" ' (p. 190).

Mistakes and self-deception in relation to contingency and the body easily turn into farce. But when the self-deception arises from relations with the reality of other people, irony is the main effect. There are so many examples in the novel I shall just mention a couple:

1 Robin Dempsey visits his ex-wife, who is now living with 'an ageing flowerchild' called Scott with the idea of taking his two children out for the day; at first the children sulk, but

> They cheered up somewhat when Robin bought them a pair of jeans and an LP each, and even condescended to talk to him over the hamburgers and chips which they demanded for lunch. This conversation, did not, however, improve his spirits, consisting as it did mainly of allusions to musicians he had never heard of, and enthusiastic tributes to Scott, who evidently had. (p. 153)

This marks several ironic contrasts between what is said and what is meant: the children are said to have 'cheered up somewhat when' Robin bought them clothes but it really means that they cheered up *because* he did so; that they 'condescended' and 'demanded' seems to be neutral description but actually implies disapproval that the proper relation between child and parent is reversed. Dempsey expects that his kids will want to talk to him and will share his dislike of Scott but in fact they are normal teenagers who want to talk about music.

2 Philip Swallow is thinking of leaving Hilary, his wife, for another woman; he makes a little speech about how his and Hilary's has not been much of a marriage, their children are grown up, they nearly separated ten years before. This concludes:

'I've stood in Hilary's way,' he said earnestly. 'She'd do better on her own' (p. 221).

The text refrains from comment except to stress that Swallow says this 'earnestly' but the insinuation is that, because of his desire for the other woman he says this in an effort to convince himself; but he is self-deceived.

Chance, the body (which just won't do what you want), mistakes, mistaken identity, errors brought about by lust and self-love (or any combination of the two) – all these are stock material for comedy in the European tradition. What makes the English sense of humour different and distinct is the way these effects rely on a sense of everyday empirical reality. And the condition for presenting this is a style which is so clear it is more or less transparent, ensuring that a reader can judge perfectly the nature of the objective situation and the subjective motive of the individual. *There* is reality; *there* is a character's idea about reality; and *there*, set out for all readers to see, is their self-delusion.

Here, for example, is what the conference-goers did on arrival at Rummidge, a university built hastily in 1969 (in England student accommodation is used during vacations by academics for conferences):

> They had appraised the stained and broken furniture, explored the dusty interiors of cupboards in vain for coat-hangers, and tested the narrow beds, whose springs sagged dejectedly in the middle, deprived of all resilience by the battering of a decade's horseplay and copulation. Each room had a washbasin, though not every washbasin had a plug, or every plug a chain. Some taps could not be turned on, and some could not be turned off. For more elaborate ablutions, or to answer a call of nature, it was necessary to venture out into the draughty and labyrinthine corridors in search of one of the communal wash-rooms, where baths, showers and toilets were to be found – but little privacy, and unreliable supplies of hot water.
>
> (p. 3)

There is some working of the language here – mock heroic vocabulary, the zeugma of 'horseplay and copulation', parallel and antithesis – but essentially this is the English commonplace style it would be hard to distinguish from that of many narratives (including, for example, *Nineteen Eighty-Four*). Played out here, in this ironically perceived description, as elsewhere in the novel, and, arguably, in the English sense of humour, is a drama of knowledge established by an empiricist opposition between the apparent and the real. On one side are the aspirations of those arriving at Rummidge; on the other the reality they actually encounter; both are explicitly displayed for the reader. Each conference-goer may think he or she is acting individually but we can see that in fact they are all doing the same thing. As readers we are placed securely outside and looking on.

What are we supposed to conclude from the paragraph describing beds and water taps at Rummidge? No satirical viewpoint is sustained, one attacking either the selfishness of the conference-goers or the impoverished condition of English universities. The writing is like that in the newspaper account of Andrew Rawnsley on the State opening of Parliament – willing to wound and yet afraid to strike, the irony exhausts itself simply in establishing an ironic viewpoint. Classic English irony always slides towards static, uncommitted ambivalence – between a Whig insight into what lies behind appearance and a conservative acknowledgement that common sense, the body and reality are forever fixed and ineluctable, so you cannot do anything about it. At one point in the novel Fulvia Morgana exclaims in exasperation, 'Ooh, the English and their ironies' (p. 120).

The pleasures of fantasy help to makes this very English brand of irony seem enough. I've not brought this out but again and again situations in *Small World*, without actually distorting empirical reality, slip over into absurdity and excess – Persse's account of his appointment by mistake, the copulating couple who land on the copies of the book on Hazlitt, the lecture notes deployed in the dark as lavatory paper, and so on. Because it is so solidly predicated *on* fact, the English sense of humour gives pleasure by escaping *from* fact.

Caricature and cartoon

Along with the sexual body, the excreting body, the body subject to need (for nourishment, shelter, warmth), *Small World* exhibits the body personalised by face, voice, gesture, clothing, accoutrements:

> Morris Zapp: 'a thickset man with a fat cigar in his mouth, and a deerstalker, with the flaps down' (p. 17).
> Robin Dempsey: 'a broad-shouldered, thickset man, with a heavy jaw that jutted aggressively, but his eyes, small and set too close together seemed to belong to some other person, more anxious and vulnerable, trapped inside the masterful physique' (p. 5).
> Ronald Frobisher: his face is 'round, fleshy, pockmarked, and peppered with tiny black specks, like grains of gunpowder. The hair is thin, dishevelled' (p. 105).
> Fulvia Morgana: she puts a book away 'along with her kidskin slippers, in her capacious burnt-orange shoulder-bag by Fendi' and 'eases her feet into the cream-coloured Armani boots, and fastens them snugly round her calves' (p. 109).
> Sy Gootblatt: 'good-looking in his slight, dark way, and a bit of a dandy, but small in stature; he keeps rising restlessly on the balls of his feet to see who is to be seen in the crowded room' (p. 234).

These descriptions are effectively verbal caricatures corresponding to the strong English graphic tradition of caricature and cartoon. Although C.R. Ashbee exaggerates when he says that 'caricature, as distinct from satire on the one hand and irony on the other, is an essentially English way of laughing' (1928, p. 10) there are discernible reasons why caricature fits in with an empiricist tradition.

Caricatura, from the Italian *caricare*, 'to load' seems to begin with Cannibale Carracci (1560–1609). England has produced a long line of famous caricaturists, including Hogarth, Gillray and Rowlandson; the tradition continued later with *Punch* (1841) and *Vanity Fair* (1862), and then, following the advent of cheap newspapers, in the cartoon directed at politics or manners. During the past decade the convention has adapted brilliantly to television in the lifelike puppets of *Spitting Image* as well as a string of comedians who imitate well-known television figures.

There are certain preconditions for the emergence of caricature. One, as E.H. Gombrich points out, is the decline of sympathetic magic (1940). In Hardy's poem 'The Photograph' the speaker burns a photograph and suddenly feels the return of an older belief that the image was the person – to destroy one was to threaten the other. Caricature cannot take hold until a culture is secular enough to treat representation of a real individual as a matter of convention, not something supernatural. From its origins, the European comic tradition usually only allowed members of the working class – servants, slaves – 'to be seen for their funny side' (p. 5). You cannot have caricature of the rich and powerful before a definite levelling impulse has taken hold. In England this has now reached a point when *Spitting Image* can portray the Royal Family in the form of soap opera.

Gombrich again: 'similarity is not essential to likeness. The deliberate distortion of single features is not incompatible with a striking likeness in the whole' (p. 12). So it becomes possible to 'transform the whole man into a completely new and ridiculous figure which nevertheless resembles the original' (p. 12). Whereas the portrait respects likeness, caricature, through exaggeration, mimics its object, calling up resemblance to demonstrate how the individuality of the original can be *cited*, reduced into equivalence with mere signs.

Secular, democratising and citational, caricature easily works to foster national feeling. Because it shows recognisable physical features, it lends itself readily to a contrast between particular ethnic and racial types. So Gillray's beefy Englishmen are opposed to scrawny, frog-eating French; and in the middle of the nineteenth century *Punch* notoriously represented Irish figures as simian and sub-human.

The English tradition

There are discernible reasons why the caricature form is specially compatible with and sympathetic to the English empiricist tradition. Jacques Lacan begins his analysis of vision by recalling how he was out fishing when a small boy in the party, seeing a sardine tin floating in the sun, said to him, '*You see that can? Do you see it? Well, it doesn't see you!*' (1977b, p. 95). In so far as caricature works with a likeness to the empirically perceived body it compels recognition of the given individuality of the subject. In so far as it distorts, stressing that the subject can never really see itself, the convention provides a position for the gaze of the Other. As with Pope's satirical portraits, caricature invites the reader or viewer into a superior knowledge of the object thus presented, a shared and knowing superiority since we have to recognise the person caricature for the image to have its proper force. Mechanical reproduction – photography and television – have enormously widened this potential audience of those who know.

Dempsey's combination of physical solidity and worried look, Gootblatt's restlessness and good looks (like Pope's Sporus with his endless smiles, squeaking voice and mincing gait) seek to present the body as moral indicator, to unite the way the individual is perceived by others with the judgement of common sense and reality. How far this is an ideological belief is clear from the fact that it is simply not true. Behind the large, avuncular moustache and twinkling eyes, who could have recognised the moral character of Stalin? Or in the banal, wide-eyed face of the Austrian find out the ethical purposes of Adolf Hitler? (See Figure 7.1.)

Treating the individual body as moral index enacts a double and

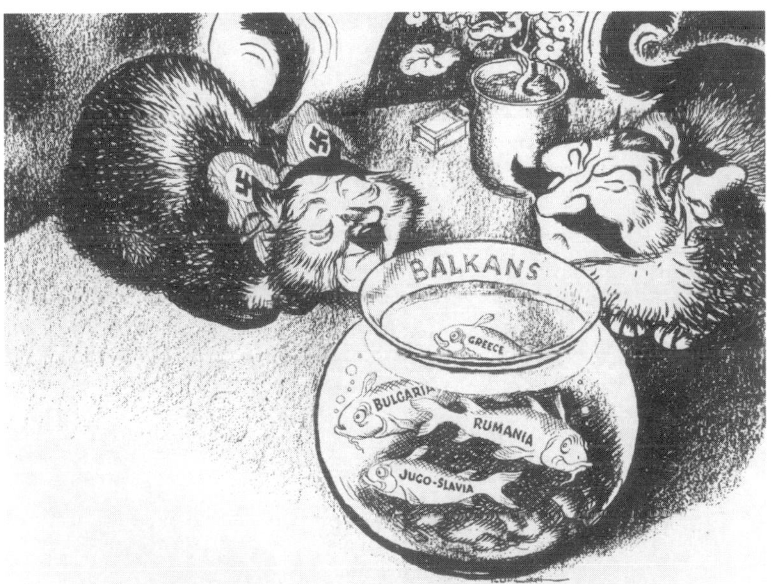

Figure 7.1 Illingworth cartoon, 'What, me? No I never *touch* goldfish!'
Source: *Daily Mail*, 17 November 1939.

contradictory desire, yet one definitely attractive to the English tradition. It realises an empiricist wish to discover morality not so much in ideas and intentions but *in reality*, in embodied 'behaviour'. At the same time staging the body as moral expression aims to contain the otherness of the body, identifying it with vice and virtue, right and wrong. Anxiety provoked by the very fact of the body, of physical existence, is there in Locke and recurs in the English mode of caricature and cartoon.

Orwell, Donald McGill and English working-class humour

It might be objected that the cluster of features advanced to describe the English sense of humour – irony, the key issue of self-deception (particularly as measured against the fact of the body), fantasy – has something to say about the comic sense of the gentry and the middle class but does not apply to English working-class humour. There is to hand a very apt example to try out this argument, in the art of Donald McGill (see Arthur Calder-Marshall 1966).

For most of this century people in England have bought rude picture postcards – usually while on holiday – and sent them to friends with the aim of amusing or embarrassing them. These are actually cartoons, showing exaggerated bodies (particularly for middle-aged women) in a design style reduced to the essential details necessary to make the joke work, in simple primary colours. Some examples:

1 An attractive young woman has been painting at an easel but the wind has blow her paper into the bushes where a man's head appears:

> 'Excuse me, have you seen a piece of paper over there?'
>
> 'No, Miss, I want a piece myself!'

(p. 83)

2 An enormously fat woman at the seaside stands looking for her son who is in fact hidden underneath her belly:

> 'I CAN'T SEE MY LITTLE CHARLIE!'

(p. 86)

3 From the street two snobbish-looking women see through a window a clergyman washing his aspidistra:

'There's the Vicar at the window sponging his Aspidistra.'

'Horrid old man! He ought to do it in the Bathroom!'

(p. 87)

4 A man lies ill in bed while the doctor speaks to his wife:

'I suppose you're giving him all he wants?'

'Oh, Doctor, he's been far too ill to think about anything of that sort!'

(p. 88)

5 A Scotsman wearing a kilt is lying asleep with his head on a tussock and his legs raised and crossed. One duck points up his kilt and tells another duck:

'There you are! What did I tell you?'

(p. 106)

6 Two men are talking cheerfully, one holding up a male toddler who is shouting:

''E don't 'arf make a row, mate!'

''E does that! 'E's got lungs like leather an' bawls like a bull!!'

(p. 117)

7 A smartly dressed woman is watching horse races through binoculars. The man beside her is looking down at her knickers, which have fallen around her feet ('panties' to American readers):

'They're off!'

(p. 121)

All of these cards were produced by a single artist, Donald McGill, who sold designs to postcard publishing companies from 1905 till his death on 13 October 1962 at the age of 87. His most popular card was the following:

8 A little girl is praying while her puppy pulls at her nightshirt to reveal her bare bottom:

> 'Please, Lord, excuse me a minute while I kick Fido!!'
> (Calder-Marshall 1966, p. 80)

According to Arthur Calder-Marshall, this sold over 2 million copies.

The tradition continues, for example in the *Carry On* series of films. In the 1950s' comedy, *Carry on Teacher*, the headmaster (Ted Ray) asks the chemistry teacher 'Are you satisfied with your equipment?' and of course receives the classic Donald McGill reply, 'I've had no complaints so far.'

In 1986 in Blackpool I bought the card reproduced in Figure 7.2.

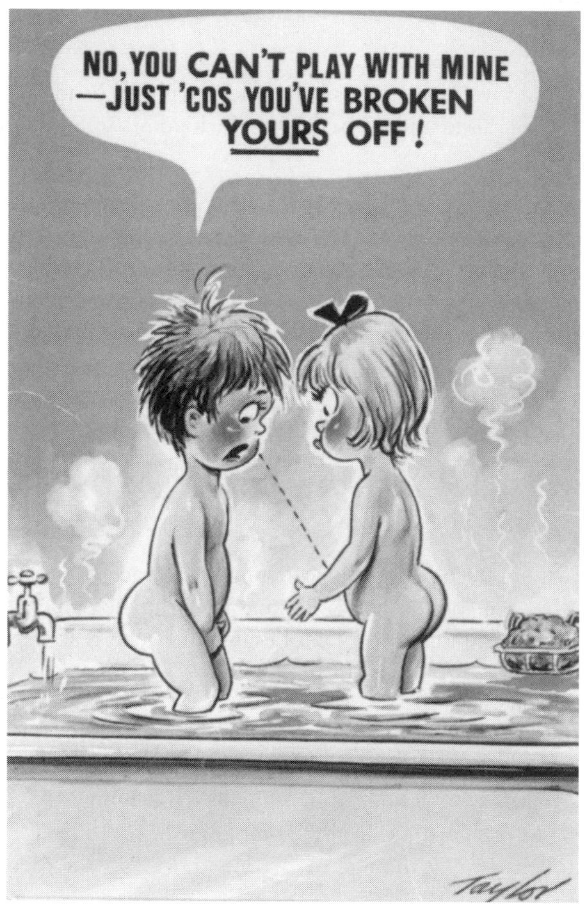

Figure 7.2 Taylor, 'No, you *can't* play with mine – just 'cos you've broken *yours* off'

Source: Postcard, Bamforth and Co, Holmfirth.

We know about Donald McGill because in 1941 George Orwell, in an essay on seaside postcards, discovered McGill's work as representing 'the norm of the comic postcard' (1968, 2, pp. 155–6). Orwell contrasts the essentially conventional values of these cards with the 'utter breakdown of all standards' he finds in the 'promiscuity' of *La Vie parisienne* (p. 159). They exhibit a transgressive humour like that of the music hall (Orwell mentions Max Miller), a sense of the comic consistent with the way Orwell describes the English working class in another essay ('The Lion and the Unicorn: Socialism and the English Genius'): 'the common people...are not puritanical. They are inveterate gamblers, drink as much beer as their wages will permit, are devoted to bawdy jokes, and use probably the foulest language in the world' (1968, 2, p. 59). The same devotion to bawdy jokes finds expression in McGill's comic postcards, with their 'overpowering vulgarity' and 'ever-present obscenity' (1968, 2, p. 156).

What is surprising is that Orwell does not search in these cards for an oppositional or alternative viewpoint on English culture (instead he refers rather lamely to their 'Sancho Panza view of life'; p. 162). If he had looked for resistance he would have found it, for the postcards constantly make jokes against the snobbery, pretentiousness and artificiality of English middle-class life, against figures who assume superiority only by contriving to ignore what is ordinary and human.

With time on his hands the vicar washes his aspidistra when a more practical viewpoint would expect him to sponge his arse. When the doctor tells the wife to care for her husband she thinks he means she should have sex with him. 'Charlie' is the name of the fat lady's child but also names her sexual organs; 'They're off' officially refers to the horses at the start of the race but actually draws attention to the displaced knickers; 'bawls like a bull', a polite meaning, also means 'balls like a bull'. The reader who gets the point must discard an apparent meaning (which is genteel) in favour of a real meaning (which is popular and vulgar). These puns or double meanings in a single word are not strictly irony, since that works with play in the meaning of a whole *phrase*. But they provide a clear equivalent in a working-class register to the more extended ironies of the middle-class tradition.

These postcards mount a lively campaign against what is felt to be the pervasive affectation of English middle-class life, and to the extent they become oppositional in theme and attitude. However, the assumptions the images depend on to make this criticism never depart from those of a thoroughly respectable empiricism. The oppositions artificial/sincere and abstract/concrete are drawn on to portray middle-class manners as a false appearance in contrast to the immediate practicality of popular attitudes – adoption of a gentrified air of superiority is seen as self-deception compared to the unassuming sincerity, directness and common sense of ordinary people. The place of reality in this appearance/reality opposition is often taken by the mere *fact* of the body (sexual, excreting, eating), the idea of the body 'itself' disclosed by nakedness ('excuse me while I kick Fido') or just size ('I CAN'T SEE MY LITTLE CHARLIE').

This sense of the body is not very different from that we find in David Lodge although in Donald McGill there is a more exclusive concentration upon it. And in these postcards there is surely again that feature of transgressive fantasy – the woman so fat she cannot see her own genitals, the vicar who might have deliberately washed his bottom by the window. In a more direct form these working-class jokes exhibit what have been put forward here as defining features of the English sense of humour: irony (or at least *double entendre*); the exposure of self-deception; fantasy.

Since discussion of the comic (as one might have expected) has touched on the question of Englishness and the body I do not want to end this chapter without some brief comment on this. Can these grotesque exaggerations be read as evidence of a celebration of the body? Or is there an undertone of horrified fascination (which would belie Orwell's view that the common people are 'not puritanical')? No doubt both, to some degree, but I would stress rather that in this very English version the body is finally moralised. The *fact* of the body, its absolute otherness so at odds with or askew to common sense and normal everyday life is presented in these images so that it becomes acknowledged and recuperated just by being brought into active relation with social life. In this sense the postcards constitute a comic rendering of the Lockeian cannonball ('Let a Cannon-bullet pass through a Room'; II.14.10).

8

CONTEMPORARY ENGLISH POETRY

> nothing is more English than the English skill at exorcising danger by making it look like someone's eccentric behaviour.…To cope with the multiple shocks of modernism, this personalising faculty had to be put into high gear, with such success that James, Ford, Yeats, Lawrence, Pound, Wells, Woolf…now seem simply occupants of more or less adjacent cells in a well-regulated Bedlam.
>
> (Hugh Kenner 1987, p. 6)

In the twentieth century, as Pierre Bourdieu has argued (1993), poetry stands out from the rest of cultural production because it is not read and does not sell. It is precisely this conspicuous distance between it and the other arts, its refusal of usefulness and the role of a commodity, which confer on poetry its quasi-transcendental status (what Bourdieu terms its 'charismatic legitimation', p. 51).

According to this logic of inversion, within England's empiricist inheritance poetry wins a special place in the cultural formation by defying utilitarianism and asserting value. If we run the analysis across the binary oppositions of empiricism it emerges that, though poetry indeed privileges the denigrated terms 'subjective' and 'fiction', risking condemnation as 'obscure' and 'silly', it can even so assert a truth *beyond* fact, an effect strengthened if poetry aligns itself with 'practice', the 'sincere' and 'amateur' over against 'theory', the 'artificial' and 'professional'. Chapter 4 argued that, from at least the time of Wordsworth, English poetry was able to install a version of empiricism within its own particular poetic practice. Although this is not the whole canonical tradition, a mainstream inheritance works by staging the presence of a speaker, who experiences reality more or less directly, and, empowered by this certainty, reflects on the implications of this active encounter.

Compared with France or Italy the cultural tradition in England can profess little in the way of painting and music. It was ready to surrender the novel as contaminated with a prosaic interest in reality, because in compensation, it could always call up one world-class author in both drama and poetry. Close to the very centre of English ideology lies a desire to add the name which, at any given time, seems able to continue the series which runs: 'Shakespeare and Milton and Wordsworth and…'. Today English culture is faced with the problem that to sustain this series into the present means negotiating it past the 'multiple shocks' of Modernism. Discussion of *Nineteen Eighty-Four* and *Small World* has already given strong hints that the English tradition feels ill at ease with Modernism and its consequences. This chapter, confining itself to contemporary poetry, will confirm that intuition.

Modernism and empiricism

Modernism and empiricism are radically incompatible. It is becoming increasingly evident that what now persists from Modernism is not the utopian and revolutionary thrust which made such impact at the time, the demand to 'MAKE IT NEW' (in Pound's phrase) and the certainty that avant-garde formal innovation – in painting, writing, music and architecture – would solve the problem of a dying culture by forging another about to be born. Hindsight reveals, rather, that *de facto* Modernism performed a critique of traditional conceptions of subjectivity, discourse and reality. Arguably, it was not until well after the event, in the 1960s, that the insights of explicit theorisation in the writing of Lacan, Foucault, Derrida, Kristeva and others began to catch up with what had been anticipated already in artistic practices of Modernism.

If the empiricist tradition affirms (1) that the subject is coherent and autonomous, (2) that discourse is in principle transparent, and (3) that reality can be experienced directly, Modernism refuses these assumptions. In 1916 Ezra Pound wrote: 'In the "search for oneself", in the search for "sincere self-expression", one gropes, one finds some seeming verity. One says "I am" this, that or the other, and with the words scarcely uttered one ceases to be that thing' (1960, p. 85).

Whatever one says about oneself, it necessarily slides away from the other self which is doing the saying, subject of enunciation unable to overtake subject of enounced. Is the subject unified or plural and dispersed? Eliot in his famous essay on 'Tradition and the Individual Talent' (1919) declares that 'the point of view which I am struggling to attack is perhaps related to the metaphysical theory of the substantial unity of the soul' (1966, p. 19). Bertolt Brecht in an interview of 1926 says that: 'The continuity of the ego is a myth. A man is an atom that perpetually breaks up and forms anew' (1964, p. 15). Doubts about the sovereignty of the ego are expressed on all sides by Modernist practitioners.

Modernism could well be characterised as 'the return of the signifier': both Pound and Eliot acknowledge that language has a self-sufficiency, a degree of autonomy as language, which can never be reduced to signified meaning. Pound endorses a slightly weird theory of the Chinese ideogram as poetic model, because it foregrounds the materiality of signification (see Fenollosa 1962); Eliot rejects the Romantic notion that poetry expresses emotions and argues that the poet, 'only a medium and not a personality' (1966, p. 20), has a neutral function like that of the catalyst in a chemical reaction – the poet's mind stores up 'numberless feelings, phrases, images, which remain there until all the particles which can unite to form a new compound are present' (p. 18). The compound resulting from this linguistic process is a new poem.

Such statements are less a programme than a way of explaining intuitions arrived at by writing poetry. If with Modernism the subject as a coherent, experiencing 'I' is felt to be unreliable, and if the means of representation by which reality is re-presented to the subject cannot be separated from some independent activity in the signifier, then the empiricist scenario – and any attempted poetic rendering of it – become radically unstable. But not in England.

'Adlestrop' and 'The Waste Land'

A clear line in the writing of empiricist poetry runs from Wordsworth in 'The Solitary Reaper' through the work of Thomas Hardy down to the Georgian poet, Edward Thomas. His poem 'Adlestrop' is a favourite anthology piece and has also been praised 'for its essential "Englishness"' (John Bayley, cited Gervais 1993, p. 58). Two preliminary points. The speaker is a voice represented in and by the poem, and should not be identified in any naive way with Edward Thomas; yet we would probably still be right to think of the speaker as male because this kind of would-be masterful and observing gaze is conventionally masculine. The poem consists of four verses in iambic tetrameter, and this metric rejoins the poem to the main English post-Renaissance tradition in which the line is organised on the basis of a regular alternation of unstressed and stressed syllables.

Adlestrop

Yes, I remember Adlestrop –
The name, because one afternoon
Of heat the express-train drew up there
Unwontedly. It was late June.

The steam hissed. Someone cleared his throat
No one left and no one came
On the bare platforms. What I saw
Was Adlestrop – only the name

And willows, willow-herb, and grass,
And meadowsweet, and haycocks dry,
No whit less still and lonely fair
Than the high cloudlets in the sky,

And for that minute a blackbird sang
Close by, and round him, mistier,
Farther and farther, all the birds
Of Oxfordshire and Gloucestershire.
(1978, pp. 71–3)

At first, when the train stops and there is no sign of life on the bare platform, the speaker feels a little crisis of subjectivity, as though meaning has dropped out of his world leaving him separated from it, facing only writing, a name, Adlestrop. Immediately, though, that crisis is overcome when he is caught up in an experience of the landscape as united with his own feelings, perceiving willows, grass and meadows as:

No whit less still and lonely fair
Than the high cloudlets in the sky.

Correspondence between subject and object restored, he accedes to a special understanding of 'Oxfordshire and Gloucestershire', presided over by the song of a blackbird, a metaphorical object whose 'song' effects a synthesis of natural and human, external and internal (perception, as Paul de Man explains in a relevant account, has ascended through a process of subjectivity into symbol, see 1983, pp. 187–228). This moment of transcendent insight justifies why Adlestrop becomes a significant memory.

'Adlestrop' represents an 'I' who is coherent and self-possessed, a unified subject, secure in its ability to affirm 'I remember', 'I saw'. The speaker does have a moment of loss – silence except for hissing steam, emptiness, the strange writing – but this is quickly recuperated into imaginary plenitude (there is a comparable effect of loss made good in Wordsworth's 'The Solitary Reaper'). And though the language of the poem is elaborate at certain points ('Unwontedly', 'No whit', 'cloudlets') this does not interfere with the overall clarity of the statement – initial hesitations and hiatuses are overcome in the fluent syntax and confident tone of the ending. This is a speaker who is sure that language can represent reality.

From the country to the city. 'Adlestrop' was written in 1915 and published in 1917; in 1922 the following lines appeared as part of Eliot's 'The Waste Land' (ll. 60–76):

> Unreal City,
> Under the brown fog of a winter dawn,
> A crowd flowed over London Bridge, so many,
> I had not thought death had undone so many.
> Sighs, short and infrequent, were exhaled,
> And each man fixed his eyes before his feet.
> Flowed up the hill and down King William Street,
> To where Saint Mary Woolnoth kept the hours
> With a dead sound on the final stoke of nine.
> There I saw one I knew, and stopped him crying: 'Stetson!
> 'You who were with me in the ships at Mylae!
> 'That corpse you planted last year in your garden,
> 'Has it begun to spout? Will it bloom this year?
> 'Or has the sudden frost disturbed its bed?
> 'Oh keep the Dog far hence, that's friend to men,
> 'Or with his nails he'll dig it up again!
> 'You! hypocrite lecteur! – mon semblable, – mon frère!'
>
> (1963, p. 65)

This is written in loose iambic pentameter tending towards free verse (it can accommodate the shortened line, 'Unreal city'). There is a represented speaker, an 'I', but the relation between object and subject, what he sees and what he feels, is uncertain. Commuters walking across London Bridge to the city appear to him as dead souls ('I had not thought death had undone so many' recalls Dante's response on first entering hell). Is this description or fantasy? The text refuses any firm distinction between external and internal.

Although there is an 'I', that ego is a point in a process, not fixed in any definite relation to London, Dante, the Punic wars (during which the battle of Mylae was fought in 260 BC) and Webster's play, *The White*

Devil (from which the warning about the dog is culled); the whole address to Stetson is unexplained and insufficiently motivated. Meaning is dislocated across syntactical oppositions: a reader is left undecided whether this is said or cited, whether a voice is represented speaking or there is rather a verbal collage from Dante, Virgil ('Mylae'), Jacobean drama and (in the last line here), Baudelaire. We are forced to become aware of the text as text.

Policing the borders

Modernist writing threatens the continuity in English poetry exemplified by what I have referred to as 'empiricist' verse. In the year of 'The Waste Land' the Modernist challenge seemed bold and inescapable – yet within two generations it was rolled back to make room for a poetry which upheld the pre-Modernist tradition from Hardy to Edward Thomas. In this process there seem to have been four main moments.

The 1930s

In 1928 T.S. Eliot declared himself 'a classicist in literature, royalist in politics, and anglo-catholic in religion' (1970, p. 7), and Pound began the move to the right which rapidly carried him into explicit support for Mussolini. This encouraged the socialist poets of the 1930s – Auden, Spender, C. Day Lewis, MacNeice – to reject Modernism as fascist and elitist. In 1936, for example, Day Lewis defends the poetry of Auden by attacking Modernism: 'Free verse, if it ever existed outside the heated imagination of reactionary writers and the parlour games of parodists, can certainly not be said to exist here' (1936, p. 72). And in 1935 Julian Bell addressed Day Lewis with the question, 'What are the proletariat to make of your patchety-hoppity following of Eliot, of Hopkins, of Yeats?' (1938, p. 326).

Modernism was rejected in favour of a left populist poetry. It is uncertain what the proletariat might have made of that but the view of one of the more acute contemporary observers was that these 'intellectual communists' were 'simply writing romantic subjective poetry about their revolutionary feelings', as Bell observed (cited Maxwell 1969, p. 55). It is ironic that writers whose avowed allegiance might have directed them to the Modernism of Brecht's poetry actually had an effect in halting the advance of Modernism in English poetry.

The Movement

Even so, in 1945 English poetry could be fairly characterised by its range and variety. However, during the 1950s a group of poets known as 'the Movement' (Robert Conquest, Elizabeth Jennings, Philip Larkin and others) were able to regulate this plurality in favour of their own kind of writing. A collection of their work was published in 1956 as *New Lines*, edited by Robert Conquest. In his 'Introduction', repudiating the Romanticism of the previous decade, Conquest advocates a poetry written in 'comprehensible language' (p. xv), which, 'empirical in its attitude to all that comes', exhibits a 'reverence for the real person or event' (p. xiv). This is an unmistakable demand for a return to the English empiricist scenario, a poetry presenting a speaker directly experiencing an external reality.

Alvarez and the 1960s

In 1962 in the 'Introduction' to his collection, *The New Poetry*, A. Alvarez attacks Larkin and the Movement (the manifesto is subtitled 'Beyond the Gentility Principle'), singles out a poem by Ted Hughes as a model for imitation, and calls for a poetry which expresses 'a more powerful complex of emotions and sensations' (1962, p. 27). However, the wished-for reorientation still excludes Modernism, on the grounds that it is *not English*: 'the experimental techniques of Eliot and the rest...were an essentially American concern' (p. 17). And such experimentalism, Alvarez insinuates, leads to right-wing politics.

Davie and Hardy

In 1973 the continuity of English poetry back to Hardy (the scenic route round Modernism) is affirmed from a surprising authority. Donald Davie had written sympathetically on a number of poets, including Ezra Pound, but his book *Thomas Hardy and English Poetry* opens with the statement that 'in British poetry of the last fifty years (as not in America) the most far-reaching influence, for good and ill, has been not Yeats, still less Eliot or Pound, not Lawrence, but *Hardy*' (1973, p. 3).

Following precedent Davie worries about the 'illiberal social and political ideas' of the great Modernists and finds Hardy in contrast recognisable as 'a "liberal"' (p. 3). Hardy's poetry is ultimately beyond analysis. Citing Irving Howe's view that, reading Hardy, the critic feels 'the grating inadequacy of verbal analysis, and the need to resort to such treacherous terms as "honesty", "sincerity", and even "wisdom"', Davie concludes, 'Unless he has felt as Irving Howe describes, no critic of Hardy's poetry is qualified to speak' (pp. 13–14). This gesture to a reality beyond language is already familiar.

That there is a continuing cultural pressure at work in these four moments is suggested by the loud inaccuracy of the reasons for dismissing Modernism. Pound and Eliot are indeed American-born, but use of experimental techniques in Braque, Webern, Kafka, Pirandello, Apollinaire and many others shows it is nonsense to think of formal innovations as 'essentially American'. Some Modernist writers were indeed on the right but even more were on the left, including Picasso, Joyce, MacDiarmid, Breton, Mayakovsky, Brecht.

These different rationalisations are designed to shove Modernism out of the way and so open the road back to Hardy. As Andrew Crozier notes in a finely perceptive essay, 'the present-day canon has its roots in the Movement' (1983, p. 207), for it was those manoeuvres in the 1950s which established hegemony for the line from Larkin through Ted Hughes to the current ascendancy of Seamus Heaney. 'Edward Thomas', comments one critic, forms 'a bridge between Hardy and Larkin' (Gervais 1993, p. 53); Seamus Heaney, writes another, displays 'a tough nostalgia for his own origins and for their rootedness, which can only be described as Romantic, and which patently looks back, though Hardy and Edward Thomas, to Wordsworth' (Larrissy 1990, p. 149). They are right. This special inheritance makes up what Charles Bernstein, the American L=A=N=G=U=A=G=E poet, has spoken of as 'The Great English High Anti-Modernist Tradition' (in conversation with the present writer, Buffalo, New York, 14 February 1991).

English High Anti-Modernism

Philip Larkin: 'The Whitsun Weddings'

Riding on the back of the set of cultural forces which brought about the Movement, Philip Larkin was acknowledged by Donald Davie in 1973 as 'the effective unofficial laureate of post-1945 England' (1973, p. 64). In 1988 his *Collected Poems* stood in the *Sunday Times* best-seller list for several weeks. And yet coming across some of the pronouncements by Larkin for the first time, a non-English European critic of poetry might well imagine they were part of a deliberate pastiche of unrepentant provincialism:

> Interviewer: I wonder if you read much foreign poetry?
> Larkin: *Foreign* poetry? *No!*
>
> (Larkin 1975, p. 249)

> Betjeman's chief significance…as a poet is that he is a writer of

> talent and intelligence for whom the modern revolution has simply not taken place. For him there has been no symbolism, no objective correlative, no T.S. Eliot or Ezra Pound.
>
> (cited Day *et al.* 1976, p. 9)

Against Eliot, Pound and Modernism – but for Betjeman – Larkin aligns himself with exactly that notion of experience found in Locke and Wordsworth: 'I write poems to preserve things I have seen/thought/felt…both for myself and for others, though I feel that my prime responsibility is to the experience itself' (cited Press 1969, p. 258).

Though the poetry and a writer's critical voice do not necessarily coincide, in Larkin's case they do. His vehement and traditionally English empiricism is well illustrated in one of his most renowned poems. 'The Whitsun Weddings' (1964, pp. 21–3) portrays an 'I' on a journey from the provinces to the metropolis who watches while the train gradually fills up with newly married couples (Whitsun being a traditional time for weddings). Seamus Heaney accurately observes that 'Larkin's England of the mind is in many ways continuous with the England of Rupert Brooke's "Grantchester" and Edward Thomas's "Adlestrop"' (1990, p. 257); it is indeed, and 'The Whitsun Weddings' recalls 'Adlestrop' not only in its railway setting but, more precisely, in the way it is structured between a carefully represented subject, a firmly experienced world of objects, and a sense of subjective loss finally overcome in a visionary apprehension of external reality.

Rhyming *abab cde cde*, the poem is presented in eight verses of iambic pentameter (except for the second line of each, which has two beats) explicitly linking the text to the canonical legacy. A coherent *persona* is dramatised by the poem, an 'I' who is 'late getting away', at first 'didn't notice' the noise of the weddings (thinking it was made by porters), then reinterprets what's happening ('I…saw it all again') until at the end what no one thought is contrasted with the insight of what this 'I' concluded from the experience. 'Scrupulously neutral' (Davie 1973, p. 65), 'a rootless observer' (Gervais 1993, p. 206), there 'as the eternal witness of the contemplative artist' (Bedient 1974, p. 92), the speaker of the poem is presented as detached, critical, not self-deceived, confident of submitting the world to a controlling gaze; in other words, very much the poised, individualised, empiricist subject whose voice has been represented as speaking in English poetry for over two centuries.

At first on the journey objects viewed from the window – knowable, reassuringly familiar – help to guarantee the mastery of the experiencing 'I': a river, canals, and then 'the next town'. However, as in

'Adlestrop', the other emerges as a threat, especially with the entry of the married couples:

All down the line
Fresh couples climbed aboard: the rest stood round;
The last confetti and advice were thrown,
And, as we moved, each face seemed to define
Just what it saw departing.

As his efforts at ironic detachment sag ('An uncle shouting smut; and then the perms'), the speaker's self-possession becomes undermined.

What the speaker noticed from the external world had already introduced a certain unease, for he found himself faced with both an English pastoral landscape and the detritus of modernity, 'industrial froth', 'dismantled cars'. Uncertainty soon develops into full-blown class anxiety when the train fills with representatives of the post-1950s' newly-rich working class wearing 'parodies of fashion' and 'jewellery-substitutes', figures who represent the social, the body, sexuality – all put at risk the control of the isolated 'I'. Subject and object threaten to lose touch with each other.

As in 'Adlestrop' the moment of alienation provides a springboard to push the poem into an apparent reconciliation, the disturbing other recuperated into a significant experience. Narrative helps here – the poem uses a 'we' which refers simply to those on the train but towards the end becomes a more inclusive plural. Marriage also helps because it shows the masses willing to submit to the customary sacrament. And then there is the speaker's change of tone, as the train hurries towards London, in a time that would seem:

Just long enough to settle hats and say
I nearly died,
A dozen marriages got under way.
They watched the landscape, sitting side by side
– An Odeon went past, a cooling tower,
And someone running up to bowl – and none
Thought of the others they would never meet
Or how their lives would all contain this hour.
I thought of London spread out in the sun,
Its postal districts packed like squares of wheat:

There we were aimed. And as we raced across
Bright knots of rail

Past standing Pullmans, walls of blackened moss
Came close, and it was nearly done, this frail
Travelling coincidence; and what it held
Stood ready to be loosed with all the power
That being changed can give. We slowed again,
And as the tightened brakes took hold, there swelled
A sense of falling, like an arrow-shower
Sent out of sight, somewhere becoming rain.

'The train journey ends apocalyptically' (Ward 1991, p. 186), 'this conclusion is magical' (Powell 1979, p. 93): those less easily persuaded may recall that in the 1950s many couples might well first have sexual intercourse on the train after the wedding. It is the thought of the young in one another's arms that enables the speaker to identify with these others in the excited rhythms of this Yeatsian ending, imagining a transcendence which unites: social and individual (them and him); body and mind ('None thought' this though he could think it for them); organic and mechanical ('knots of rail'); pastoral and urban ('postal districts packed like squares of wheat'); England's past and its present (the orgasmic 'arrow-shower' recalls the battle of Crecy in the 1944 film of *Henry V*, as Holbrook argues; 1977, p. 266); and of course, subject and object.

'The Whitsun Weddings' presents what is in many ways a 'Modernist' moment of alienation but does so in what is emphatically not Modernist discourse. Confronted with the married couples the speaker's situation is not so far from that of the speaker of 'The Waste Land' disabled by the London commuters. Perhaps the poem could have developed otherwise but not while holding on to its version of the empiricist subject. Everything in the poem – train journey, landscape and townscape, the couples, the concluding vision – is constructed by a script which represents a speaker who experiences all this for us. And the condition for that is an effacement of the materiality of language, to give the effect of someone 'really' speaking.

The language of the poem is written to appear almost invisible, a plain transcription of reality ('fathers with broad belts under their suits', etc.). This was what Larkin said he aimed at, in another of those invocations of a reality beyond language:

> You couldn't be on that train without feeling the young lives all starting off, and that just for a moment you were touching them....It was wonderful, a marvellous afternoon. It only needed writing down. Anybody could have done it.
>
> (cited Gervais 1993, pp. 206–7)

For Donald Davie it is utterly persuasive:

> Some have criticised what Larkin does with the truths he discovers, what attitudes he takes up to the landscapes and the weather of his own poems; but those landscapes and that weather – no one, I think has failed to recognise them. And this is just as true if we think of landscapes and weather metaphorically; we recognise also the seasons of an English soul – the moods he expresses are our moods too, though we may deal with them differently.
>
> (1973, p. 64)

Two points. This process of understanding is effectively telepathic, since recognition of 'the English soul' takes place outside any means of representation operating to make a version of anything recognisable to anyone. Second, the 'we' Davie calls up and equates with 'the English soul' is quite as dubious in its claim to national universality as the repeated 'we' of 'The Whitsun Weddings'.

Ted Hughes: hawks real and symbolic

Wordsworth, Hardy, Larkin – and Ted Hughes. By the 1960s a change in sensibility dictated the relegation of Larkin from the number-one slot as guardian of the English High Anti-Modernist tradition and the promotion of Ted Hughes. As Alvarez pointed out in 1962, the conjuncture called for something more sensational, more Lawrentian and macho. If the provincial securities of Larkin were supported by the continuity from England's imperial war-time mission into the immediate post-war period, the exorbitance of Ted Hughes answered better to a post-imperial moment of decolonisation and a sense of what the war had meant outside England. In Hughes, Larkinesque reflection gave way to a sense of participation. While Larkin seemed complacently bounded by the ordinary, Hughes offered the promise of big themes – 'the forces of the Universe' (Ekbert Faas, cited Bedient 1974, p. 98), 'the nature of existence' (Swinden 1972, p. 397), a 'visionary, revelatory poetry that sees into the life of things' (Sagar 1975, p. 3). Davie notes that Hughes's 'large and loyal public has been recruited largely in the classroom' (1989, p. 129). In December 1984 he was declared Poet Laureate.

A number of Hughes's poems represent a speaker having an intense experience of an external object. So it is in 'The Hawk in the Rain' (1957, p. 11):

I drown in the drumming ploughland, I drag up
Heel after heel from the swallowing of the earth's mouth,
From clay that clutches my every step to the ankle
With the habit of the dogged grave, but the hawk

Effortlessly at height hangs his still eye.
His wings hold all creation in a weightless quiet,
Stead as a hallucination in the streaming air.
While banging wind kills these stubborn hedges,

Thumbs my eyes, throws my breath, tackles my heart,
And rain hacks my head to the bone, the hawk hangs
The diamond point of will that polestars
The sea drowner's endurance: and I,

Bloodily grabbed daze last-moment-counting
Morsel in the earth's mouth, strain towards the master-
Fulcrum of violence where the hawk hangs still.
That maybe in his own time meet the weather

Coming the wrong way, suffers the air, hurled upside down,
Fall from his eye, the ponderous shires crash on him,
The horizon trap him; the round angelic eye
Smashed, mix his heart's blood with the mire of the land.

The poem works with a binary opposition between earth and air. The speaker contrasts his own situated materiality and time-bound contingency with the apparently ideal and eternal world he imagines for the hawk – effortless, weightless, virtually without position (a 'diamond point') – though in the last stanza he also foresees that even the hawk may fall and fail. The regular four-line verses, unrhymed, are written in a loose six-beat line that keeps recalling an iambic norm ('His wings hold all creation'). This serves, as ever, to attach the poem to the main poetic body, as does the theme, which refers it to a whole series of individual voices enraptured by intensely perceived birds, from Shelley's skylark, Keats's nightingale and Hopkins' windhover to Yeats' swans.

Compared to 'The Whitsun Weddings', Hughes' poem seems to be much more openly stylised, foregrounding awareness of its own language and carefully worked use of metaphor. This is certainly writing which has acquired some formal explicitness from Modernism but Modernist it is not. Though Hughes's poetry is 'densely encrusted with metaphor' (Swinden 1972, p. 393), these take a traditional form. In 1802 Coleridge proposed that 'a Poet's *Heart & Intellect* should be *combined*, *intimately* combined & *unified*, with the great appearances in

Nature' and not merely mixed with them through 'formal Similies (*sic*)' (letter of 10 September 1802 in 1956, 2, p. 459). The principle is to avoid shared and conventional comparisons, and seek out ones without obvious precedent. The idea of clay as a hand which 'clutches' the foot or rain as a blade which 'hacks' a head 'to the bone' are fresh comparisons, able to give the effect of an individual experiencing clay and rain for the first time, so bringing subject and object into determinate relation. In this way formal trope is made over into an expression of personal feeling.

So also with the worked poetic language in Hughes, which might seem to accord autonomy to the signifier. In fact, though, the phonemes are organised into patterns of alliteration and assonance – 'drown'/ 'drumming'/'drag', 'clay'/'clutches' – with the effect of making over the material force of language into an expression of intensity of feeling so that, in a manner traditional in English poetry since Shakespeare, the sound may seem an echo to the sense. With the materiality of the text thus moved to the periphery (it cannot be eradicated), a sense of the empiricist subject comes to rest in the centre.

Elsewhere Hughes's poetry presents a natural object – a pike, a cat, an otter, a crow – and suppresses the viewpoint of a perceiving speaker, poems therefore which might be thought to develop at a tangent to poetic empiricism and which require a little exploration. 'Hawk Roosting' is an example:

> I sit in the top of the wood, my eyes closed.
> Inaction, no falsifying dream
> between my hooked head and hooked feet:
> Or in sleep rehearse perfect kills and eat.
>
> (1960, p. 26)

The hawk is not observed by a human being, rather, it is construed anthropomorphically as if 'in this hawk Nature is thinking' (Faas, cited Bradshaw 1983, p. 53), seeing the whole world as arranged for its benefit: 'it is all mine', he says, the 'high trees', 'the air's buoyancy':

> I kill where I please because it is all mine.
> There is no sophistry in my body:
> My manners are tearing off heads –
>
> The allotment of death.
> For the one path of my flight is direct
> Through the bones of the living.

> No arguments assert my right:
>
> The sun is behind me.
> Nothing has changed since I began.
> My eye has permitted no change.
> I am going to keep things like this.
>
> (1960, p. 26)

There is a critical consensus that this is a poem about a hawk:

> No poet has observed animals more accurately.
>
> (Sagar 1983, p. 37)

> the voice heard in 'Hawk Roosting' is that of nature.
>
> (Bradshaw 1983, p. 217)

> in 'Hawk Roosting' we find words and statements suggesting animal consciousness.
>
> (Dyson 1975, p. 427)

If 'Hawk Roosting' did aim to present something like the hawkness of a hawk it would surely conform to the principle of Modernism Ezra Pound put forward in 1912 in his account of 'Symbols':

> I believe that the proper and perfect symbol is the natural object, that if a man use 'symbols' he must so use them that their symbolic function does not obtrude; so that *a* sense, and the poetic quality of the passage, is not lost to those who do not understand the symbol as such, to whom, for instance, a hawk is a hawk.
>
> (1954, p. 9)

This could hardly be more apposite though turns out to be less straightforward than it sounds.

A hawk (for example) is to be conceded a literal meaning as an object in reality *apart* from the usual connotations it has acquired subjectively for human beings (ferocity, rapacity, nobility, and so on). But there is a problem here. Both the 'literal' meaning (a hawk as a hawk) and the 'symbolic' meaning (hawk as rapacity) exist as they are constructed within human experience, so how could a poem fulfil Pound's manifesto requirement to discriminate them? How could poetry render hawk as hawk?

A fine poetic response to that question (and perhaps to the Hughes poem) is made in Charles Tomlinson's poem 'Hawks' (1972, p. 25). Around the topic of a pair of hawks hovering together, this keeps moving between an assertion of 'what we share with them', on the one hand, and the difference between hawk and human, on the other. Against the usual idea that the cruelty of hawk nature mirrors human nature it is affirmed that what we share with them is a biological necessity to mate and rear young – the pair of hawks 'After their kind are lovers'. Having noted a common genetic disposition between us and them, the poem goes back the other way to assert 'we cannot tell what it is they say'. It thus unfolds in the belief that the best sense one can get of reality as reality is to establish a sense of expectation and then countermand it (a strategy with precedents in both Pound and Wallace Stevens).

From this perspective Hughes' animal poems appear almost programmatically anti-Modernist. 'Hawk Roosting' is not about a hawk. Mixed with a certain crude Nietzscheianism ('I kill where I please'), the poem surely expresses the moment of primary narcissism when the infant still finds no distinction between itself and the world ('it is all mine') though begins to fear this may not last ('I am going to keep things like this'). It expresses desire for a world unmediated by language even if, contradictorily, the voice of the poem admits the possibility of such mediation by denying it ('no sophistry'). In using a hawk – the *idea* of hawk – as vehicle for such feelings (or something like them), the poem effortlessly unites object and subject, as in the ending of 'Adlestrop' and 'The Whitsun Weddings'.

How has the poetry of Hughes been able to support its inflated reputation? In the England of the 1970s and 1980s what are we to make of a poetry centred around images of hawks, pikes, cats, otters and crows?

> contemporary English verse has borrowed little from foreign sources; it is almost politically English; *these poets* insist upon the English countryside, and are even positively patriotic. When, therefore, they turn to the common object, to the animal or flower or hearth-rug, it is in the mood not of Dostoevski but of Wordsworth.

In this quotation, to make a point, I have replaced the words 'the Georgian poets' in the first sentence with 'these poets'. For the judgement was made by T.S. Eliot in 1917 (cited Press 1969, p. 117). Those who find the poetry of Hughes interesting, original, or in any significant sense contemporary might refer back to the portrayal of hawks in Dylan Thomas' 'St John's Hill' or re-read Gerard Manley Hopkins'

'The Windhover'; they should compare Hughes' 'Pike' with Edmund Blunden's 'The Pike' (1920).

Seamus Heaney

Hardy, Larkin, Hughes – and Seamus Heaney. As the sensational 1960s faded, Hughes' tenure of the canonical patronage became less secure. In 1985 one critic likened the writing of 'Crow' to 'the technique of the horror-comic, with its crude devices of BAM! SPLAT! ZOWY!' (Thwaite 1985, p. 85), implying a preference for the urbanities of Larkin. Then there was the problem of the rampant sexism in Hughes's poetry, which came to look increasingly out of key as the 1970s turned into the 1980s. And Hughes's politics were either undefinable or a bit fascistic.

The quest was on to find a protagonist without these limitations but who still wrote in a pre-Modernist fashion. In the postmodern England of the 1980s Neo-Georgian writers were hard to find (Hughes had come from Yorkshire) but one might still be uncovered in the recesses of rural Ireland (it was there that David Lodge recruited his innocent poet, Persse McGarrigle). Mossbawn in County Derry supplied a poet capable of such reassuringly agricultural titles as *Wintering Out* (1972), *Field Work* (1979) and *The Haw Lantern* (1987) ('Adlestrop' at least had a steam train).

At the same time, however, Heaney's pastoralism could make a claim to be political, for it expressed muted sympathy with the Catholic community and deplored the atrocities which followed the arrival of the British Army in Northern Ireland in 1969. Harsh as the truth may be, for most people on the mainland – and for most readers of Heaney – the 'Troubles' of Northern Ireland constitute a television war showing events almost as securely far away as Bosnia (if not, would it have lasted so long?). The present conflict in Northern Ireland originated in the seventeenth century as a struggle between native Irish, who were Catholic, and Protestant *pieds-noirs*, who had been encouraged to settle there by an imperial power. Politically, it exemplifies a form of social action significant in the 1960s, the struggle against colonialism in Algeria, Kenya and other parts of the world. Thirty years later political attention concerns other things – the shift from smaller to larger blocs, globalism, tensions between nations and supra-national organisations. Terrible as the situation has been in Northern Ireland, it remains something outmoded and atavistic, not a genuinely contemporary form of politics.

Drawing on this subject matter Heaney's poetry was able to sound high serious and authoritative without treading on anyone's toes. Again and again his political gestures, calling up ancient wrong, unconscious tradition and the living past, have invoked the old fantasy about pre-modernity, the organic community. That stance is well suited to a 'poetry of the self'.

For these reasons – though the man himself would repudiate the distinction – Seamus Heaney has been adopted as an honorary Briton. Celebrating his 1995 award of the Nobel Prize for Literature as though he was native-born, Blake Morrison provides a convenient summary of the virtues usually ascribed to his writing (*Guardian*, 6 October 1995). It is, says Morrison, a poetry of 'blood and soil', yielding a sense of 'the primal sources of the self'; Heaney understands the 'ugly blooms of tribal and religious conflict' yet writes a poetry affirming 'something more visionary, ecstatic and transcendental'. Heaney's poetry is widely taught in schools and universities. Reviewing Heaney's collection *Seeing Things*, an Oxford professor was moved to exclaim that 'Reading these and several other poems, you feel what the first readers of, say, Keats's odes or Milton's 1645 collection must have felt' (John Carey, *Sunday Times*, 2 June 1991).

Blake Morrison elsewhere notes that Heaney learned to write 'a poetry that combined the wit and metrical tightness of the Movement with the power and physicality of Ted Hughes' (1982, p. 29). After the excesses of Hughes, Heaney restores the sobriety of the full, English empiricist mode. Sixty years after the event, a typical Heaney poem plays out very much the same scenario as 'Adlestrop'. An example would be the poem specially praised by Morrison and Motion in their 1982 'Introduction' to *Contemporary British Poetry*, 'The Grauballe Man'. The poem is organised in loose two- and three-beat lines never far from the iambic norm and carefully arranged into four-line unrhymed stanzas ('Heaney was never tempted by the modernist attack on the iamb and the pentameter'; O'Donoghue 1994, p. 41). 'The Grauballe Man' represents a speaker describing a mummified body, one of the bog people who was ritually murdered (1975, pp. 36–7):

As if he had been poured
in tar, he lies
on a pillow of turf
and seems to weep

the black river of himself.
The grain of his wrists
is like bog oak,
the ball of his heel

like a basalt egg.
His instep has shrunk

cold as a swan's foot
or a wet swamp root.

The speaker reflects on the figure, thinking of the classical statue of a northern hero, and then of sectarian murder in Northern Ireland:

Who will say 'corpse'
to his vivid cast?
Who will say 'body'
to his opaque repose?

And his rusted hair,
a mat unlikely
as a foetus's.
I first saw his twisted face

in a photograph,
a head and shoulder
out of the peat,
bruised like a forceps baby,

but now he lies
perfected in my memory,
down to the red horn
of his nails,

hung in the scales
with beauty and atrocity:
with the dying Gaul
too strictly compassed

on his shield,
with the actual weight
of each hooded victim
slashed and dumped.

There is the same three-part movement as in the Edward Thomas poem. An object, the Grauballe Man, is initially alien and self-defining, seeming 'to weep/the black river of himself', but then, under the persisting gaze of the observer, this is made over from an outward perception ('I first saw his twisted face/in a photograph') into an inward experience ('now he lies/perfected in my memory').

Subject and object brought together, the experience can support a moment of transcendent understanding. The Grauballe Man comes to represent a truth about the human being as victim, a truth eternally the same whether as the primitive suffering of a bog person, of 'the Dying Gaul', or of someone assassinated in the Bogside. The poem is constructed to give the effect of an experiencing ego as its source and speaker. First person pronouns ('I first saw', 'in my memory'), demonstratives ('now he lies'), direct address ('Who will say…?') make up a script for a consistently developing 'I' who 'speaks' to us in fluent and sustained syntax across the twelve verses.

One more example. 'From the Frontier of Writing' recalls the repeated event of being in a car stopped at a road block by soldiers (Heaney 1987, p. 6):

as one bends his face
towards your window, you catch sight of more
on a hill beyond.

Again, the experience leads at first to disabusement and loss, 'The tightness and the nilness round that space/when the car stops in the road'. But after the incident, waved on by a rifle, 'you' drive on to what is termed 'the frontier of writing' where the scene at roadblock is replayed, though at a metaphorical level, perception again acceding to symbol. On this basis, the incident reappears but transformed:

the posted soldiers flowing and receding
like tree shadows into the polished windscreen.

The soldiers have been safely converted into a vision of pastoral beauty far from modernity, the city, and the forces of the state. Heaney's poetry, it is said, makes 'an affirmation of self, of individual autonomy and separateness in a world where self is constantly threatened' (Foster 1989, p. 134).

A poem cannot dramatise a version of the empiricist self unless it can contain the force of the signifier, hold in place the materiality of the text as figure and phoneme. Heaney's metaphors and similes have been widely acclaimed as deliberate and adventurous: 'the ball of his heel/ like a basalt egg' ('The Grauballe Man'), 'their blunt heads farting' (frogs in 'Death of a Naturalist'), 'those brats of showers' ('Hailstones'). 'Strange Fruit' opens with three comparisons:

Here is the girl's head like an exhumed gourd.
Oval-faced, prune-skinned, prune-stones for teeth.

So we have: (1) a head (cut off as part of an ancient ritual and preserved in a museum) is like a gourd; (2) a head with black, wrinkled skin is like a prune or dried plum; (3) dead teeth are like small, black prune-stones. The two lines are stuffed with efforts to come up with original comparisons for aspects of the perceived world and so support the effect of individual experiencing the described object 'personally', for themselves, as no one else has.

Sympathetic critics applaud Heaney's poetry on the grounds that it *does* in fact draw attention to its own writing: 'he delights in language, relishing it' (Morrison and Motion 1982, p. 13); 'few books touch so directly upon particular words as *words*' (Harold Bloom on *Wintering Out*, 1986, p. 2). A fairly random list might include phrases such as 'elvers tails my hair' ('Toome'), 'palpable, lithe/Otter' ('The Otter'), 'slabbed passage' ('In Memoriam: Robert Fitzgerald'), or 'the squelch and slap/ Of soggy peat' ('Digging'). Although these assign the phonetic a place which would not have been acceptable before Modernism, they do not – as does the extract from Eliot's 'The Waste Land' cited earlier – open the writing to a sense of textuality. Far from it: each turns the sound of words as words to expressive purposes.

Conventional discussion of Heaney's 'language' has lingered on what he does in some poems by concentrating on the sound of particular words unfamiliar to English readers, 'Anahorish', 'Toome' and 'Broagh'. But the concentration aims precisely to recuperate the phonetic materiality of sound (the signifier as arbitrary signifier) and render it as far as possible into a source of meaning. Bernard O'Donoghue points out, 'the lexical items in "Broagh" become "a perfect symbol of difference"' (1994, p. 64) (regional or national difference, that is), they become *thematised*. There is 'creative tension between the wish to be faithful to origin and the wish to aspire to transparency in lyric utterance remains constant in Heaney's writings' (p. 21). He concludes that Heaney is 'not a modernist' (p. 153), nor is he a postmodernist because his poetry is too 'strongly informed by spoken forms' (p. 154), by the dramatisation of the effect of a voice 'really' speaking. Sure enough, Heaney has himself made the old empiricist claim that some of his poems are 'poems which in a sense *anybody* could write' (cited Corcoran 1986, p. 122).

In England now

Like his predecessors Larkin and Hughes, Heaney does not try to engage his reader with a poetry which is complex and difficult, a poetry uncertain, in fact, whether it is poetry or not. In the bardic, uplifted tone of every line Heaney's writing proclaims that poetry matters and that it can hearten its reader with a vision and an understanding beyond the ordinary. The superficial concern with 'language' should not hide the way its deeper structures repeat accustomed effects. Andrew Crozier remarks of Heaney's poetry, 'Everything is of a piece, irrespective of what is being said' (1983, p. 230), and indeed Heaney's poetry is wonderfully fluent, deft, poised, verbally accomplished and professional. As one would expect since the forms it works with are long familiar.

If the poetry of Larkin, Hughes and Heaney does indeed recirculate an old-fashioned poetic empiricism, the question is how it has maintained its almost exclusively privileged position within English culture. It seems unaccountable that a sensitive writer and critic such as Donald Davie should praise Heaney's capacity 'to contribute to international modernism' (1989, p. 245), incredible that Morrison and Motion can refer to Heaney as one of the contemporary British poets who exhibit 'the spirit of postmodernism' (Morrison and Motion 1982, p. 20).

An answer must lie, first, in the dovetailing complicity between this kind of writing and the empiricist assumptions of current criticism discussed in Chapter 5. Such poetry confirms literary journalism and in turn is supported by it. A larger reason must be the intimate and seemingly spontaneous compatibility between the dominant poetry and the ancient power of the English empiricist tradition. Poetry, because it works on the verbal signifier, goes deep. For British culture to persist in honouring this backward-looking Neo-Georgian verse is not a symptom of vitality.

Meanwhile, the wide promotion of the Larkin/Hughes/Heaney ascendancy has occluded and pushed to the margins the exciting and varied range of English writing which accepts the Modernist revolution, poetry which indeed has a serious claim to engage with the contemporary (for appropriate collections, see Allnutt *et al.* 1988; Crozier and Longville 1990; Hampson and Barry 1993; also the journal *fragmente*). Here is one brief and slight example, first published in 1968, to stand for a larger number of writers:

Shoes

shoes come from leather leather
comes from cows come from milk no
no milk comes from cows come
from shoes baby shoes
                    come
from there to here hear

the shoes of blind children shoes
shuffling tripping a blind child falls into a cement mixer
a deaf child is crushed by the ambulance racing to the
    blind child who is the child of some dumb man who
    makes shoes

that evening he cries over a piece of leather stained with
                                                  [milk
the tear marks make a pattern he tries to read to read
he wants to cut the leather into the shape of a gingerbread
                                                  [man

he wants very much to have his child back
to ride on the cows back

(Raworth 1988, p. 38)

Although having a strong rhythmic drive which owes something to nursery rhymes and tongue twisters ('Red leather yellow leather'), 'Shoes', published by Tom Raworth in 1968, is written in free verse. This feature locates the poem firmly outside the traditional canon while it enormously facilitates the associative and unpremeditated shifts of tone across which the text moves, as words repeat, interrupt and suggest each other. For example, 'tripping' (with its double sense of prancing and falling over) pulls the poem suddenly into the absurdly exaggerated horror of the blind child falling into a cement mixer, though almost as quickly the tone can swerve into the idea (at once childish and surrealist) of reading the pattern made by one's own tears and then on to the pathos of the last two lines.

A typical progression, 'here hear', is entirely homonymic: because the phonetic materiality of language is openly avowed as the basis for the text, there can be no question of sustained imitation of an empiricist subject experiencing this, that, or the other. Rather, the text acknowledges the act of speaking as an effect that emerges from sound before it enters into meaning, this poem knows it is a poem. Recalling the stories of the gingerbread boy and of Pinocchio (narratives which share the image of children produced by an act of will) it invites us to consider a link between paternal grief and the fantasy of paternal conception. 'Shoes' is not a major poem but, because it locates itself in direct relation to Modernism, it represents a different *kind* of poem from those in the Hardy/Thomas tradition.

9

NATION: IDENTITY AND DIFFERENCE

> England is perhaps the only great country whose intellectuals are ashamed of their own nationality.
>
> (George Orwell 1968, 2, p. 75)

Empiricism revisited

Discursive differences

The four examples of discourse considered – literary journalism, history-writing, tragic and comic novels, poetry – are marked in different ways by the main features of empiricist discourse (the assumption that reality is essentially unproblematic and self-interpreting, that discourse is in principle transparent and that the subject, typically a moral subject, can find a place safely outside the process which affords knowledge and experience). The aim has been to demonstrate a deep structural continuity between the founding moment of English national culture and contemporary expression (of course some other examples could have been found which would not have confirmed this hypothesis). The recurrence of a sense of weakness or limitation in English empiricist discourse today tempts generalisation. Making a judgement is difficult, however, for a number of reasons.

In the first place, the various forms, discourses and practices of a nation, though acting in relation to each other, proceed according to their own specificity and autonomy. The four discussed here differ considerably in their force and effect. Literary journalism takes the form of newspaper reviewing, history-writing is an academic discipline, tragic and comic were illustrated mainly from the novel, a form of artistic practice itself distinct from the poetry discussed afterwards.

In different ways each of the four examples suggested the desirability of change, that their empiricist commitment had now become – for contrasted reasons – inadequate, provincial, obsolete, backward-looking. Even if this were agreed, I do not think we should anticipate rapid alteration in the near future. The empiricism of literary journalism – at least, on my showing – is at some distance from (for example) the modernist and postmodernist concerns of much architectural reviewing. Newspapers can live with this kind of disparity, and the traditionalism of literary pages often contrasts with a more informed and theoretical approach found elsewhere in the same issue. The attitudes of literary journalism are so entrenched, it is hard to imagine them catching up with the level of analysis offered in (for example) the economics pages apart from some much more widespread change in English cultural life.

Despite its role as guardian of the national narrative, history-writing, to the extent that it is separated off as an academic discourse, should be more ready for a break with its own prevailing empiricism. Within the past two decades another university discipline alongside it, literary criticism, has been largely transformed into a version of literary and cultural theory (much to the scorn of literary journalism). It is now a question how long history-writing in England can hold out when it is already reacting nervously to 'postmodernism' and the so-called 'linguistic turn' for, as Keith Thomas acknowledges, in this restricted arena 'cultural lag does not last forever' (*Guardian*, 6 September 1994).

Aesthetic texts, such the novels and poetry examined, have a more intimate connection with ordinary life than an academic discourse such as history-writing. Even if novel-writing and poetry with a Modernist/postmodernist tendency did come to an accepted prominence, it would almost certainly be by elevating itself above a mainstream writing which would probably persist anyway, recycling 'the rhetoric of pathos' and empiricist narrativisation commented on in le Carré and Orwell. These tropes and effects have firm roots in 'common sense' and everyday life, as does the 'English sense of humour', exemplified in one novel and some picture postcards, and are thus much less susceptible to change.

A discursive formation, in so far as it is anchored in the operation of the signifier, resists transformation. One way to document this (it's not easy) would be to think of the different ways post-structuralism (an essentially Parisian intellectual movement after 1965) was taken up in England and in the United States. In England it was pulled into the orbit of the prevailing radical discourse, 'New Left' Marxism, in terms that allowed many of the old empiricist themes to reappear under new management. An opposition between 'theoretical practice' and 'ideological practice' was able to support:

1 a confident appeal to reality (albeit a reality acknowledged as a constructed one);
2 a capacity to discriminate between a true discourse of knowledge and one that was manifestly non-transparent (referred to as 'ideology' rather than as 'jargon');
3 a heavily moralised view of the subject (though officially this was a subject-in-process).

All carried on in a traditional tone of high seriousness. Simultaneously, the same post-structuralist ideas – though no longer the same by the time they had been translated – were incorporated according to the protocols of the national tradition of the United States and reproduced across the Atlantic as the playful subversiveness of 1970s American-style 'deconstruction'. Despite surface adaptations discursive formations do not change unless they have to. In 1999 it is hardly possible to imagine a 'non-empiricist' England, and certainly not for an English writer who has himself failed to escape an empiricist idiom (irony, colloquial appeals to the real and no doubt more than a touch of covert moralising) even when writing in criticism of it.

Assessing empiricism

Apart from the inconclusive debate between Nairn–Anderson and Edward Thompson recapitulated at the beginning of Chapter 3 I am not aware of any attempt to *assess* the English empiricist tradition. There is indeed the warning from Ellen Meiksins Wood that Nairn–Anderson feel empowered to mount their critique of empiricism because they have before them the counter-instance of France, with its rationalist tradition, radicalised intelligentsia and institutionalised discourse of theoretical critique. Wood exposes this overvaluation by showing that in France 'deep structural continuities' run between absolutism, rationalism and the strongly undemocratic character of its post-revolutionary state (1991, p. 76). Even if it were on offer, that would be (or would have been) a heavy price to pay for another England, a 'rationalist' England.

What could one say, in general terms, to assess the English tradition there is? That belief in a self-evidencing reality which you can retrieve if you rid yourself of fantasy has fostered negotiation and compromise since every dispute is framed by belief that a solution consistent with the self-interest of all parties must be available somewhere (the essential Englishness of this belief being demonstrated every time the English try to intervene in Northern Ireland)? That anxiety about the capacity of the gaze of the Other to expose one's own self-deceptions has encouraged democratic feeling by encouraging doubt whether anyone's claim to authority was not in fact based on wish-fulfilment prompted by their will to power? That the tendency towards individual submission to the gaze of the Other has promoted a distrust of pleasure along with the duty to work hard but by the same token introduced a likeable readiness towards self-depreciation?

In the other direction it would be as easy to enter corresponding reservations. That compromise always entails evasion ('when in doubt, the English imagine a pendulum', as Raymond Williams says) (1961, p. 69). That belief you really have escaped self-deception is only a greater self-deception (in Lacan's disconcerting account, it is what 'renders modern man so sure of being himself even in...the mistrust he has learned to practise against the traps of self-love'; 1977a, p. 165). That empiricist scepticism can play over everything except its own procedures for eliciting truth. That the habit of self-mockery is a way to put yourself centre-stage.

It does seem that in many aspects of contemporary England the empiricist inheritance has now become a clog rather than a spur to clear and decisive thinking about the present. But we do not have access to a fixed point on which we might stand to draw up an appropriate reckoning for and against that inheritance. Every form of discourse states only by repressing, making inclusions only by keeping something out. A better move, then, may be to try to think of what the empiricist tradition today inhibits and excludes from proper expression.

Exclusions

Modernism

Contextualising reality, insisting on the signifier, relativising subjectivity, Modernism threatens empiricist discourse, a threat apparent in the way the English tradition attempts a commination of Modernism in the figures of O'Brien in *Nineteen Eighty-Four* and Morris Zapp in *Small World*. As was argued, Modernism, in its theoretical manifestation as post-structuralism, keeps nipping at the heels of literary journalism, which in turn keeps trying to see off this adversarial discourse. Only in poetry does English High Anti-Modernism seem authentically confident it can by-pass Modernism without qualm ('*Foreign* poetry? *No!*'; Larkin 1975, p. 249). Rather the same story about empiricist procedures in contemporary poetry could be told about the dominant mode of the English novel since 1945 as represented in a series of Booker prize winners. Modernist (or rather, now, postmodernist) writing in poetry and the novel does happen in England but not so that many people notice. And there was a decisive Modernist intervention in drama by Pinter, Arden and others in the 1950s, which has transformed a small area of the theatrical tradition. But this kind of minority, ghettoised situation is at odds with what has happened in visual representation, where English painting and sculpture have had to come to terms publicly with Modernism and its consequences, and done so very well (is this why contemporary visual art retains an unusual aura of excitement and transgression in English culture?).

Constitutional reform

There is one important area in contemporary English life which certainly will have to be reinvented in the immediate future because of the force of current events, that of constitutional reform. Strictly, as political practice, it lies at a tangent to the main topic of this present study though, as I shall argue, attitudes mobilised against reform do invite understanding in relation to empiricism.

I am a subject of Her Majesty the Queen and not a citizen of the United Kingdom; if I were a citizen I would have rights under a written constitution. As it is I am subject to the sovereign power of the monarch, which, following the settlement of 1689, means subject to monarchical power as exercised through Parliament. In practice this means that Parliament can do almost anything it wants (for example, during the Gulf War of 1990 hundreds of Iraqis living in England and who were *opponents* of Saddham Hussein were imprisoned without trial on the basis of parliamentary prerogative).

There is more than one reason why this situation will have to be modified. Britain's membership of the European Union has meant that the European Convention on Human Rights has applied *de facto* and is being codified into English law. The Labour government elected on 1 May 1997 is committed to some devolution of power to Scotland and Wales, as well as radical reform of the House of Lords. All this will open the door to constitutional changes which the organisation Charter 88 has been lobbying for over the past ten years – an explicit, written constitution, a Bill of Rights, a Freedom of Information Act. The effect would be to redefine the English not as subjects but as citizens.

So far, despite influential support, Charter 88 has not been able to break out of its strangely marginal position. Antagonism to constitutional reform appears mainly in two forms. A left opposition says 'Writing on bits of paper is illusory – what matters is the exercise of political power' while hostility from the right expresses itself in the view that 'We don't need to have our rights written down because we've got them already.'

Both arguments appeal to a sense of empirical reality conceived in a binary opposition to the apparent. The left position tends to be Hobbesian–Marxist, believing that instinct, aggression and power are real, while institutions, legislation and law are superficial and false. The right-wing position trusts that what happens in practice is real, so any attempt to change it in the name of programmatic theory or dogma is merely fanciful (Michael Oakeshott would be the relevant name to document the associated view that theory is only a derivation of practice anyway; see 1967).

In this specific arena of constitutional reform empiricism blocks the view, activating the seventeenth-century English tradition of 'common sense' and occluding an eighteenth-century vision of universal reason, explicit Constitutions and 'the Rights of Man'. Charter 88 would be naive if it failed to see it represents a challenge not simply to certain existing political institutions but, at a deeper level, to the prevailing forms and traditions of political culture in England. Nevertheless, constitutional reform is now inevitable, and with it some shift in empiricist attitudes, at least in so far as these are focused by constitutional questions.

Blindness and insight

I will turn finally to an example, one to match against the imaginary conversation between the two English people abroad with which I began. The experiment is meant to suggest how empiricist discourse lets us see what it shows us only by hiding something. It is also intended to draw attention to the empiricist effect as present not just in a text but in the interpretation of a text. The passage is quite long:

> Hence the reversals which constitute Alice's adventures: the reversal of becoming larger and becoming smaller – 'which way, which way?' asks Alice, sensing that it is always in both directions at the same time, so that for once she stays the same, through an optical illusion; the reversal of the day before and the day after, the present always being eluded – 'jam tomorrow and jam yesterday – but never jam *to-day*'; the reversal of more or less: five nights are five times hotter than a single one, 'but they must be five times as cold for the same reason'; the reversal of active and passive: 'do cats eat bats?' is as good as

> 'do bats eat cats?'; the reversal of cause and effect: to be punished before having committed a fault, to cry before having pricked oneself, to serve before having divided up the servings.
>
> All these reversals as they appear in infinite identity have one consequence: the contesting of Alice's personal identity and the loss of her proper name. The loss of the proper name is the adventure which is repeated throughout all Alice's adventures. For the proper or singular name is guaranteed by the permanence of knowledge. The latter is embodied in general names designating pauses and rests, in substantives and adjectives, with which the proper name maintains a constant connection. Thus the personal self requires God and the world in general. But when substantives and adjectives begin to dissolve, when the names of pause and rest are carried away by the verbs of pure becoming and slide into the language of events, all identity disappears from the self, the world, and God. This is the test of knowledge and recitation which strips Alice of her identity. In it words may go awry, being obliquely swept away by the verbs. It is as if events enjoyed an irreality which is communicated through language to knowledge and to persons. For personal uncertainty is not a doubt foreign to what is happening, but rather an objective structure of the event itself, insofar as it moves in two directions at once, and insofar as it fragments the subject following this double direction. Paradox is initially that which destroys good sense as the only direction, but it also that which destroys common sense as the assignation of fixed identities.

For the moment I shall conceal the name of the author so that the native reader may experience the full, estranging shock of these sharp-heeled footsteps on the April fields of Lewis Carroll's Alice. I wanted a limit case, something well loved and intimately familiar to many English people but treated in a very unEnglish manner. Though the writer could conceivably be English (such is literary criticism today), the passage and its reading of Carroll are not. Perhaps examination of a native's seemingly instinctive outrage ('this is all wrong') will suggest what empiricism represses.

Like the givenness of the reality empiricism presupposes, being English means you know that the work of Lewis Carroll is self-evidently *silly*, that it is a series of jokes, a premeditated transgression, which delightfully plays with impossibilities known to be impossibilities from the perspective of common sense (the genre inscribes madness 'the better to contain it', as Lecercle asserts, 1994, p. 208). For English culture it is acceptable if mathematicians or philosophers who claim a sense of humour pull out a couple of apposite sentences from Alice for the head of a chapter but this writer has engaged in a determined misreading, imposing an unrelentingly humourless, abstract and theoretical dogma about reversal on the common-sense comedy of the text.

So every detail inspires contestation. 'Do cats eat bats?' and 'Do bats eat cats?' are *not* 'the reversal of active and passive' but a play on words appropriate to Alice's youth (and the fact that she is 'dozing off'); the idea that 'five nights are five times hotter than a single one' is another joke of that special 'logical' kind the English have traditionally ascribed to the Irish (an Irish bull in fact). Far from being 'the reversal of the day before and the day after, the present always being eluded', the reference to 'jam tomorrow and jam yesterday – but never jam *today*' is a sad, witty and knowing admission that pleasure is always past or to come but never actually available in the here and now (and this reading is confirmed by the way the phrase has passed into common English discourse).

Besides missing the humour because he (or she) is so pleased with their own cleverness, in the second paragraph the writer plays fast and loose with the argument, constantly overstating assertions and claiming things follow perfectly when they don't or don't obviously. No, 'all these reversals' do not have 'one consequence' – they have lots of consequences. Yes, there are lots of jokes about personal identity but Alice's identity is contested only to be reaffirmed in a common-sense manner (she *imagines* getting so big that she would have to write a letter to her feet but is fully aware that she is talking nonsense). The 'proper name maintains a constant connection' with 'general names' (it does? why?); 'the personal self requires God' (you could say this but it hardly follows as a 'Thus'); 'when the names of pause and rest are carried away by the verbs' (wait a minute – when was that?); this 'strips Alice of her identity' (but it doesn't, see above); it is 'as if events enjoyed an irreality' (as if pigs could fly). And so on.

But these blunt, common-sensical objections (somewhat unnervingly for the English reader the passage supposes there is 'good sense' *as well as* 'common sense') completely miss the point of this account of Alice, one which is working within the protocols of another, more rationalist discourse, in which the burden is not on the writer to indicate reality but rather on the reader to follow a logic. It is not necessary to confront the complexity of the argument that language enacts temporality as a becoming which simultaneously sets limits to identity and transcends them to appreciate that it is the argument which is given precedence by

Gilles Deleuze (1990, p. 3), for he it is, so confirming for some their worst suspicions – foreign and Catholic and French (though actually Deleuze was not a Catholic).

Empirical reality does not come first (Deleuze feels no discomfort in assimilating the 'facts' of Lewis Carroll's texts to the purposes of his own theorisation) – the line of argument comes first, its premisses explicit, its assumptions pushed home, its consequential statements confrontationally thrown at the reader and opened for challenge ('Thus'). Discourse of this kind invites – deliberately provokes – reply, it does not gesture in silent consensus towards a supposedly given reality ('whether this be so, or no, I will not here determine, but appeal to every one's own Experience').

What this analysis may let one appreciate is the major limitation on the empiricist method – its inability to interrogate its own epistemology, its own method (which is not to say that the discursive tradition Deleuze represents does not have its own limitations). Since (at least in its widespread, informal versions) empiricist discourse claims not to have a method or procedure for constructing knowledge of reality, it is not possible for it to question the very conceptual framework within which it works and on which its insights depend. Everything can appear in question – the continuous obligation to avoid self-deceit energises that – except what makes the questions available in the first place. In a post-modern world, where everything, even the reading of *Alice in Wonderland*, may be radically contested, the inbuilt tendency of empiricism towards premature and unacknowledged closure, its philosophic pretension to non-philosophy, must put it at an increasing disadvantage as a means of understanding the world.

Nation reconsidered

After nation?

Charles Tilly categorised the growth of nation in three periods (1994, p. 253):

1 1500–1700: 'the formation and consolidation of the first great national states'.
2 1650–1850: 'the regrouping of the remainder of Europe into a system of states, accompanied by the extension of European political control into most of the non-European world'.
3 1800–1950: 'extension of the state system to the rest of the world'.

Tilly himself is not so sure but other commentators are confident that globalisation, the intensifying of social relations on a world-wide scale, is leading to the demise of the nation-state, to what Paul Gilroy welcomes as 'the postmodern eclipse of the modern nation-state as a political, economic, and cultural unit' (1992, p. 188).

There is a risk here of submitting too quickly to an unqualified opposition according to which there is either the nation-state or globalisation. Capitalism has operated on a global scale since at least the late nineteenth century – the fact that since 1945 this process has been further extended does not necessarily mean that we are witnessing 'the emergence of a truly global, as distinct from highly interdependent, international economy' (Bromley 1996, p. 3). And though it is certainly the case that no individual nation today can act in the spirit of careless independence which characterised nations a century ago, this does not prove the nation-state has now disappeared: reactions to the war between the United States and Vietnam (1965–75) showed the effect of the immense international pressure brought to bear against even the most powerful nation in the world when it tried to relive in the post-war world a dream of nineteenth-century imperial freedom of action.

In globalisation a number of factors act together. The system of capitalist economy works increasingly to exploit markets on an international scale, supported by the post-war development of international agencies (the International Monetary Fund, World Bank). At the same time there is a globalisation of communications (grounded in the technology of satellite communication, and exemplified in CNN and a revitalised Hollywood with television and film interests world-wide). Recently computer technology has begun to operate globally via the Internet. In political relations there has been an internationalisation of 'peace-keeping', with United Nations' interventions in the Gulf (1990), Somalia (from 1992), Haiti, and former Yugoslavia. Culturally, global awareness is promoted by such events as the Olympic Games and the Football World Cup.

Yet in none of these does nation vanish, far from it. The great international conglomerates (Standard Oil, Sony, Boeing) repatriate profits to the country in which they are owned and its foreign policy is influenced by that fact; CNN (as any non-American immediately knows) gives world news with an American slant; international film and television – as well as the music business – have their commercial roots as solidly in Hollywood, USA, as they ever did (though the world-wide success of this extraordinary square mile may owe less to some actual globalisation of consciousness than a thirst for the modernity America signifies). 'International peacekeeping' follows the agreement (and in some cases the interests) of nation-states – even under the blue berets of the United Nations the soldiers remain members of a national military. International sport (it goes without saying) consists of fierce competition between nations.

Simon Bromley concludes that 'the expansion of liberal states in the world economy, their participation in international organisations, and the development of international law are not threats to sovereignty, but rather the forms of its consolidation on an increasingly global basis' (p. 4). In fact, in certain respects tendencies towards globalisation have actually stimulated a defensive turn towards national identity, encouraging nations to foreground their distinctiveness (if so, the recalcitrance of the signifier, concretised in national discourses, may have actually buttressed such resistance). It is possible that the development of nation-states and their situation since the nineteenth century have evidenced some shift of emphasis in the definition of nation, from the importance of state to the role of culture.

If the European Union moves (as seems likely) towards a version of federalism, this might pose some threat to the persistence of the United Kingdom as a nation-state (a threat felt strongly by a minority of people in England). In his *Reflections on Today's Europe* (1992b) Derrida gives cautious endorsement to the possibility of a united Europe on condition it avoids the dangers of cultural nationalism and remains an open rather than closed structure. At present, as Michael Mann notes, the European Union 'does not really cultivate a real sense of European identity' (1996, p. 304) though it very easily could. If in the next century the 'United States of Europe' comes about, it might well reproduce the old issues around nation at a higher level. Orwell in *Nineteen-Eighty Four* prophesies a world divided between Eurasia, Eastasia and Oceania.

In the meantime and for the obviously foreseeable future most people will find their main collective identity in the nation-state. In the rest of this section I shall return to the problematic issues around the kind of identity afforded by nation that were anticipated in the first chapters.

The two sides of nation

The 'temporal' account

It is now widely conceded that nation emerges in a double potentiality. Anthony Giddens refers to 'what so many students of nationalism have pointed to', namely 'its Janus-faced character, as generating both virulent forms of national aggressiveness, on the one hand, and the democratic ideals of the enlightenment (*sic*) on the other' (1985, p. 218). Janus, the Roman god of beginnings and war, had two faces, looking both backwards and forwards. And so, in this emphasis, does national possibility. Speaking 'On National Culture' in 1959, Frantz Fanon rejects the view that anti-colonial struggles in Africa should be undertaken against a blanket notion of white domination or in the name of an African consciousness. Rather, it is his view that it would be a mistake to wish 'to skip the national period' (1967, p. 198) and he goes on to endorse belief that 'every culture is first and foremost national' (p. 174), so that nation must be the primary arena for contestation. On this basis Fanon plots a number of stages through which an independence movement must develop, starting with a 'passionate search for a national culture which existed before the colonial era' (p. 168) in order to find empowerment and legitimation for the effort to move forward into modernity, using the past 'with the intention of opening the future, as an invitation to action and a basis for hope' (p. 187).

In *The Break-Up of Britain* Tom Nairn reworked this account of anti-colonialist nationalism as a general theory of nation. He thus set himself the uncomfortable task of explaining how nationalism, if it began in the colonised peripheries, could then reappear in the old, imperialist nations at the metropolitan centre (it is said to be due to a process of uneven development). What is particularly valuable in Nairn's analysis is his insistence on the necessary co-presence of 'negative' and 'positive' nationalism. For 'human society' in 'its passage to modernity' nation is constituted in a double effect, like 'the old Roman god, Janus' (1981, p. 348), compelled in the same gesture to look back to some irrationally conceived national tradition so it can gather strength for the ordeal of reaching forward to the most modern forms of production.

The 'spatial' account

While these accounts from Fanon and Nairn, recognising two sides of nation, seek to mark one off from the other on a temporal line extending from past to future (so keeping open a utopian possibility), others aim to draw the line in a spatial dimension. They pick up the lead of Friedrich Meinecke in discriminating between nation as state and nation as culture, between civic and ethnic nation, going on then to describe these as good and bad nation respectively, often in the hope that the bad side may be discarded or superseded altogether.

Writing in 1951 Hannah Arendt celebrates the originally progressive potential of nation through its commitment to the 'rights of Man' and so to a certain universality. But if this democratic force lies on the side of nation as state and its members as citizens, from the first another eventuality loomed because of competition between nations: 'Whenever the nation-state appeared as conqueror it aroused national consciousness and desire for sovereignty among the conquered people' (1951, p. 127). Desire aroused like this, from 1789, effected a slide from nation to nationalism, from state to culture, for 'nationalism is essentially the expression of the perversion of the state into an instrument of the nation and the identification of the citizen with member of the nation' (p. 231).

Arendt's position has come to represent something of an orthodoxy in accounts of nation. Eric Hobsbawm in a recent lecture attacked 'identity politics' as divisive in contrast with the political project of the left, which is universalist in that 'it is for *all* human beings' (1996, p. 43). He went on to find a degree of such democratic universality in nation:

> However, there is one form of identity politics which is actually comprehensive, inasmuch as it is based on a common appeal, at least within the confines of a single state: citizen nationalism. Seen in the global perspective this may be the opposite of a universal appeal, but seen in the perspective of the national state, which is where most of us still live, and are likely to go on living, it provides a common identity.
>
> (p. 45)

A generally more positive response to nation by Hobsbawm than previously, this predictably lays stress on the benefits of the civic nation.

As does Jürgen Habermas when he argues that the democratic possibility of nation can be hived off from its ethnic and cultural collateral:

> the bonding power of a republican community of free and equal members is supposedly insufficient to assure the political stability of a state. I consider this assumption – that democracy needs to be backed up by the bonding energy of a homogeneous nation – to be both empirically false and politically dangerous.
>
> (1996, p. 10)

Politically dangerous because the state will have to enforce homogeneity in a diverse population; empirically false because, in principle, state and culture are not the same thing.

In some contrast to this view of Habermas, a recent book by David Miller, *On Nationality* (1995) affirms bonding in a relatively homogeneous nation is desirable while at the same time it makes one of the strongest possible cases for the nation as an institution compatible with the principles of rationality and liberalism. Miller keeps emphasising the fundamentally democratic tendency structured into the collectivity of national identity, arguing that the national community promotes the self-agency of its members through national sovereignty. The assertion is made precisely and explicitly when Miller states, 'The principle of nationality points us towards a republican conception of citizenship and towards deliberative democracy as the best means of making political decisions' (p. 150). As part of this case Miller refers the modern development of the nation-state not to modernity and desire but to a predominantly rational and democratic reality: 'What was new was the belief that nations could be regarded as active political agents, the bearers of the ultimate powers of sovereignty' (p. 31). He even justifies the way that national identities 'contain a considerable element of myth' (p. 35) on the grounds that even if such myth is false it has a rational purpose in holding the community together.

What makes Miller particularly relevant for the present discussion is that he is directly critical of the tradition of 'civic nationalism' and a narrowly 'rational-individualist' view of citizenship. Against the endorsement of such figures as Arendt, Hobsbawm and Habermas, Miller asserts that if national identity is considered only as something consciously chosen by individuals, this assumes nation as socially atomised; if groups are thought of as tied to one another by nothing beyond the practice of citizenship 'they would insist on strict reciprocity' and 'each would expect to benefit from their association in proportion to his or her contribution' (pp. 71–2). Nations, he proposes, are not and should not be like this. Nations are 'ethical communities' (p. 11) and encourage their members to care for each other in an unchosen relation which goes beyond any purely contractual exchange.

In this aim Miller faces a significant dilemma. From Benedict Anderson he has learned that nation is not an ideology or a club one decides to join but a lived experience. So Miller writes persuasively of national identity as 'intuitive' (p. 27), as hidden 'in the deeper recesses of the mind' (p. 18), formed out of 'mainly subterranean loyalties' (p. 15) and 'implicit understandings' (p. 41). Nation is based on shared loyalties and obligations derived from the way people 'identify' (p. 65) with other members of a group though Miller fails to offer an explanation of how this process of this identification might work (his example is an Oxford college). Thus, *de facto* Miller's account recognises the force and consequence of nation as an unconscious effect though it beats a rapid retreat from any thought of nationalism 'as something to be explained in terms of the subconscious [*sic*] needs of individuals' (p. 6).

Miller wants to discriminate between 'defensible and indefensible versions of the principle of nationality' (p. 40), to advocate a national identity which excludes 'the strident, sometimes almost racist, form that nationalism often takes' (p. 1). He therefore skims off a notion of identity which suits with his liberal purposes while forgetting about any potentially noxious residue. From this thoughtful and good-hearted but ultimately rather provincial defence of nation we must turn to Kristeva to begin to appreciate the price that has to be paid for any kind of identity, including national identity.

Kristeva and 'Esprit général'

Julia Kristeva followed her first book on nation, *Strangers to Ourselves* (discussed in Chapter 2) with another short and finely suggestive essay, *Nations without Nationalism* (1993). Referring back to Hannah Arendt, this once again speaks for the civic nation associated with 1789 and *The Declaration of the Rights of Man and Citizen*. But in a way which is particularly important for my own argument Kristeva's affirmation is undermined when she turns to psychoanalytic sources – here the opposition between civic and ethnic nation begins to be deconstructed.

Kristeva begins with the irrational, pointing out that the feeling for nation can easily regress into a hatred for '*those others* who do not share my origins' (1993, p. 2) modelled on archaic feelings from childhood and attachment to closest relatives. But that 'glorification of origins' correlates to an opposite, a 'hatred of origins' expressed by those 'who repress their roots, who don't want to know where they come from, who detest their own' (p. 2) and think they can 'settle matters by fleeing' (p. 3). This denial, Kristeva implies, arises from the same feeling about origins as that expressing itself in glorification, and she goes in search of an alternative to it.

She finds it in nation considered as an *esprit général*, a term borrowed from Montesquieu, which Kristeva wants to contrast with the notion of *Volksgeist* developed by Herder and later by Hegel. Kristeva's wish is to define nation on the basis of what she refers to as 'the French national model stemming from the Enlightenment' in opposition to the German Romantic tradition in which nation is revered because of its irrational power to issue 'mystical calls' and 'cast a spell on the masses', the *Volk* (p. 45). Collective identity of the kind she prefers would promote citizenship over rooted community and, so Kristeva hopes, be more open to strangers and modernity. Desirable as it may be – a collectivity ('tomorrow, perhaps') in which 'the *esprit général* wins overs the *Volksgeist*' (p. 63) – this recommendation does not correspond to nation as experienced since 1789. It hopes to fillet the bones of nation as state (citizenship, rights, etc.) and leave behind the flesh of nation as culture and lived experience.

As Kristeva knows perfectly enough, for she opens the other side of the argument herself. The possibility of the unconscious cuts across social organisations as conventionally understood and cannot be ignored: 'The complex relationships between cause and effect that govern social groups obviously do not coincide with the laws of the unconscious regarding the subject, but these unconscious determinations remain a constituent part, an essential one, of social and therefore national dynamics' (p. 50). And what the theory of the unconscious has to tell us is that it may not be so easy to separate attractive and unattractive features in nation, to dissolve the subjective glue holding state and culture together. 'Yes', cries Kristeva in a stirring passage,

> let us have universality for the rights of man, provided we integ rate into that universality not only the smug principle according to which 'all men are brothers' but also that portion of conflict, hatred and violence, and destructiveness that for two centuries since the *Declaration* has ceaselessly been unloaded upon the realities of wars and fratricidal closeness and that the Freudian discovery of the unconscious tells us is a surely modifiable but yet constituent portion of the human psyche.
>
> (p. 27)

Kristeva's assured grasp of psychoanalysis does not sit on all fours with her hopeful advocacy of nation as *esprit général*. It is not simply that in human identity and human community irrationality and hatred are present *as well as* reason and love but that these obvious opposites are brought about *together* in a simultaneous process:

> Freud has demonstrated to what extent the conglomeration of men and women into sets is oppressive and death-bearing. 'Society is founded on a common crime', he wrote in *Totem and Taboo*, and the exclusion of 'others', which binds the identity of a clan, a sect, a party, or a nation, is equally the source of the pleasure of identification ('this is what *we* are, therefore it is what *I* am') and of barbaric persecution ('that is foreign to me, therefore I throw it out, hunt it down, or massacre it').
>
> (p. 50)

On similar grounds – that in the human subject the pleasures of identification spring from the same source as a lust for persecution –

Chantal Mouffe has maintained we must surrender all hope of a non-conflictual politics:

> When we accept that every identity is relational and that the condition of existence of every identity is the affirmation of a difference, the determinates of an 'other' that is going to play the role of a 'constitutive outside', it is possible to understand how antagonisms arise. In the domain of collective identification, where what is in question is the creation of a 'we' by the definition of a 'them', the possibility always exists that this 'we/them' relation will turn into a relation of the friend/enemy type.
>
> (1993, pp. 2–3)

Once the question of fantasy and unconscious motivation is broached, identification and hostility appear as different sides of a single piece of paper. This effect is constitutive for any collectivity such as nation, and cannot be evaded.

Nation on the dark side

Freud's reactions to Leninism and the Russian Revolution deserve to be more widely known. In the *New Introductory Lectures* of 1933 he comments on the Marxist theory that operation of the economic 'base' determines the ideological 'superstructure' and on contemporary Soviet belief that changing the economic structure would necessarily lead to changes in ideology. Freud points out that since the child's superego is modelled on that of their parents, each subject becomes 'the vehicle of tradition'. He continues:

> It seems likely that what are known as materialist views of history sin in underestimating this factor. They brush it aside with the remark that human 'ideologies' are nothing other than the product and superstructure of their contemporary economic conditions. That is true, but very probably not the whole truth. Mankind never lives entirely in the present. The past, the tradition of the race and of the people, lives on in the ideologies of the superego, and yields only slowly to the influences of the present and to new changes; and so long as it operates through the superego it plays a powerful part in human life, independently of economic conditions.
>
> (1973–86, 2, p.99)

There's more than one implication in this rich passage.

The terms in which Freud refers here to the superego undoes the inherited opposition between rational and irrational. The voice of conscience which works to impose social order on the human animal does not consist of some kind of free-floating 'rationality' since it is itself in part an unconscious effect. Civilisation is founded when the superego acquires from the unconscious enough force to match animal instinct. By the same logic those seemingly rational aspects of the state emphasised by advocates of civic nationalism (civil rights, the claims of the individual, independent citizenship) do not emerge in a skyey domain beyond the unconscious; charged with narcissism, they are expressions of the ego, which is a function of the unconscious subject. Even the far-seeing 'universality' of reason itself manifests *Bemächtigungstrieb*, 'the drive to mastery'.

Second, Freud's pessimistic sense of temporality – of the past living on into the present – must frustrate hopes that society might ever become essentially non-conflictual. The effects of the unconscious may be 'modifiable', as Kristeva says, but will never go away. Marxism is a product of the Enlightenment, represents an optimistic view that the right application of theory to practice – in this case, correct economic management – will bring about a transformed, just and harmonious society. But psychoanalysis puts in question some of the most cherished expectations of the Enlightenment: rationality and utopia.

Far from being tangential to nation, these reflections have a direct impact on it. It is Hegel, the great philosophic proponent of the nation-state, who foresees it as the highest achievement of an unfolding spirit of rationality as well as the perfect form for collective human freedom. But there is a problem lying at the centre of the idea of nation, something Hegel tries but fails to resolve convincingly.

In *The Philosophy of History* Hegel admits that one nation can only be itself at the expense of other nations equally engaged in a rightful struggle to be themselves. His attempted solution is to draw on the distinction between spirit and its realisation in order to discriminate between nation as universal and nation as particular:

> On the one hand, the spirit of the nation is in essence particular, yet on the other, it is identical with the absolute universal spirit – for the latter is One.... The particular spirit of a particular nation may perish, but it is a link in the chain of the world spirit's development, and this universal spirit cannot perish. The spirit of the nation is therefore the universal spirit in a particular form.
>
> (1975, pp. 52–3)

If Hegel's envisaged reconciliation of universal and particular is not available, then the identity of one nation is endangered by the very existence of another. Conflict leading to a nationalism which jeopardises the democratic promise of nation is not one outcome of the history of nation (as Arendt suggests) but inherent in a situation where there is more than one nation.

Reasons for this are suggested by Paul Ricoeur:

> When we discover that there are several cultures instead of just one and consequently at the time when we acknowledge the end of a sort of cultural monopoly, be it illusory or real, we are threatened with the destruction of our discovery. Suddenly, it becomes possible that there are just *others*, that we are ourselves an 'other' among others.
>
> (1965, p. 278)

The nature of the danger – that if there is an other like me, there is otherness at the heart of myself – is well stated but not adequately explored. The 'cultural monopoly' nation enjoys when it seems to be alone in the world ('Sinn Féin', 'Ourselves Alone'), like that of the infant when it still thinks it's everything, ensues from the sense of presence afforded by imaginary identity. Experience of difference follows from the existence of the symbolic order of which any individual identity is an effect, from the discovery that 'every identity is relational' (in Mouffe's phrasing), that there is alterity at the nucleus of our sense of being ourselves, that ' "I is an other" ' (Lacan 1977a, p. 23). The result tends towards catastrophe.

Lacan, identity and aggression

Leaning on Freud's concept of the subject as constructed as a split between conscious and unconscious, Lacan works out the implications of the view that imaginary and symbolic turn on each other – identity and difference, self and Other, are equally inescapable and inseparable. In 'The Mirror Stage' (as was considered in Chapter 1) the identity of the individual is constituted by being borrowed from the Other. Subsequently, by repeating this internalisation of an idealised reflection of itself the subject aspires to a homogeneity and permanence which will make good its lack, identifying its unity (above all) in an image of the body as a unified whole and fearing (above all) a corresponding image of the body in pieces ('images of castration, mutilation, dismemberment, dislocation, evisceration, devouring, bursting open of the body'; 1977a, p. 11).

> It is in this erotic relation, in which the human individual fixes upon himself an image that alienates him from himself, that are to be found the energy and the form on which this organisation of the passions that he will call his ego is based.
>
> (p. 19)

Since the ego was never *there* in the first place it has to be organised out of fragments bound together to make up a unity, and the active energy that holds it together is always likely to be released against anything that threatens to pull it to pieces. In an essay written just after the Second World War Lacan discusses 'Aggressivity in Psychoanalysis', using the term to look beyond direct acts of aggression to more general feelings present even in what may appear outwardly gestures of human kindness (philanthropy, giving to charity). His argument is that the ego and aggressivity are born together since aggressivity is 'the correlative tendency of a mode of identification that we call narcissistic' (p. 16).

Everything not the I endangers the I – flux challenges its permanence, spatial difference its fixity of position, any alterity its identity, any outside its inside. Desire arises beyond the subject and so the subject's desire always overflows its ego – 'That is why', Lacan writes,

> man's ego can never be reduced to his experienced identity; and in the depressive disruptions of the experienced reverses of inferiority, it engenders essentially the moral negations that fix it in its formalism. 'I am nothing of what happens to me. You are nothing of value.'
>
> (p. 20)

The subject would preserve its coherence by denying what undermines it and projecting internal threat on to the outside. Developing in a 'paranoiac structure' through such acts of negation the ego throws 'back on to the world the disorder' from which it is composed (p. 20). At worst, in its ultimate expression, the logic of aggressivity correlative to the ego must be: 'If I'm taking you to pieces, nothing can be taking me to pieces.'

What is the case for individual identity must hold equally for collective identity, for those groups whose members identify with a common object and so find identification with each other. All collective identity (clan, nation, region, ethnic group) identifies self by denying the other, demarcates inside from outside, stretches a distance between 'us' and 'them'. The condition for collective identification – 'my blood, my family, my kin, my clan, my nation, my race' – is an ever-present and potentially violent expulsion of those who are *not* 'my blood, my family, my kin, my clan, my nation, my race'.

Žižek and 'the Thing'

At this point I shall turn aside to confront a major counter-theorisation of nation, with the intention of rebutting it and so confirming my own account. Slavoj Žižek's casually brilliant theory of nation (see 1991a but especially 1994, pp. 200–37) is a rival which also draws authority from Lacanian psychoanalysis: 'national identity constitutes itself through resistance to its oppression – the fight for national revival is therefore *a defence of something which comes to be only through being experienced as lost or endangered*' (citing Hegel in the italicised words, 1991b, p. 802). What he sees as endangered, though, is not collective identity in a narcissistic organisation but a love object. In *Tarrying with the Negative* Žižek draws on Lacan's account of 'the Thing' (*das Ding*) to argue that at the heart of nation there is what he christens the Nation-Thing: 'The element which holds together a given community cannot be reduced to the point of symbolic identification: the bond linking together its members always implies a shared relationship towards a Thing, towards Enjoyment incarnated' (p. 201; 'enjoyment' is the Lacanian *jouissance*).

In support of his view that 'National identification is by definition sustained by a relationship towards the Nation qua Thing' (p. 201), Žižek adduces four main arguments:

1 the Nation-Thing 'is present in that elusive entity called "our way of life"...the way our community organises its feasts, its rituals of mating, its initiation ceremonies, in short, all the details by which is made visible the unique way a community *organises its enjoyment*' (p. 201);
2 this way of life is elusive, invisible, defies enumeration by features because 'the national Thing exists as long as members of the community believe in it' (p. 202); the character of this belief is tautological having a form in which '"I believe in the (national) Thing" equals "I believe that others (members of my community) believe in the Thing"' (p. 202); the 'structure' of this belief is the same as belief in 'the Holy Spirit in Christianity' (p. 202);
3 no 'deconstructionist' account of nation as 'pure discursive effect', as 'a contingent discursive construction, an overdetermined result of textual practices', is sufficient since it 'overlooks the remainder of some *real*, non-discursive kernel of enjoyment which must be present' (p. 202) for nation to have the substance it does;

4 we impute excessive enjoyment to the other and fear 'he wants to steal our enjoyment' (p. 203), so treating our Thing as 'accessible only to us', something 'they' cannot grasp but which is none the less 'constantly menaced by "them"' (p. 201).

A preliminary point: Žižek bases his account on Lacan's theory of *La chose* though this figures mainly in his book on ethics (1960/1992) and is rethought as *objet petit a* by the time of Seminar 11 (1964/1977b), as Dylan Evans brings out (see 1996, p. 205)]. Overall, I would reply that Žižek's first argument (1) is a debating move. It prevents me (or anyone) from naming national activities in which the pleasure is the narcissistic one of collective identification because, in advance, it has defined *all* the collective activities of a community as ways of organising enjoyment. Point (2) does no more than re-phrase around 'the Thing' what Freud says about the organisation of collective identification in relation to a shared object: that the individual's identification with nation becomes an identification with others. What Žižek says about the structure of belief and the Holy Spirit assimilates perfectly to Freud's account of common identification with the shared object of Jesus (and if the Holy Spirit is thought of as a less concrete object than Jesus we should recall Freud's claim that for a shared object such as this 'an idea, an abstraction' will do just as well).

It would be possible to accept (3) that *some* affect in nation ensues from 'the Thing' (or something like it) while maintaining the priority of nation as a consequence of identification (Lacan after all speaks of the 'organisation of the passions' in the ego as an 'erotic relation'). Žižek insists on an improper either/or. He fails to address the relation of identity assumed by all the 'we's' and 'our's' in his own account (how did this identity get to be there?). In dismissing 'deconstructionist' accounts of nation (such as that offered in these pages) because they see nation as a 'pure discursive effect' he overlooks the fact that there can be no such thing as a *pure* discursive effect since every discursive effect is an effect in and for a subject (Lacan declares more than once that 'a signifier is that which represents the subject for another signifier'; 1977a, p. 316).

As for (4), the relation between self and other described, what is 'accessible only to us' but menaced by them, can be understood in terms of projection and paranoia without necessarily invoking 'the Thing' at all. It is Lacan who insists on the 'paranoiac structure of the ego' (and so, by implication, of the collective ego of the nation), for the I trusts to an identity accessible only to itself while being endlessly sabotaged by the fact that this identity is stolen from the Other whose very existence is a constant menace. If aggressivity is to characterise nation, then it would be closer to the teaching of Lacan to regard it as likely to arise from a narcissistic structure. Žižek's account defines nation as continuously trembling on the edge of violence against those who seem to steal its enjoyment. What needs to be explained is how the sunny and transparent appearance of nation, which may last for years, even decades, as a relaxed group collectively in love with ordinary common objects (a sporting event, the ritual change of president, a weather report on television) and so in love with each other, can with suave and unnerving continuity suddenly move into hatred if it comes to feel the other as a threat which puts in question its own identity and existence.

Nation and aggressivity

If all human identities – individual and collective – can become what they are only because of their inescapable dependence on what we might like to think of as 'inhuman' possibilities, nation will not be immune from this law. For those writing on nation in the West in the years after 1945 – Arendt and many others (see discussion Chapter 1, pp. 6–12) – the excesses of nationalism were a scandal. How could the civic nation of citizens, with its origins in modernity, rationalism and the Enlightenment, become so easily perverted into nationalism? Yet one might easily contend that nation is *more* likely than other comparable collectivities to slide towards the dark side contained within its otherwise bright identity.

For that possibility one could argue like this. As a product of modernity nation arises more on the side of *Gesellschaft* than *Gemeinschaft*, is more obviously 'constructed' and has a less definite claim on 'nature' than pre-national collectivities. And while pre-national collectivities (clans, regional groupings) might well feel their own identity was simply incommensurate with that of potentially competing groups around them – might even think they were unique – nation cannot similarly evade dangerous comparisons. In virtue of its more conscious construction and seeming universality, the existence of one nation presupposes other identical nations, with the consequences that cause Hegel such anxiety and which might be phrased as: 'if the other is so like me, the other is within'.

The intensity with which nation has been embraced – that recorded, for example, by Stendhal – does not speak of the solidity and strength of nation but rather of its fragility. Nation is almost certain to be actually more heterogeneous in its membership than a pre-national grouping, more mixed by race, class, gender, regional loyalty, etc. At the same time, and unlike collectivities before modernity, nation is composed of two separate aspects, a modern state and a culture, which can never in fact become unified though their difference provokes the wish that they may be. Again, because of its origin with modernity, the signifiers in the symbolic order which members of a particular nation identify with are harder to bury away in the imaginary, they are just more apparent (the flag in the sequence from *Drums along the Mohawk*).

But it is not difficult to argue back the other way, reading every term in an opposing direction. While nation is more obviously constructed than pre-national collectivities, it has by the virtue of the same effect discovered equivalent and appropriate ways to maintain its own stability, of which the most evident is the modern state as it ramifies through the whole apparatus of society and culture. Pre-national collectivities may seem more homogeneous than nation but they do not have nation's developed capacity to produce the effect of homogeneity through citizenship and state institutions. And nation has the unprecedented historical feature that it can command the allegiance of its members on the basis of a claim to democratic participation.

Beside the fact that we are still rather too close to nation to gain adequate analytic distance on it, the obstacle in judging whether nation is more precarious than other collectivities is that nation is the product of modernity and so, in contemporary conditions, little alternative to it can be imagined. In this respect, as Marx suggested, history sets us only the problems we can solve. If the lack at the heart of nation is greater than in comparable historical organisations, then this absence will incite a correspondingly greater desire for the presence and plenitude of national identity. If on one side nation is structured by modernity with a passionate frailty, on the other, it is cemented together by its special purchase on modernity.

Like every human collectivity nation cannot insulate itself from the fear of coming to pieces and the desire to contain that threat by directing violence at another. This possibility will never go away, if, that is, the argument deriving aggression from identity is correct.

A lucid pessimism

Between 23 April and 6 May 1994 fighting between the Hutu and Tutsi clans in Rwanda led to the extermination of what at first was thought to be 200,000 and later revised upwards to over a million civilians. In the years after 1992 and the collapse of Yugoslavia as many as 200,000 have died, often in terrible ways, through 'ethnic cleansing'. Many have been tempted to lay these atrocities once again at the door of nation as revealing the bloody face and true nature of nationalism.

This is too easy, as Tom Nairn has explained. Even if one sets aside the view that the conflict in Rwanda has not really concerned nation at all but clans, neither that situation nor Yugoslavia disclose what nation is really like since both concern what may happen if nation is *not* in place. 'Ethnic nationalism erupted because civic-democratic nationalism was never given a chance', as Nairn puts it (1995, p. 102); disaster overcame people in situations where the structures of the nation-state were not already solidly entrenched.

Two inferences may be drawn from this. The first is that – as Arendt and the others foresee – the 'rational' possibilities secured in the civic and state feature of nation may mitigate the risk attending national identity through its aggressive correlate. Mitigate but not remove. And this opens on to what is, arguably, the central topic of our time, one which re-emerges in every discussion of gender, race, ethnicity, class, sexuality, nation, Eurocentrism and Orientalism. How can there be identity which does not disparage, deny and – in the worst form of its rationale – seek to annihilate the Other which that same identity produces along with itself? How (to change the register) can there be presence *and* difference, a necessary presence which is not won at the expense of difference?

Any conclusion from the preceding argument has to concur with Kristeva and with Chantal Mouffe. No utopian programme can extricate the construction of human identity from its interweaving with atrocious possibilities. There is no non-conflictual resolution of the opposition between self and Other, no foundational sanction inclining us once and for all towards the human rather than the 'inhuman'.

Nairn has countenanced this eventuality, interestingly, by referring to the same political events as does Freud in the passage where he insists that a distant human past lives on into the present, the Soviet Revolution. In so far as the aspiration to world communism was a child of the Enlightenment and an alternative to the sectarian irrationalities of nation, that hope could not survive 1989 and the collapse of the Soviet regime (accompanied, as it was, when the People's Republic of China surrendered most of state control of the economy to market forces). Nairn writes:

> The persisting spirit of the European Enlightenment has always been terribly disappointed by its firstborn, Capitalism. Its eldest son, Nationalism, remains even more of a nuisance. But it no longer has the faintest hope of getting rid of either of them. It was this hope which ended around 1989, not history.... One reaction to post-1989 events is a lucid pessimism, the

> abandonment of hope by all who have approached them via this particular intellectual portal.
>
> (p. 96)

To accept that we can't get rid of capitalism is not to give up all attempts to inflect and control a capitalist system. Nation, besides being historically necessary in present conditions, has a strongly progressive aspect (as is well argued by David Miller and, elsewhere, by Nairn himself). As for the Enlightenment, this has not been wholly abandoned in a pessimism which claims to be lucid.

England now

In 1995 the radical think-tank, Demos, published a report, *Freedom's Children* detailing attitudes to work, relationships and politics among England's 18- to 34-year-olds (Wilkinson and Mulgan 1995). This analysis of 'Thatcher's Generation' resulted from a year-long project involving a large number of researchers in different universities and drawing on group discussions as well as surveys carried out by MORI *Socioconsult.* Under the heading '*Hostility to the system and the nation*' the report described how 'young people now take pride in being out of the system' (p. 106) and displayed the results of a 'disconnection index'. This was arrived at by aggregating responses to a number of statements:

> agreement with the statements 'I do not feel that I'm part of the British system and I'm proud of it' and 'if I had the chance I would emigrate' and disagreement with the statements 'I feel that I really belong to this neighbourhood' and 'on the whole I prefer to buy British'.

Only 8 per cent of those aged 65+ felt disconnected, rising on an even line to 37 per cent for 25- to 34-year-olds and 54 per cent for the 18–24 age group. The Demos document was reported in the press as showing 'a diminishing attachment to any national identity' among the young (*Guardian*, 25 September 1995).

These sociological findings pose the usual problems of interpretation. What about the 36 per cent of the 18–24 age group who presumably *did* feel connected to the nation, some of whom were only too conspicuous during England's European Cup run in the summer of 1996? Can we be sure the statement 'I do not feel part of the British system' is not made from the bravura of youth? It may be these young people in Britain answered as they did because they just felt disconnected or it may be that, unlike their French equivalents, they had never been formally taught the virtues of their nation.

Even more problematic, in the context espoused by the present discussion, is an assumption that adults give valid answers to questions because self-reflection reveals to them the full contents of their own minds. One could read the Demos conclusions at face value. Or one could interpret them as a symptom of the ambivalence about nation acutely diagnosed by Kristeva. A traditional nationalistic 'glorification of origins' corresponds negatively to a denial of origins from those 'who repress their roots, who don't want to know where they come from, who detest their own' and think they can 'settle matters by fleeing' (Kristeva 1993, p. 2). Before coming back to these avowedly 'a-national' under-25s, I want to make a short detour.

Something similar to this contradictory formation of assertion and denial of nation said to be evident in the generation that matured under Thatcher also figured, though in a much more charged version, in German discussions of the Nazi period in the so-called 'Historians' Debate'. During the 1980s certain conservative writers took up the question of 'coming to terms with the past' by seeking to normalise German responsibility by arguing, for example, that the Nazi Holocaust had to be measured against Stalin's Gulag, or that any historian faced with choice as it appeared in 1945 – between Hitler, the victorious Red Army, or the German army – would opt for the brave German soldiers defending the civilian population. The position taken attempted to relativise German accountability and by this move open a way back to a persisting and still honourable German national identity. It is like the manoeuvre Kristeva refers to but in inverse form – retreat from contemporary identity and responsibility corresponds to a covert attempt to reconsecrate past honour.

In a series of newspaper articles in 1986 Habermas intervened directly in this debate, addressing the question 'Can one become the legal successor to the German Reich and continue the traditions of German culture without taking on historical liability for the form of life in which Auschwitz was possible?' (1989, p. 236).

Despite his proclaimed commitment to nation as republican community rather than homogeneous culture, in the context of this argument Habermas angrily rejected the tactic of maintaining continuity by denying unattractive aspects of the full historical narrative. In a powerful passage he argued instead for the necessity to accept good and bad in a national identity together, a necessity which persuasively carries him far from the idea of the civic nation and the bonding of the 'republican community' into a recognition of the deep roots of national culture and of the nation as libidinal relationship:

> there is the simple fact that subsequent generations also grew up within a form of life in which *that* was possible. Our own life is linked to the life context in which Auschwitz was possible not by contingent circumstances but intrinsically. Our form of life is connected with that of our parents and grandparents through a web of familial, local, political, and intellectual traditions that is difficult to disentangle – that is, through a historical milieu that made us what and who we are today. None of us can escape this milieu, because our identities, both as individuals and as Germans, are indissolubly interwoven with it. This holds true from mimicry and physical gestures to language and into the capillary ramifications of one's intellectual stance. As though when teaching at universities outside Germany I could ever disclaim a mentality in which the traces of a very German intellectual dynamic from Kant to Marx and Max Weber are inscribed. We have to stand by our traditions, then, if we do not want to disavow ourselves.
>
> (pp. 232–3)

Nation, on this showing, offers not just a citizenship but an identity into which (to use a term from Heidegger) one is thrown and in which certain responsibilities inhere.

Here Habermas does not think of nation as consisting just of some knowable, conscious viewpoints and themes. He recognises that beyond these identity presents itself through identification with what he lists (a little uneasily) as 'mimicry', 'physical gestures', 'language', 'the traces of a very German intellectual dynamic'. I am compelled to claim that this cluster can be better understood as effects of national identity in the form of a specific discursive formation, what Habermas realises he could never disclaim because it writes him when he thinks he is speaking in his own voice.

For the English as we approach the new millennium an acceptance of national identity along the lines set out by Habermas would entail finding a responsible position towards Empire and the loss of Empire (including what could reasonably be described as an act of genocide towards the Irish people in 1847). And it would require an attempt to step aside from the contradiction in which glorification and hatred of origins together form a pair of opposites (one which seems very much alive in some current English attitudes towards the European Union).

With these questions in mind I would return to the English 18- to 24-year-olds. That many of them feel alienated from the official world of Englishness is hardly surprising since it has let many of them down bitterly over the past decade and a half through unemployment and cuts in the welfare state. But I wonder if their flight from national roots may not mean something more.

David Miller summarises shrewdly three main reasons why the attractions of English identity have been eroded in the post-war period: Britain's 'relatively dismal economic performance'; increasing evidence of Britain's constitution (or lack of it) as 'a ramshackle contrivance' compared with that of the United States or Germany; the manifest refusal of ex-colonies to sustain political institutions modelled on the 'Mother of Parliaments' (pp. 170–2). Beneath all these lies the end of Empire, so that England today is only too well caricatured by Christine Brooke-Rose when she describes the country as 'a crotchety old lady backside to the continent with stretched legs driving a motorcar into the Atlantic, Ireland as the wheel' (1996, p. 11).

Could it be that the 54 per cent who led their interviewers to believe they felt 'disconnected' from Englishness did not in fact feel so differently from the 36 per cent who did not get classified as disconnected? On one side there is an assembly of relatively naive youth who exalt a glorification of England as they have been taught it by mainly right-wing celebrants, while on the other there are the disaffected young. But could it be that those fleeing from their origins, in a classic expression of *denial*, are active in rejecting English national identity because it cannot measure up to the imperial visions they have inherited, as though to say 'If I cannot have Great Britain I don't want England at all'?

If that were the case it would not be the end of the story or at least the story I've given prominence to. For, surely, whether they do feel connected to Englishness or not, almost all these youthful subjects will have been produced within and will unconsciously be reproducing the inherited English discourse? They will speak and write in a discursive form with almost the full range of ironies, jokes, empiricist tropes and gestures, including what I have referred to as 'The Great Oppositions', all as natural as driving a car. And along with that interwoven identity, whether they acknowledge it or not, they inherit responsibilities.

This may indicate one last, significant possibility for speculation. Even in their avowed disaffection from the state and official Englishness these young English people cannot flee from a particular set of discourses in which they find their identities. Could it be that a post-modern subject for nation may be emerging for whom nation as independent nation-state matters somewhat less than nation as culture?

If a subject were to be constituted in a more open avowal of its dependence on a particular set of signifiers, it would be more dispersed; a different economy could have been at work in the correlation of identity and aggression necessary to its formation. An identity might begin to develop which, though still a national identity, held a much reduced potential for moving on to the dark side, into the bad excesses of nationalism.

BIBLIOGRAPHY

Allnutt, Gillian *et al.* (eds) (1988) *The New British Poetry*, London: Paladin.

Althusser, Louis (1977) 'Ideology and Ideological State Apparatuses', in *Lenin and Philosophy*, 2nd edn, London: Verso, pp. 121–73.

Althusser, Louis and Balibar, Etienne (1970) *Reading Capital*, trans. Ben Brewster, London: New Left Books.

Alvarez, Al (ed.) (1962) *The New Poetry*, Harmondsworth: Penguin.

Anderson, Benedict (1991) *Imagined Communities: Reflections on the Origin and Spread of Nationalism*, revised edn, London: Verso.

Anderson, Perry (1964) 'Origins of the Present Crisis', *New Left Review*, 23 (January/February), pp. 26–53.

—— (1966) 'Socialism and Pseudo-Empiricism', *New Left Review* 35 (January/February), pp. 2–42.

—— (1968) 'Components of the National Culture', *New Left Review* 50 (July/August), pp. 3–58.

—— (1979) *Lineages of the Absolutist State*, London: Verso.

Arendt, Hannah (1951) *The Origins of Totalitarianism*, New York: Harcourt Brace.

Ascham, Roger (1570) *The Scholemaster*, in William Wright (ed.), *English Works*, Cambridge: Cambridge University Press, 1904.

Ashbee, C.R. (1928) *Caricature*, London: Chapman and Hall.

Aubrey, John (1972) *Aubrey's Brief Lives*, Harmondsworth: Penguin.

Ayers, Michael (1991) *Locke*, 2 vols, London: Routledge.

Bacon, Francis (1857–74) *The Works*, eds James Spedding, Robert Ellis, Douglas Heath, 14 vols, London: Longman.

—— (1974) *The Advancement of Learning*, ed. Arthur Johnson, Oxford: Clarendon Press.

Balakrishnan, Gopal (1995) 'The National Imagination', *New Left Review* 211 (May/June), pp. 56–69.

—— (ed.) (1996) *Mapping the Nation*, London: Verso.

Baldick, Chris (1983) *The Social Mission of English Criticism, 1848–1932*, Oxford: Blackwell.

Balibar, Etienne (1991) 'The Nation Form: History and Ideology', in Etienne

Balibar and Immanuel Wallerstein (eds), *Race, Nation, Class*, trans. Chris Turner, London: Verso, pp. 86–106.

Barthes, Roland (1975) *S/Z*, trans. R. Miller, London: Cape.

— (1977) 'Introduction to the Structural Analysis of Narratives', in *Image-Music-Text*, London: Collins, pp. 79–124.

—— (1981) 'The Discourse of History', trans. Stephen Bann in Elizabeth Schaffer (ed.), *Comparative Criticism: A Yearbook III*, Cambridge: Cambridge University Press, pp. 3–20.

Bauer, Otto (1996) 'The Nation', in Gopal Balakrishnan (ed.), *Mapping Nation*, London: Verso, pp. 39–77.

Beckett, Samuel (1963) *Watt*, London: John Calder.

Bedient, Calvin (1974) *Eight Contemporary Poets*, London: Oxford University Press.

Bell, Julian (1938) *Essays, Poetry and Letters*, London: Hogarth.

Belsey, Catherine (1985) *The Subject of Tragedy*, London: Methuen.

Bennington, Geoff (1987) 'The Perfect Cheat: Locke and Empiricism's Rhetoric', in Andrew Benjamin, Geoffrey Cantor and John Christie (eds), *The Figural and the Literal*, Manchester: Manchester University Press, pp. 103–23.

Benveniste, Emile (1971) *Problems in General Linguistics*, Miami: University of Miami Press.

Bergonzi, Bernard (1990) *Exploding English*, Oxford: Clarendon Press.

Birch, Anthony H. (1989) *Nationalism and National Integration*, London: Unwin Hyman.

Blake, William (1966) *Complete Writings*, ed. Geoffrey Keynes, London: Oxford University Press.

Bloom, Harold (1986) 'Introduction', in H. Bloom (ed.), *Seamus Heaney*, New Haven: Chelsea House, pp. 1–10.

Booth, Wayne C. (1961) *A Rhetoric of Fiction*, Chicago, IL: University of Chicago Press.

Boswell, James (1945) *Life of Dr Johnson*, New York: Scribners.

Bourdieu, Pierre (1993) *The Field of Cultural Production*, ed. Randal Johnson, Cambridge: Polity.

Bradshaw, Graham (1983) 'Creative Mythology in *Cave Birds*', in Keith Sagar (ed.), *The Achievement of Ted Hughes*, Manchester: Manchester University Press, pp. 210–38.

Braudel, Fernand (1988) *The Identity of France*, 2 vols, London: Collins.

Brecht, Bertolt (1964) *Brecht on Theatre*, ed. J. Willett, London: Methuen.

—— (1965) *The Messingkauf Dialogues*, trans. John Willett, London: Methuen.

Breuilly, John (1982) *Nationalism and the State*, Manchester: Manchester University Press.

Bromley, Simon (1996) 'Globalisation?', *Radical Philosophy* 80 (November/December), pp. 2–5.

Brooke-Rose, Christine (1996) *Remake*, Manchester: Carcanet.

Calder-Marshall, Arthur (ed.) (1966) *Wish You Were Here: The Art of Donald McGill*, London: Hutchinson.

Carr, E.H. (1945) *Nationalism and After*, London: Macmillan.
—— (1964) *What is History?*, Harmondsworth: Penguin.
Carroll, Lewis (1952) *Alice's Adventures in Wonderland*, London: Dent.
Cohen, G.A. (1985) *History, Labour, and Freedom*, Oxford: Clarendon Press.
Coleridge, Samuel Taylor (1907) *Biographia Literaria*, ed. J. Shawcross, 2 vols, London: Oxford University Press.
—— (1956) *Collected Letters*, ed. E.L. Griggs, 6 vols, London: Oxford University Press.
Colley, Linda (1992) *Britons: Forging the Nation, 1787–1837*, New Haven, CT and London: Yale University Press.
Conquest, Robert (ed.) (1956) *New Lines*, London: Macmillan.
Corcoran, Neil (1986) *Seamus Heaney*, London: Faber.
Crowley, Tony (1989) *The Politics of Discourse*, London: Macmillan.
Crozier, Andrew (1983) 'Thrills and Frills: Poetry as Figures of Empirical Lyricism', in Alan Sinfield (ed.), *Society and Literature 1945–1970*, London: Methuen, pp. 199–233.
Crozier, Andrew and Longville, Tim (eds) (1990) *A Various Art*, London: Paladin.
Darwin, Charles (1970) *The Origin of Species*, Harmondsworth: Penguin.
Davie, Donald (1973) *Thomas Hardy and English Poetry*, London: Routledge and Kegan Paul.
—— (1989) *Under Briggflats: A History of Poetry in Great Britain 1960–1988*, Manchester: Carcanet.
Davis, Horace. B. (1978) *Towards a Marxist Theory of Nationalism*, New York: Monthly Review Press.
Day, Roger *et al.* (1976) 'Philip Larkin', Unit 28, *Twentieth Century Poetry* (A 306), Milton Keynes: Open University Press.
Day Lewis, C. (1936) *A Hope for Poetry*, Oxford: Blackwell.
Debray, Régis (1977) 'Marxism and the National Question', *New Left Review*, 105 (September/October), pp. 25–41.
de Certeau, Michel (1988) *The Writing of History*, trans. T. Conley, New York: Columbia University Press.
Deleuze, Gilles (1990) *The Logic of Sense*, trans. Mark Lester, London: Athlone Press; *Logique du sens*, Paris: Minuit, 1969.
de Man, Paul (1983) *Blindness and Insight*, 2nd edn, London: Routledge.
Derrida, Jacques (1976) *Of Grammatology*, trans. Gayatri Spivak, Baltimore, MD: Johns Hopkins University Press.
—— (1978) *Writing and Difference*, trans. Alan Bass, London: Routledge and Kegan Paul.
—— (1980) *The Archaeology of the Frivolous: Reading Condillac*, trans. John P. Leavey, Jr, Lincoln, NB and London: University of Nebraska Press.
—— (1981) *Dissemination*, trans. Barbara Johnson, London: Athlone Press.
—— (1982) *Margins of Philosophy*, trans. Alan Bass, Brighton: Harvester.
—— (1984) *Otobiographies*, Paris: Galilée.
—— (1987) 'The Laws of Reflection: Nelson Mandela, in Admiration', in *For Nelson Mandela*, ed. Jacques Derrida and Mustapha Tlili, New York: Henry Holt, pp. 13–42.

—— (1992a) *Given Time: I. Counterfeit Money*, trans. Peggy Kamuf, Chicago and London: University of Chicago Press.

—— (1992b) *The Other Heading: Reflections on Today's Europe*, trans. Pascale-Anne Brault and Michael B. Naas, Bloomington, IN: Indiana University Press.

—— (1992c) 'Onto-Theology of National-Humanism (Prolegomena to a Hypothesis)', *Oxford Literary Review* 14: 1–2, pp. 3–23.

—— (1993) *Aporias*, trans. Thomas Dutoit, Stanford, CA: Stanford University Press.

—— (1994) *Specters of Marx*, trans. Peggy Kamuf, New York and London: Routledge.

—— (1997) *Politics of Friendship*, trans. George Collins, London: Verso.

Doyle, Brian (1989) *English and Englishness*, London: Routledge.

Dryden, John (1962) *Poems and Fables*, ed. James Kinsley, London: Oxford University Press.

Dunn, John (1984) *Locke*, Oxford: Oxford University Press.

Durozoi, Gérard and André Roussel (1987) *Dictionnaire de philosophie*, Paris: Natten.

Dyson, A.E. (1975) 'Ted Hughes', in Graham Martin and P.N. Furbank (eds), *Twentieth Century Poetry*, Milton Keynes: Open University Press, pp. 423–31.

Eagleton, Terry (1976) *Criticism and Ideology: A Study in Marxist Literary Theory*, London: Verso.

—— (1984) *The Function of Criticism*, London: Verso.

—— (1988) 'The Silences of David Lodge', *New Left Review* 172 (November/December), pp. 93–102.

Eley, Geoff and Nield, Keith (1995) 'Starting Over: The Present, the Post-Modern and the Moment of Social History', *Social History* 20: 3 (October), pp. 355–64.

Eliot, T.S. (1957) *On Poetry and Poets*, London: Faber.

—— (1963) *Collected Poems 1909–1962*, London: Faber.

—— (1966) *Selected Essays*, London: Faber.

—— (1970) *For Lancelot Andrewes*, London: Faber.

Elliott, Gregory (1995) 'Olympus Mislaid? A Profile of Perry Anderson', *Radical Philosophy* 71 (May/June), pp. 5–19.

Engels, Frederick (1969) *The Condition of the Working Class in England*, St Albans: Granada.

Evans, Dylan (1996) *An Introductory Dictionary of Lacanian Psychoanalysis*, London: Routledge.

Fanon, Franz (1967) *The Wretched of the Earth*, Harmondsworth: Penguin.

Fenollosa, Ernest (1962) 'The Chinese Written Character as a Medium for Poetry', in Karl Shapiro (ed.), *Prose Keys to Modern Poetry*, New York: Harper and Row, pp. 136–55.

Fish, Stanley (1967) *Surprised by Sin: The Reader in 'Paradise Lost'*, London: Macmillan.

—— (1974) *Self-Consuming Artifacts*, Berkeley, CA: University of California Press.

—— (1989) *Doing What Comes Naturally*, Oxford: Oxford University Press.

Forrester, John (1990) *The Seductions of Psychoanalysis*, Cambridge: Cambridge University Press.

Foster, Thomas C. (1989) *Seamus Heaney*, Boston, MA: Hall.

Foucault, Michel (1979) *Discipline and Punish*, Harmondsworth: Penguin.

Freud, Sigmund (1953–74) 'A Difficulty in the Path of Psycho-Analysis', in *Standard Edition*, 24 vols, London: Hogarth Press and the Institute of Psycho-Analysis, 17, pp. 136–44.

—— (1973–86) *Pelican Freud Library*, 15 vols, Harmondsworth: Penguin.

Frye, Northrop (1947) *Fearful Symmetry: A Study of William Blake*, Princeton, NJ: Princeton University Press.

Gardner, Helen (1982) *In Defence of the Imagination*, London: Oxford University Press.

Gates, Henry L. (1988) *The Signifying Monkey*, New York: Oxford University Press.

Gellner, Ernest (1964) *Thought and Change*, London: Weidenfeld and Nicolson.

Gervais, David (1993) *Literary Englands*, Cambridge: Cambridge University Press.

Giddens, Anthony (1985) *The Nation-State and Violence*, Cambridge: Polity.

Gilroy, Paul (1992) 'Ethnic Absolutism', in Cary Nelson, Paula A. Treichler and Lawrence Grossberg, (eds), *Cultural Studies*, New York and London: Routledge, pp. 187–98.

—— (1993) *Small Acts*, London: Serpent's Tooth.

Gombrich, E.H. (1940) *Caricature*, Harmondsworth: Penguin.

Gray, Frances (1994) *Women and Laughter*, London: Macmillan.

Gross, John (1969) *The Rise and Fall of the Man of Letters*, London: Weidenfeld and Nicolson.

Guibernau, Montserrat (1996) *Nationalism*, Cambridge: Polity.

Habermas, Jürgen (1989) 'On the Public Use of History', in *The New Conservatism*, trans. Shierry Weber Nicholsen, Cambridge: Polity, pp. 228–40.

—— (1996) 'National Unification and Popular Sovereignty', *New Left Review* 219 (September/October), pp. 3–21.

Hampson, Robert and Barry, Peter (1993) *The New British Poetries*, Manchester: Manchester University Press.

Harris, Nigel (1992) *National Liberation*, Harmondsworth: Penguin.

Heaney, Seamus (1975) *North*, London: Faber.

—— (1987) *The Haw Lantern*, London: Faber.

—— (1990) 'Englands of the Mind', in Dennis Walder (ed.), *Literature of the Modern World*, Oxford: Oxford University Press, pp. 250–7.

Hegel, G.W.F. (1956) *The Philosophy of History*, trans. J. Sibree, New York: Dover.

—— (1975) *Lectures on the Philosophy of World History*, 'Introduction' (second draft, 1830), trans. H.B. Nisbet, Cambridge: Cambridge University Press.

Heidegger, Martin (1962) *Being and Time*, trans. J. Macquarrie and E. Robinson, Oxford: Blackwell.

Himmelfarb, Gertrude (1992) 'Telling It as You Like It: Post-modernist History and the Flight from Fact', *TLS*, 16 October, pp. 12–15.

Hirst, Paul Q. and Woolley, Penny (1982) *Social Relations and Human Attributes*, London: Macmillan.

Hobbes, Thomas (1908) 'Preface to Homer', in J.E. Spingarn (ed.), *Critical Essays of the Seventeenth Century*, 3 vols, Oxford: Clarendon Press.

—— (1991) *Leviathan*, ed. Richard Tuck, Cambridge: Cambridge University Press.

Hobsbawm, Eric (1992) *Nations and Nationalism since 1780*, 2nd edn, Cambridge: Cambridge University Press.

—— (1996) 'Identity Politics and the Left', *New Left Review* 217 (May/June), pp. 38–47.

Hobsbawm, Eric and Ranger, Terence (eds) (1983) *The Invention of Tradition*, Cambridge: Cambridge University Press.

Holbrook, David (1977) *Lost Bearings in English Poetry*, London: Vision Press.

Holmes, Frederick M. (1990) 'The Reader as Discoverer in David Lodge's *Small World*', *Critique* 32: 1 (Fall), pp. 47–57.

Hughes, Ted (1957) *The Hawk in the Rain*, London: Faber.

—— (1960) *Lupercal*, London: Faber.

Hutcheon, Linda (1991) *Splitting Images: Contemporary Canadian Ironies*, Toronto, Ont.: Oxford University Press.

—— (1994) *Irony's Edge: The Theory and Politics of Irony*, London and New York: Routledge.

Hutchinson, John and Smith, Anthony D. (eds) (1994) *Nationalism*, Oxford: Oxford University Press.

Huxley, T.H. (1879) *Hume* (English Men of Letters), London: Macmillan.

James, Paul (1996) *Nation Formation*, London: Sage.

Jenkins, Keith (ed.) (1997) *The Postmodern History Reader*, London: Routledge.

Joyce, Patrick (1993) 'The Imaginary Discontents of Social History', *Social History* 18: 1 (January), pp. 82–5.

—— (1995) 'The End of Social History?', *Social History* 20: 1 (January), pp. 72–91.

Joyce, Patrick and Kelly, Catriona (1991) 'History and Post-modernism I and II', *Past and Present* 133 (November), pp. 204–13.

Jung, C.G. (1953–77) *Collected Works*, trans. R.F.C. Hull, 20 vols, London: Routledge and Kegan Paul.

Kamenka, Eugene (ed.) (1976) *Nationalism*, London: Arnold.

Kedourie, Elie (1961) *Nationalism*, revised edn, London: Hutchinson.

Kenner, Hugh (1987) *A Sinking Island: The Modern English Writers*, London: Barrie and Jenkins.

Kettle, Arnold (1976) 'Literature and Ideology', *Red Letters* (Communist Party Literature Journal) 1, pp. 3–5.

King, Richard (1991) 'The Discipline of Fact/The Freedom of Fiction?', *Journal of American Studies* 25: 2, pp. 171–88.

Kirk, Neville (1994) 'History, Language, Ideas and Post-modernism: A Materialist View', *Social History* 19: 2 (May), pp. 221–40.

Kohn, Hans (1965) *Nationalism: Its Meaning and History*, revised edn, New York and Cincinnati, OH: Van Nostrand.

Kristeva, Julia (1991) *Strangers to Ourselves*, trans. Leon Roudiez, London: Harvester Wheatsheaf.

—— (1993) *Nations without Nationalism*, trans. Leon S. Roudiez, New York: Columbia University Press.

Lacan, Jacques (1977a) *Ecrits*, trans. Alan Sheridan, London: Tavistock.

—— (1977b) *The Four Fundamental Concepts of Psycho-Analysis*, London: Hogarth.

—— (1988a) *The Seminar of Jacques Lacan: Book I*, trans. John Forrester, Cambridge: Cambridge University Press.

—— (1988b) *The Seminar of Jacques Lacan: Book II*, trans. Sylvana Tomaselli, Cambridge: Cambridge University Press.

—— (1992) *The Ethics of Psychoanalysis, 1959–60*, trans. Dennis Porter, London: Tavistock/Routledge.

LaCapra, Dominick (1989) *Soundings in Critical Theory*, Ithaca, NY: Cornell University Press.

Lakoff, George and Johnson, Mark (1980) *Metaphors We Live By*, Chicago, IL: University of Chicago Press.

Laqueur, Thomas (1990) *Making Sex: Body and Gender from the Greeks to Freud*, Cambridge, MA: Harvard University Press.

Larkin, Philip (1964) *The Whitsun Weddings*, London: Faber.

—— (1975) 'Interview' (1964), in Graham Martin and P.N. Furbank (eds), *Twentieth Century Poetry*, Milton Keynes: Open University Press, pp. 243–54.

Larrissy, Edward (1990) *Reading Twentieth Century Poetry*, Oxford: Blackwell.

Leavis, F.R. (1937) 'Literary Criticism and Philosophy: A Reply', *Scrutiny* 6: 1 (June), pp. 59–70.

le Carré, John (1964) *The Spy who Came in from the Cold*, London: Pan.

Lecercle, Jean-Jacques (1990) *The Violence of Language*, London and New York: Routledge.

—— (1994) *Philosophy of Nonsense*, London: Routledge.

Locke, John (1975) *An Essay Concerning Human Understanding*, ed. Peter H. Nidditch, Oxford: Oxford University Press.

Lodge, David (1985) *Small World*, Harmondsworth: Penguin.

Louvre, Alf (1988) 'Reading Bezer', *Literature and History* 14: 1 (Spring), pp. 23–36.

Lowe, E.J. (1995) *Locke on Human Understanding*, London: Routledge.

Lyotard, Jean-François (1984) *The Postmodern Condition*, trans. Geoff Bennington, Manchester: Manchester University Press.

MacCabe, Colin (1985) *Theoretical Essays*, Manchester: Manchester University Press.

Mann, Michael (1996) 'Nation-states in Europe and Other Continents', in Gopal Balakrishnan (ed.), *Mapping the Nation*, London: Verso, pp. 295–316.

Marx, Karl and Engels, Frederick (1950) *Selected Works*, 2 vols, London: Lawrence and Wishart.

—— (1974) *The German Ideology*, London: Lawrence and Wishart.

Maxwell, D.E.S. (1969) *Poets of the 'Thirties*, London: Routledge and Kegan Paul.

Meinecke, Friedrich (1907) *Cosmopolitanism and the National State*, trans. Felix Gilbert, Princeton, NJ: Princeton University Press, 1970.

Metz, Christian (1975) 'The Imaginary Signifier', *Screen* 16: 2 (Summer), pp. 14–76.

Mill, J.S. (1910) *Utilitarianism, Liberty, Representative Government*, London: Dent.

Miller, David (1995) *On Nationality*, Oxford: Clarendon Press.

Milton, John (1958) *The Poetical Works*, ed. Helen Darbishire, London: Oxford University Press.

Minogue, K.R. (1967) *Nationalism*, London: Batsford.

Močnik, Rastko (1993) 'Ideology and Fantasy', in E. Ann Kaplan and Michael Sprinker (eds), *The Althusserian Legacy*, London: Verso, pp. 139–56.

Morrison, Blake (1980) *The Movement*, Oxford: Oxford University Press.

—— (1982) *Seamus Heaney*, London: Methuen.

Morrison, Blake and Motion, Andrew (1982) 'Introduction', *Contemporary British Poetry*, Harmondsworth: Penguin, pp. 11–20.

Moscovici, Serge (1985) *The Age of the Crowd*, trans. J.C. Whitehouse, Cambridge: Cambridge University Press.

Mouffe, Chantal (1993) *The Return of the Political*, London: Verso.

Muecke, D.C. (1982) *Irony and the Ironic*, London and New York: Methuen.

Mulhern, Francis (1979) *The Moment of 'Scrutiny'*, London: New Left Books.

Nairn, Tom (1964a), 'The British Political Elite', *New Left Review* 23, (January/February), pp. 19–25.

—— (1964b) 'The English Working Class', *New Left Review*, 24 (March/April), pp. 43–57.

—— (1977) *The Break-Up of Britain*, 2nd edn, London: Verso, 1981.

—— (1995) 'Breakwaters of 2000: From Ethnic to Civic Nationalism', *New Left Review* 214 (November/December), pp. 91–103.

Nimni, Ephraim (1994) *Marxism and Nationalism*, London: Pluto.

Oakeshott, Michael (1967) *Rationalism in Politics*, London: Methuen.

O'Connor, D.J. (1952) *John Locke*, Harmondworth: Penguin.

O'Donoghue, Bernard (1994) *Seamus Heaney and the Language of Poetry*, Hemel Hempstead: Harvester.

Orwell, George (1968) *Collected Essays*, ed. Sonia Orwell and Ian Angus, London: Secker and Warburg, 4 vols.

—— (1949) *Nineteen Eighty-Four*, Harmondsworth: Penguin, 1983.

Parker, Andrew *et al.* (eds) (1992) *Nationalism and Sexualities*, New York: Routledge.

Pascoe, David (1990) 'Brickbats and Masters', *Essays in Criticism* 40: 4 (October), pp. 347–58.

Patterson, Thomas C. (1989) 'Post-structuralism, Post-modernism: Implications for Historians', *Social History* 14: 1 (January), pp. 83–8.

Peters, Richard (1979) *Hobbes*, Westport, CT: Greenwood.

Pope, Alexander (1965) *Poems*, ed. John Butt, London: Methuen.

Pound, Ezra (1954) *Literary Essays*, London: Faber.

—— (1960) *Gaudier-Brzeska: A Memoir*, Hessle, Yorkshire: Marvell.

Powell, Neill (1979) *Carpenters of Light: A Critical Study of Contemporary British Poetry*, Manchester: Carcanet New Press.

Press, John (ed.) (1969) *A Map of Modern English Verse*, London: Oxford University Press.

Priest, Stephen (1990) *The British Empiricists*, Harmondsworth: Penguin.
Quinton, Anthony (1980) *Bacon*, Oxford: Oxford University Press.
Raworth, Tom (1988) *tottering state: Selected Poems 1963–1987*, London: Paladin.
Renan, Ernest (1990) 'What is a Nation?', in Homi K. Bhabha (ed.), *Nation and Narration*, London: Routledge, pp. 8–22.
Ricoeur, Paul (1965) 'Universal Civilisation and National Cultures', in *History and Truth*, trans. Charles A. Kelbley, Evanston, IL: Northwestern University Press, pp. 271–84.
Rorty, Richard (1994) *Philosophy and the Mirror of Nature*, Oxford: Blackwell.
Royal Institute of International Affairs (RIIA) (1963) *Nationalism*, London: Cass, 1939.
Sagar, Keith (1975) *The Art of Ted Hughes*, Cambridge: Cambridge University Press.
—— (1983) (ed.) *The Achievement of Ted Hughes*, Manchester: Manchester University Press.
Said, Edward (1985) *Orientalism*, Harmondsworth: Penguin.
Samuel, Raphael (ed.) (1989) *Patriotism*, London: Routledge & Kegan Paul.
—— (1991) 'Reading the Signs: I', *History Workshop Journal* 32 (Autumn), pp. 88–109.
—— (1992) 'Reading the Signs: II', *History Workshop Journal* 33, (Spring), pp. 220–51.
Sandison, Alan (1986) *George Orwell: After 1984*, London: Macmillan.
Seton-Watson, Hugh (1977) *Nations and States*, London: Methuen.
Simpson, David (1993) *Romanticism, Nationalism and the Revolt against Theory*, Chicago, IL: Chicago University Press.
Skinner, Quentin (1996) *Reason and Rhetoric in the Philsophy of Hobbes*, Cambridge: Cambridge University Press.
Smith, Anthony D. (1973) '*Nationalism*, A Trend Report', *Current Sociology* 21: 3, The Hague: Mouton.
—— (1986) *The Ethnic Origins of Nation*, Oxford: Blackwell.
—— (1991) *National Identity*, Harmondsworth: Penguin.
—— (1993), 'The Nation: Invented, Imagined, Reconstructed?', in Marjorie Ringros and Adam J. Lerner (eds), *Re-Imagining the Nation*, Milton Keynes: Open University Press, pp. 9–28.
Spiegel, Gabrielle M. (1990) 'History, Historicism, and the Social Logic of the Text in the Middle Age', *Speculum* lxv, pp. 59–86.
—— (1992) 'History and Post-modernism IV', *Past and Present* 135 (May), pp. 194–208.
Stalin, Joseph (1973) 'Marxism and the National and Colonial Question', in Bruce Franklin (ed.), *The Essential Stalin*, London: Croom Helm, pp. 57–61.
Stone, Lawrence (1958) 'The Inflation of Honours 1558–1641', *Past and Present*, 14 (November), pp. 45–70.
—— (1991) 'History and Post-Modernism', *Past and Present* 131 (May), pp. 217–18.
—— (1992) 'History and Post-Modernism III', *Past and Present* 135 (May), pp. 189–94.

Swinden, Patrick (1972) 'English Poetry', in C.B. Cox and A.E. Dyson (eds), *The Twentieth Century Mind III: 1945–1965*, London: Oxford University Press, pp. 386–413.

Tennyson, Alfred (1969), *The Poems*, ed. Christopher Ricks, London: Longman, Green.

Thomas, Edward (1978) *Collected Poems*, Oxford: Clarendon Press.

Thompson, Edward (1978) *The Poverty of Theory*, London: Merlin.

Thwaite, Anthony (1985) *A Critical Guide to British Poetry 1960–1984*, London: Longman.

Tilly, Charles (1994) 'Western State-Making and Theories of Political Transformation', in John Hutchinson and Anthony D. Smith (eds), *Nationalism*, Oxford: Oxford University Press, pp. 251–4.

Tomlinson, Charles (1972) *Written on Water*, London: Oxford University Press.

Tönnies, Ferdinand (1887) *Community and Association*, trans. Charles P. Loomis, London: Routledge & Kegan Paul, 1955.

Walker, William (1994) *Locke, Literary Criticism, and Philosophy*, Cambridge: Cambridge University Press.

Ward, John Powell (1991) *The English Line: Poetry of the Unpoetic from Wordsworth to Larkin*, London: Macmillan.

Wasserman, Earl (1964) 'The English Romantics', *Studies in Romanticism* 4: 1 (Autumn), pp. 17–24.

Watkins, John (1989) *Hobbes's System of Ideas*, 2nd revised edn, Aldershot: Gower.

Waugh, Evelyn (1951) *Brideshead Revisited*, Harmondsworth: Penguin.

Weber, Max (1948) 'The Nation', in *From Max Weber: Essays in Sociology*, trans. H.H. Gerth and C. Wright-Mills, London: Routledge & Kegan Paul, pp. 171–9.

White, Hayden (1973) *Metahistory*, Baltimore, MD: Johns Hopkins University Press.

—— (1978) *Tropics of Discourse*, Baltimore, MD: Johns Hopkins University Press.

—— (1987) *The Content of the Form*, Baltimore, MD: Johns Hopkins University Press.

—— (1995) 'Response to Arthur Marwick', *Journal of Contemporary History* 30: 2 (April), pp. 233–46.

Wilkinson, Helen and Mulgan, Geoff (1995) *Freedom's Children*, London: Demos.

Willey, Basil (1962a) *The Seventeenth-Century Background*, Harmondsworth: Penguin.

—— (1962b) *The Eighteenth-Century Background*, Harmondsworth: Penguin.

—— (1964) *Nineteenth-Century Studies*, Harmondsworth: Penguin.

Williams, Raymond (1961) *Culture and Society, 1780–1950*, Harmondsworth: Penguin.

—— (1975) *The Country and the City*, London: Granada.

—— (1983) *Towards 2000*, London: Chatto and Windus.

Wittgenstein, Ludwig (1968) *Philosophical Investigations*, Oxford: Blackwell.

Wood, Ellen Meiksins (1991) *The Pristine Culture of Capitalism*, London: Verso.

Woolf, Virginia (1992) *A Room of One's Own; Three Guineas*, Oxford: Oxford University Press.

Wordsworth, William (1952–9) *Poetical Works*, ed. Ernest de Selincourt and Helen Darbishire, 5 vols, Oxford: Oxford University Press.
—— (1979) *The Prelude, 1799, 1850, 1850*, eds Jonathan Wordsworth, M.H. Abrams and Stephen Gill, New York: Norton.
Žižek, Slavoj (1989) *The Sublime Object of Ideology*, London: Verso.
—— (1991a) *Looking Awry*, Cambridge, MA: MIT Press.
—— (1991b) *For They Know Not What They Do*, London: Verso.
—— (1994) *Tarrying with the Negative*, Durham, NC: Duke University Press.

INDEX